STUDY GUIDE
Dan Martinez
Salt Lake Community College

Macroeconomics
Principles, Applications, and Tools
Fifth Edition

O'Sullivan/Sheffrin/Perez

Upper Saddle River, New Jersey 07458

VP/Editorial Director: Jeff Shelstad
AVP/Executive: David Alexander
Senior Development Editor: Lena Buonanno
Associate Director, Manufacturing: Vincent Scelta
Production Editor & Buyer: Carol O'Rourke
Printer/Binder: Bind-Rite Graphics, Robbinsville

Copyright © 2007 by Pearson Education, Inc., Upper Saddle River, New Jersey, 07458.
Pearson Prentice Hall. All rights reserved. Printed in the United States of America. This publication is protected by
Copyright and permission should be obtained from the publisher prior to any prohibited reproduction, storage in a
retrieval system, or transmission in any form or by any means, electronic, mechanical, photocopying, recording, or
likewise. For information regarding permission(s), write to: Rights and Permissions Department.

Pearson Prentice Hall™ is a trademark of Pearson Education, Inc.

10 9 8 7 6 5 4 3 2 1
ISBN-13: 978-0-13-232931-6
ISBN-10:   0-13-232931-X

Contents

Preface   v

1   Introduction: What Is Economics?   1

2   The Key Principles of Economics   17

3   Exchange and Markets   32

4   Demand, Supply, and Market Equilibrium   43

5   Measuring a Nation's Production and Income   62

6   Unemployment and Inflation   77

7   The Economy at Full Employment   93

8   Why Do Economies Grow?   108

9   Aggregate Demand and Aggregate Supply   127

10   Fiscal Policy   142

11   The Income-Expenditure Model   155

12   Investment and Financial Markets   173

13   Money and the Banking System   187

14   The Federal Reserve and Monetary Policy   201

15   Modern Macroeconomics: From the Short Run to the Long Run 217

16   The Dynamics of Inflation and Unemployment   233

17   Macroeconomic Policy Debates   248

18   International Trade and Public Policy   262

19   The World of International Finance   276

Preface

This Study Guide was written to be used with *Macroeconomics: Principles, Applications, and Tools, 5th Edition,* by O'Sullivan, Sheffrin, and Perez. If used consistently, the Study Guide will aid your understanding of the main book's content and give you additional problems and exercises to help you apply economic concepts to various situations and interpret graphs.

Study Guide Features

Each chapter of the Study Guide contains the following features:

Chapter Summary

Summarizes the main points of the chapter and corresponds to the summary that appears at the end of each chapter of the main book.

Applying the Concepts

Lists the key questions that are answered by the Applications in the main book.

Section-by-Section Overview

Highlights important concepts, principles, definitions, and figures in each numbered section of the main book.

Extra Examples

Provides short, additional examples not found in the main book. These extra examples are identified with the following icon: ☞

Study Tips, Cautions, Key Equations, and Remember Boxes

Highlight important items to remember. The Caution boxes warn you against common mistakes that students make. The Remember boxes highlight material that is particularly important.

Application Summary

Provides an overview of the Applications used to answer the key questions that open the chapter.

Activity and Answer

Helps you complete an activity to further build your understanding of economic concepts.

Key Terms

Provides all the terms and definitions that appear in the margin of the chapter.

Practice Quiz

Helps you prepare for exams. There are multiple-choice questions and short-answer questions. Several questions ask you to interpret a graph. Several questions also support the Applications you learned about in the chapter. Answers are provided so you can confirm your understanding.

Use the Study Guide to Do Better on Tests

1. Figure out what you don't know. Often students spend time studying everything, when there are some things they actually know very well and some things that they need to work on. Use the exercises in the Study Guide and on **www.myeconlab.com** to help you figure out what you know well and what you need to spend extra time on. See the section entitled "Other Learning Resources" for more about MyEconLab.
2. Practice in a test environment. Often when working problems you may have the text or notes and use those resources to help get the right answer. That's a good thing, that's how you learn. At test time, however, you don't realize how much you depended on those resources. Also, you sometimes know how to solve a problem, but don't solve problems quickly and feel rushed in a test environment. Here's a suggestion. Use the Study Guide as a source of questions to mimic a test environment. Set a timer for 15 minutes and answer 15 multiple-choice questions without using any study aid. This will let you know what things you really know and will also help you feel comfortable with a time constraint.

Study Tips

1. The Study Guide doesn't replace the text! The Study Guide is intended to be used *along with* the text. It has been written to provide an overview of the key topics, but you should always read the text chapter first. In addition, the Study Guide references figures and graphs that are found in the text. To get the most out of the Study Guide, you really need to use it alongside the text.
2. Attend class and read chapters before you go to class. Reading the chapter first will give you an idea of what your instructor will discuss in class. Often you will find that you are able to understand many basic ideas simply from your reading of the text. You can then use class time to learn how to apply those basic ideas, to understand more difficult concepts, and to ask questions.
3. See economics in the world around you. Almost every decision you make has an economic component to it. Suppose that you watched the Golf Channel every day or read all you could about playing the piano, but you never went to the golf course or sat down at a piano. All the knowledge in the world doesn't benefit you much if you never put it into practice. It is the same with economics. Don't just learn the material; put it into practice as you go about your daily routine.
4. Do extra exercises. Economics is a problem-solving discipline. The more problems you do, the better you will understand the material and the more comfortable you will be working with the material. The activities and exercises in the Study Guide are a great practice ground. Also visit **www.myeconlab.com** to complete more exercises and get tutorial help.

Other Learning Resources

Here are two other resources you can use in addition to this Study Guide to help you understand economic concepts and build your skills solving problems and exercises:

Get Ahead of the Curve

You can arrive to class with confidence and take exams with confidence if you build your skills in applying the economic concepts in the text. MyEconLab (**www.myeconlab.com**) is the only online assessment system that gives you the tools you need to learn from mistakes. Here are the features of MyEconLab:

Problem Solving

Each chapter in the main text ends with a wide selection of summary and practice exercises. You have the option of completing these exercises online at www.myeconlab.com. MyEconLab identifies your weak areas and provides tutorial help to master those areas.

Tests and Quizzes

MyEconLab comes with two preloaded Sample Tests for each chapter so you can assess your understanding of the material. Your instructor can assign the Sample Tests. Many Sample Test problems contain algorithmically generated values to increase practice opportunities.

Study Plan

MyEconLab generates a Study Plan from your results on assigned exercises and Sample Tests. You can clearly see which topics you have mastered—and more importantly, where you need remediation. The Study Plan links you to additional practice problems and tutorial help on those topics.

Unlimited Practice

Study Plan exercises and instructor-assigned Homework problems provide you with valuable opportunities for practice and remediation. Each problem includes links to learning resources so that you can focus on the concepts you need to master.

Learning Resources

You can get help from a host of interactive, targeted resources. Links to eText pages secure the connection between online practice and key chapter concepts. MyEconLab also has a suite of graphing tools that help you draw and interpret graphs and chapter-specific, current news articles that tie economic concepts to everyday topics.

Hear it. Get it.

www.vangonotes.com

You can study on the go with VangoNotes—chapter reviews from the text in downloadable MP3 format from **www.vangonotes.com**. Now wherever you are—whatever you're doing—you can study by listening to the following for each chapter of the book:

- **Big Ideas.** The "need to know" for each chapter.
- **Practice Tests.** A gut check for the Big Ideas—tells you if you need to keep studying.
- **Key Terms.** Audio "flashcards" to help you review key concepts and terms.
- **Rapid Review.** A quick drill session that you can use right before a test.

VangoNotes are **flexible**. You can download all the material directly to your MP3 player or only the chapters you need. VangoNotes are also **efficient**. You can use them in the car, at the gym, walking to class, wherever you want to go.

Learning economics can be interesting and rewarding. The skills you develop in your economics class will be with you throughout your life. Enjoy the class, the book, and this Study Guide.

Dan Martinez
Salt Lake Community College

1

Introduction: What Is Economics?

Chapter Summary

This chapter explains what economics is and why it is useful. Here are the main points of the chapter:

- Most of modern economics is based on positive analysis, which answers the question "what is?" or "what will be?" Economists contribute to policy debates by conducting positive analyses about the consequences of alternative actions.
- The choices made by individuals, firms, and governments answer three questions: What products do we produce? How do we produce the products? Who consumes the products?
- Normative analysis answers the question "what ought to be?"
- To think like economists, we (a) use assumptions to simplify, (b) use the notion of *ceteris paribus* to focus on the relationship between two variables, (c) think in marginal terms, and (d) assume that rational people respond to incentives.
- We use macroeconomics to understand why economies grow, to understand economic fluctuations, and to make informed business decisions.
- We use microeconomics to understand how markets work, to make personal and managerial decisions, and to evaluate the merits of public policies.

Applying the Concepts

After reading this chapter, you should be able to answer these two key questions:
1. Do people respond to incentives?
2. What is the role of prices in allocating resources?

1.1 What Is Economics?

Economics is the study of how people, businesses, governments, and other organizations make choices when there is scarcity. **Scarcity** means that the resources we use to produce goods and services are limited. Human wants, however, are unlimited. For instance, you may earn enough money each month to make a lease payment on a Lexus, but if you do that you won't have money to pay for rent and buy food. Because your resources are limited, you have to choose between a nice car, and food and a place to sleep.

We call the resources used to produce goods and services **factors of production** and typically think of five types of factors:

- **Natural resources**, which are provided by nature and include land, mineral deposits, oil and gas deposits, and water.
- **Labor**, the physical and mental effort people use to produce goods and services.
- **Physical capital**, the stock of equipment, machines, structures, and infrastructure that is used to produce goods and services.
- **Human capital**, the knowledge and skills acquired by a worker through education and experience.
- **Entrepreneurship**, the effort to co-ordinate the factors of production to produce and sell products.

☞ Think about the factors of production needed to open a coffee shop near your campus. You would need some physical capital such as a building, an espresso machine, tables, and chairs. You would need labor, workers who would make the coffee drinks and who, hopefully, could suggest and help develop new recipes as they learn what your customers like. You would provide the entrepreneurial ability as you find a location and make decisions on the best way to use the resources at your disposal.

Economic analysis takes on two primary forms: **positive analysis,** which answers the question "What is?" or "What will be?" and **normative analysis,** which answers the question "What ought to be?"

An example of a positive question is "Why do athletes make more money than schoolteachers?" A related normative question would ask "Should athletes make more money than schoolteachers?" Another positive question is "How does a monopoly affect market outcomes?" A related normative question is "Should society regulate monopolies?"

📄 Remember

Most of what is covered in this book will take the form of positive analysis, trying to understand the world the way it is, not the way we might like it to be.

Economics seeks to answer three primary questions:
- What products do we produce? Should a coffee shop sell breakfast food and lunch food along with coffee?
- How do we produce the products? Should the coffee shop hire bakers to make breakfast pastries or should they buy pastries from someone else?
- Who consumes the products? Should prices determine who buys coffee or should the coffee shop use some other mechanism?

Most of the time markets will provide the answers to these three questions. There are times when legal or regulatory restrictions are imposed on the market. We will explore how those impact economic outcomes. We will also see that there are times when legal or regulatory action improves market outcomes.

To simplify analysis, we use **economic models.** A model is a simplified representation of an economic environment. At this level, our models will often employ a graph. A model focuses on the main issues in an economic situation. Most of our models ignore certain aspects of real markets, but the models do contain the essential features that let us understand how markets work. For example, we might assume in a model that firms sell identical goods. In most cases we know that the goods offered by different companies are not technically identical. However, if most consumers don't care what color facial tissues they buy, we can simplify analysis by assuming that all facial tissues are the same. By making this assumption we remove a factor that would add a great deal of complexity to the analysis, but little understanding.

1.2 Economic Analysis and Modern Problems

Policy makers, economists, company executives, and you can use the tools of economic analysis to understand and solve a variety of problems in the world. For instance, we might ask "What is the best way to reduce pollution?" and even "What is the right amount of pollution?" Economic analysis is often used to provide answers to these questions.

We can also use the tools of economics to measure the level of economic activity and to examine how changes in policy or education affect the level of economic activity and the amount of economic growth in a country.

Your book provides three examples of real-world problems that can be addressed by economics:
- Traffic congestion: How do you help people realize the true cost of driving on a road, and will this reduce congestion?
- Poverty in Africa: As economies grow, the poorest households share in the prosperity. A key source of economic growth missing from this is a well-functioning legal and regulatory system.
- Japan's economic problems: How can changing the financial system revitalize one rapidly growing economy?

These will be used as examples in more detail in later sections of the book.

1.3 The Economic Way of Thinking

In many cases multiple things are happening at once. Most economic analysis attempts to understand how changing one **variable**, a measure of something that can take on different values, changes the economic outcome. To do this we often assume that all other variables are held constant in the analysis. *Ceteris paribus* is the Latin expression that means "to hold other variables fixed."

Perhaps the most important thing to remember about the economic way of thinking is that economics focuses on the **marginal change**, that is, a small, one-unit change. Even though we may not consciously make decisions in this manner, it provides a very nice framework to understand decision making. Decisions made by individuals and institutions are usually very close to the decisions predicted by marginal analysis.

☞ As an example of a marginal change, suppose that a store is selling sweaters for $40 each, two for $70 and three for $85. To find the marginal cost of each sweater, we ask, "How much more do we have to spend to buy an additional sweater?" For the first sweater, we must spend $40. The marginal cost of the second sweater is only $30. Why? We have already spent $40 to purchase one sweater. Since we can buy two sweaters for $70 we need to spend only an additional $30 to acquire the second sweater. The third sweater will only cost us only $15 because we have paid $70 for two sweaters and to purchase the third we must increase our payments to $85.

> ## ᧡ **Study Tip**
>
> Throughout your study of economics, you will use the concept of a marginal change. Be sure that you understand that a marginal change considers how a small change in economic activity affects some other economic variable. For instance, marginal cost tells us how the production of one more unit of output changes our total costs. The marginal benefit of a slice of pizza is the change in satisfaction that comes from eating one more slice of pizza.

There are four main elements to the economic way of thinking:

1. **Use assumptions to simplify**: In any problem there are certain key elements we need to understand along with other elements that don't affect the current decision. We use assumptions to eliminate the other elements so we can focus on the key elements for the decision.

☞ For example, when you decide which road to take to travel from Seattle to San Francisco, you don't take into account the curvature of the earth or all the smaller side roads along the path. You examine a flat highway map that shows only main roads. You have assumed away factors that don't affect the decision at hand.

2. **Isolate variables**: Examine how a change in one factor (say, the price of apples) affects another (say, the quantity of apples a person purchases) while assuming all other factors, such as income, remain unchanged. We can then ask how a change in income affects the quantity of apples purchased, assuming the price of apples remains constant.

3. **Think at the margin**: Analyze a problem by asking, "What happens if we make a small change from our current point?"

☞ For instance, a firm might ask, "If we hire one more worker, how will our output change, holding everything else constant?" Or consider that no one tries to decide whether they should drop out of high school or become a doctor. In part because those aren't the two options available. A marginal decision would be "do I drop out of high school or do I graduate?" The next decision would be "do I go to college or not?" Only after you graduate from college can you decide to go to medical school to be a doctor.

4. **Rational people respond to incentives**: People will change their behavior as the benefits and costs of their actions change.

☞ Imagine how your behavior would change if police could confiscate your car if they catch you speeding. Since the price of speeding would increase, you would be more careful to drive the speed limit. Some states will confiscate your car if you are caught driving under the influence.

Let's review two Applications that answer the key questions we posed at the start of the chapter:

1. Do people respond to incentives?

APPLICATION 1: PEDALING FOR TELEVISION TIME

In this Application, researchers increased the cost of watching TV by making children ride a bike to power the TV. Children that didn't have to pedal to watch TV watched 21 hours per week. For the children who had to pedal the bike to watch TV, this higher cost reduced their TV viewing time to only 2 hours per week. This is a nice example of people responding to incentives—as the cost of watching TV increased (because now the person had to work to power the TV), the amount of TV viewing decreased.

2. What is the role of prices in allocating resources?

APPLICATION 2: LONDON SOLVES ITS CONGESTION PROBLEM

To solve the problem of traffic congestion, we first assume that all drivers and all cars have the same effect on congestion. This is an important simplifying assumption. We then examine how a government policy of charging a toll to drive on the road will affect the number of cars, holding constant things such as income and the price of gasoline. This assumption lets us focus on just the policy variable. To determine how well the toll works, we examine the effects of adding only one more car to the highway, that is, we think at the margin. In the book example, an additional car added two seconds to the travel time for each of the 900 other cars on the road. This amounted to 30 minutes of additional travel time. London decided to charge a tax of $8 per day to drive in the city between 7AM and 6:30PM. This higher price led some people to avoid driving in the city during the day, thus easing congestion.

1.4 Preview of Coming Attractions: Macroeconomics

Macroeconomics is the study of the nation's economy as a whole. Macroeconomists study questions of inflation, unemployment, and economic growth. These are the economic issues you frequently hear about on the news or read about in the paper and on the web. Macroeconomics answers questions such as "What makes economies grow?" "How can we smooth out business cycles?" "How does the Federal Reserve affect economic performance?"

Three important reasons for studying macroeconomics are:
*   To understand why economies grow.
*   To understand economic fluctuations.
*   To make informed business decisions.

1.5 Preview of Coming Attractions: Microeconomics

Microeconomics studies the choices of individual economic agents such as households, firms, and governments. Microeconomics also studies how the choices made by these agents affect the market for goods and services. Questions of output and pricing would be microeconomic questions. Some questions addressed by microeconomics might be "How will a hurricane in Florida affect the price of citrus fruits?" "Who pays when a tax is imposed in a market?" "When will a new business enter a market?" "Why does the price of bottled water rise after a hurricane?"

Three important reasons for studying microeconomics are:
- To understand markets and predict changes.
- To make personal and managerial decisions.
- To evaluate public policies.

ᕲᕒ **Study Tip**

Economics is a way of looking at the world and understanding how the world works. To be successful in this class you must become comfortable thinking like an economist. While this may seem difficult at first, as with many things, practice will help this become second nature. That is one of the reasons it is important to work a lot of problems as you try to learn economics. Working the problems helps you to begin to see the world as an economist.

Activity

An important concept introduced in this chapter is that people respond to incentives. You can see this around you every day. As an example, think about all of the lectures and other campus events students attend because they are given extra credit. The incentive (extra credit) has changed their behavior. How incentives affect behavior is an important part of understanding economic decisions.

List a few ways that you and your fellow students respond to incentives. A good place to start is to ask yourself if you have ever attended a campus function that you normally wouldn't attend to earn extra credit points. If you have, you have changed your behavior in response to the incentives offered.

Key Terms

Ceteris paribus: The Latin expression meaning other variables being held fixed.

Economics: The study of choices when there is scarcity.

Economic model: A simplified representation of an economic environment, often employing a graph.

Entrepreneurship: The effort used to coordinate the factors of production—natural resources, labor, physical capital, and human capital—to produce and sell products.

Factors of production: The resources used to produce goods and services; also known as production inputs.

Human capital: The knowledge and skills acquired by a worker through education and experience.

Labor: The physical and mental effort people use to produce goods and services.

Macroeconomics: The study of the nation's economy as a whole; focuses on the issues of inflation, unemployment, and economic growth.

Marginal change: A small, one-unit change in value.

Microeconomics: The study of the choices made by households, firms, and government and how these choices affect the markets for goods and services.

Natural resources: Resources provided by nature and used to produce goods and services.

Normative analysis: Answers the question "What ought to be?"

Physical capital: The stock of equipment, machines, structures, and infrastructure that is used to produce goods and services.

Positive analysis: Answers the question "What is?" or "What will be?"

Scarcity: The resources we use to produce goods and services are limited.

Variable: A measure of something that can take on different values.

Appendix: Using Graphs and Percentages

Graphs are a visual way of representing a relationship between variables. The relationship is usually either a **positive relationship**, meaning that the two variables move in the same direction, or a **negative relationship**, meaning that the two variables move in opposite directions. Figure 1A.4 shows a graph of a positive relationship. Figure 1A.6 shows a graph of a negative relationship. Graphs, particularly graphs of two variables, are used extensively in economics and a good understanding of the material in the appendix is needed for success.

> ## ᏗᎠ Study Tip
>
> We will use graphs throughout the text. Now is the time to make sure you understand how to understand information presented in a graph. In particular, understand the difference between those factors that cause us to move between two points on a fixed curve and those factors that cause the position of the curve to shift. Being able to work with graphs will be particularly important in Chapter 4 when you study supply and demand.

The **slope of a curve** tells us by how much a change in one variable affects the value of another variable. You can find the slope by dividing the vertical difference between two points (the rise) by the horizontal difference between the two points (the run). A graph of two variables with a positive relationship will have a positive slope. A graph of two variables with a negative relationship will have a negative slope. The slope answers questions in economics such as, "By how much does quantity demanded fall when the price of a good increases by $1?"

We move along a curve when we move from one point on a graph to another point on the same graph. This would be a movement from point *f* to point *g* in Figure 1A.5. You can see that both hours and income have changed along the line representing income with a $90 allowance. We shift the curve when one of the variables changes while the other variable stays the same. This would be a shift from point *f* to point *b*. Our income per week now takes on a different value at the same number of hours worked per week.

☑ Key Equations: Finding the slope of a line

$$\text{slope} = \frac{\text{vertical distance between two points}}{\text{horizontal distance between two points}}$$

$$\text{slope} = \frac{\text{rise}}{\text{run}}$$

$$\text{slope} = \frac{\Delta y}{\Delta x}$$

The equations above all represent the same concept.

☑ Key Equations: Calculating percentage changes

$$\text{Percentage change} = \frac{(\text{new value} - \text{initial value})}{\text{initial value}} \times 100$$

In some cases, we will use the midpoint formula:

$$\text{Percentage change} = \frac{(\text{new value} - \text{initial value})}{\text{average value}} \times 100$$

where the average value is:

$$\frac{(\text{new value} + \text{initial value})}{2}$$

Key Terms for Appendix

Negative relationship: A relationship in which two variables move in opposite directions.

Positive relationship: A relationship in which two variables move in the same direction.

Slope of a curve: The vertical difference between two points (the rise) divided by the horizontal difference (the run).

Practice Quiz

(Answers are provided at the end of the Practice Quiz.)

1. Economics is the study of choice under conditions of:
   a. supply.
   b. scarcity.
   c. opportunity.
   d. abundance of resources.

2. Which of the following terms would best describe the consequence of scarcity?
   a. Limited resources
   b. Tradeoffs
   c. Unlimited wants
   d. Poverty and possibly starvation

3. The resources provided by nature and used to produce goods and services are also known as:
   a. factors of production.
   b. natural resources.
   c. physical capital.
   d. productive inputs.

4. Select the best answer. Which questions usually lie at the heart of policy debates?
   a. Positive questions
   b. Normative questions
   c. All economic questions, both positive and normative
   d. Questions about the choices made by individuals

5. If the president of Colombia commented that "we should do something to reduce inflation in Colombia," this would be an example of:
   a. a normative statement.
   b. a positive statement.
   c. a statement that has both positive and normative components.
   d. neither positive analysis nor normative analysis.

6. Economic decisions are made at every level in society. When we try to decide which production method to use among several alternatives, which of the key economic questions are we trying to answer?
   a. What products do we produce?
   b. How do we produce the products?
   c. Who consumes the products?
   d. Which government agency should supervise the production of goods?

7. Economic models are:
   a. precise representations of reality that include as many details as possible in order to accurately predict behavior.
   b. simplifications of reality that focus only on key relationships and ignore less relevant details.
   c. presentations of all the possible outcomes under all real world circumstances.
   d. analytical interpretations of economic behavior involving a good deal of the surrounding social and political structure of society.

8. Economists develop analytical tools to deal with specific problems. Which of the problems below is an economist prepared to discuss?
   a. The economic view of Japan's economic problems
   b. The economic view of poverty in Africa
   c. The economic view of traffic congestion
   d. All of the above

9. A roadmap is a good example of one of the four elements of economic thinking. Which one?
   a. Using assumptions to simplify
   b. Isolating variables—*ceteris paribus*
   c. Thinking at the margin
   d. Acting rationally and responding to incentives

10. This question tests your understanding of Application 1 in this chapter, *Pedaling for television time.* Do people respond to incentives? To illustrate the notion that people are rational and respond to incentives, an experiment was conducted by researchers at St. Luke's Roosevelt Hospital in New York City. Which of the following best illustrates the findings of that experiment?
    a. Children are rational and respond to incentives in the manner we would expect any rational person to respond.
    b. Children don't seem to respond to incentives in the same manner as adults do.
    c. Sometimes children act in a manner consistent with the incentives provided to them, but other times they don't seem to pay attention to incentives.
    d. Adult behavior is closely linked to childhood development.

11. Macroeconomics can be used to understand all of the topics below, EXCEPT:
    a. how the national economy works.
    b. how consumers decide which car to buy based on their preferences vs. prices.
    c. what causes economic booms and downturns.
    d. how to make informed business decisions.

12. In which of the following situations can we use economic analysis?
    a. To determine how well the government performs its roles in the market economy and to examine the tradeoffs associated with various public policies
    b. To answer many practical questions about markets and how they operate
    c. To explain why some resources increase over time and how an increase in resources translates into a higher standard of living
    d. All of the above

13. If Y = 600 - 3X, what is the slope of this line?
    a. -1/3
    b. 1/3
    c. 3
    d. -3
    e. 600

14. Refer to the graph below. The solid line can be expressed algebraically as $Y = a + bX$. What causes the line to shift, from the solid line to the dashed line?

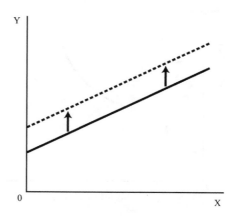

    a.   A change in the value of a
    b.   A change in the value of b
    c.   A change in the value of X
    d.   A change in the value of bX

15. Refer to the graph below. Which move describes the impact of an increase in the preference for consumer goods during the Christmas season?

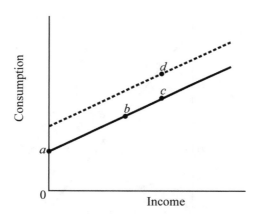

    a.   The move from *b* to *c*
    b.   The move from *c* to *d*
    c.   The move from *d* to *c*
    d.   A simultaneous move from *b* to *c*, and from *c* to *d*

16. Refer to the graph below. The relationship between output produced and cost of production can be described as follows:

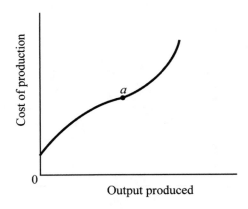

a. The cost of production decreases up until point *a*, then it increases.
b. The cost of production increases rapidly up until point *a*, then it increases slowly.
c. The cost of production increases at a decreasing rate up until point *a*, then it increases at an increasing rate.
d. The cost of production equals zero if there is no output produced.

17. Refer to the graph below. Which of the following statements is true about the value of the slope of this line?

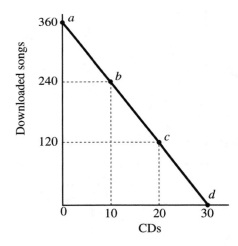

a. The value of the slope is greater between points *a* and *b* than between points *c* and *d*.
b. The value of the slope is smaller between points *a* and *b* than between points *c* and *d*.
c. The value of the slope is the same between points *a* and *b* and points *c* and *d*.
d. The value of the slope increases as the value of the variable along the horizontal axis increases.

18. Refer to the graphs below. Which graph shows a negative and increasing relationship between X and Y?

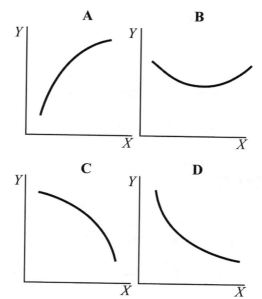

a. A
b. B
c. C
d. D

19. Refer to the figure below. The expression for the slope of this line between points a and b equals:

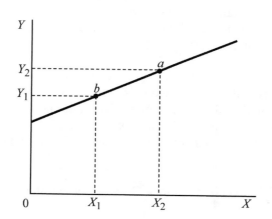

a. $\dfrac{Y_2 - Y_1}{X_2 - X_1}$

b. $\dfrac{Y_2 - X_2}{Y_1 - X_1}$

c. $\dfrac{X_2 - X_1}{Y_2 - Y_1}$

d. $\dfrac{X_2 - Y_1}{Y_2 - X_1}$

20. The sale price of a shirt is $40. There is a sign on the clothing rack that states "price marked is 20% off original price." What was the original price of the shirt?
    a. $70
    b. $60
    c. $65
    d. $50

21. Define "economics" and explain the most fundamental economic problem.

22. Relate the concept of the "invisible hand" to the way in which decisions are made in a market economy.

Answers to the Practice Quiz

1. b. Scarcity is a situation in which resources are limited in quantity and can be used in different ways. Economics is the study of choice under conditions of scarcity.

2. b. Economists are always reminding us that there is scarcity—that there are tradeoffs in everything we do.

3. b. Natural resources are provided by nature. Some examples are fertile land, mineral deposits, oil and gas deposits, and water. Some economists refer to all types of natural resources as *land*. Factors of production refers to all of the resources, not only natural resources but also labor, physical capital, human capital, and entrepreneurship, used to produce goods and services; also known as production inputs. Physical capital is the stock of equipment, machines, structures, and infrastructure that is used to produce goods and services. Some examples are forklifts, lathes, computers, factories, airports, roads, and fiber-optic cables. Productive inputs are all of the resources, not only natural resources but also labor, physical capital, human capital, and entrepreneurship, used to produce goods and services; also known as factors of production.

4. b. Correct. Normative economics answers the question: What ought to be? Normative questions lie at the heart of policy debates. Positive economics only lays out the possibilities and their likely consequences; it does not suggest decisions among these alternatives which are based on values and priorities. Policies often do influence how individuals make choices but policy debates are centered around the choices made by policy makers based on their judgments on which policy will be best for society.

5. a. The word "should" implies a value judgment. Only normative statements involve value judgments.

6. b. When we try to decide which production method to use among several alternatives, we ask questions such as: Should power companies use coal, natural gas, or wind power to produce electricity? Should professors teach in large lecture halls or small classrooms?

7. b. Abstraction and simplification, as opposed to concrete and complex information, are the preferred characteristics of economic models. Models ignore all non-essential elements of real world complexity. They also ignore a good deal of the social and political reality in order to study the underlying economic concepts.

8. d. Economic analysis provides important insights into real-world problems. Economists attempt to diagnose and provide solutions to problems such as traffic congestion, pollution, taxation, or the problems of an entire economy.

9. a. Economists use assumptions to make things simpler and focus attention on what really matters. If you use a road map to plan a car trip from Seattle to San Francisco, you make two unrealistic assumptions to simplify your planning: The earth is flat: The flat road map doesn't show the curvature of the earth. The roads are flat: The standard road map doesn't show hills and valleys. Instead of a map, you could use a globe that shows all the topographical features between Seattle and San Francisco, but you don't need those details to plan your trip. A map, with its unrealistic assumptions, will suffice, because the curvature of the earth and the topography of the highways are irrelevant to your trip.

10. a. In the experiment, kids responded to incentives as expected, watching less TV when the cost of watching is higher. The experiment does not differentiate between children and adults, nor does it establish a relationship between child behavior and subsequent adult behavior.

11. b. The decision between two types of cars is an individual choice. This is a topic of microeconomics.

12. d. Economic analysis includes all of the above. Economics is divided into two categories: macroeconomics and microeconomics. Macroeconomics is the study of the nation's economy as a whole; it focuses on the issues of inflation, unemployment, and economic growth. Macroeconomics explains why economies grow and change and why economic growth is sometimes interrupted.

13. d. The slope of this line is -3. You can calculate this by finding any two points on the line and remembering that the slope is the change in Y divided by the change in X. Alternatively, for any linear function of the form $Y = a + bX$, b is the slope.

14. a. The value of a represents the Y-intercept. An increase in the value of the intercept causes the upward, parallel shift of the line. The value of b represents the value of the slope of the line. A change in the value of the slope makes the solid line steeper or flatter, but it does not shift the line. A change in the value of X causes a move along the solid line, not a shift to the dashed line. Only a change in a would result in a parallel shift of the line.

15. b. Christmas is a factor, other than income, which causes consumption to rise. When variables other than income change, the curve shifts.

16. c. The relationship is first positive and decreasing, then positive and increasing.

17. c. The value of the slope is the same between any two points along a line.

18. c. As the value of X increases, the value of Y decreases at an increasing rate.

19. a. The difference between Y2 and Y1 is the vertical distance, or the change in Y. The difference between X2 and X1 is the horizontal distance, or the change in X. The ratio of the changes is commonly called "rise over run."

20. d. A reduction of 20% means that the new price is 80% of the old price. If $40 equals 80%, then how many dollars are equivalent to 100%? The answer is (40 x 100)/80 = 50.

21. Economics studies the choices that can be made when there is scarcity. Scarcity is a situation in which resources are limited in quantity and can be used in different ways. Because our resources are limited, we must sacrifice one thing for another. Economists are always reminding us that there is scarcity—that there are tradeoffs in everything we do.

22. The "invisible hand" explains how people acting in their own self-interest may actually promote the interest of society as a whole. In modern economies, most of the decisions about what to produce, how to produce it, and how much to produce are made in markets. The decisions made in markets result from the interactions of millions of people, each acting in his or her own self-interest. There is no coordinating authority. A key assumption of most economic analysis is that people act rationally, meaning that they act in their own self-interest. Rational people respond to incentives.

2

The Key Principles of Economics

Chapter Summary

This chapter introduces five key principles of economics. You'll see these principles again in each chapter of the book. The five key principles are:

- **Principle of Opportunity Cost:** The opportunity cost of something is what you sacrifice to get it.
- **The Marginal Principle:** Increase the level of an activity as long as its marginal benefit exceeds its marginal cost. Choose the level at which the marginal benefit equals the marginal cost.
- **Principle of Voluntary Exchange:** A voluntary exchange between two people makes both people better off.
- **Principle of Diminishing Returns:** Suppose that output is produced with two or more inputs, and we increase one input while holding the other inputs fixed. Beyond some point—called the point of diminishing marginal returns—output will increase at a decreasing rate.
- **The Real–Nominal Principle:** What matters to people is the real value of money or income—its purchasing power—not the face value of money or income.

Applying the Concepts

After reading this chapter, you should be able to answer these seven key questions:
1. What is the opportunity cost of running a business?
2. What are society's tradeoffs between different goods?
3. How do firms think at the margin?
4. What is the rationale for specialization and exchange?
5. Do farmers experience diminishing returns?
6. How does inflation affect the real minimum wage?
7. How does inflation affect lenders and borrowers?

ᎾᏆ Study Tip

While the concepts introduced in this chapter may seem very elementary, they are quite important. In fact, the rest of the book is an application of the principles in this chapter. As you go through the text, you may wish to look back and see how different topics are examples of these five principles.

2.1 The Principle of Opportunity Cost

To make a good decision we must compare the benefits of the decision with the costs. The important cost concept for decision making is that of the **opportunity cost**, what you sacrifice to get something. It is important to recognize that opportunity costs often don't involve spending money. Waiting in line is a cost: You sacrifice time you can't get back. Would you wait in line for 15 minutes at a gas station to save $1 on a tank full of gas instead of paying $1 more at a gas station with no line? In this case you need to recognize that sacrificing your time is part of the cost of the gasoline. Only if you value 15 minutes of time at less than $1 would you want to wait in line.

An opportunity cost can involve both time and money. When evaluating the costs of college, some costs, such as tuition and books, are obvious because they involve spending money. Some costs are not obvious, because they don't involve spending money. The income you give up by going to college instead of taking a full-time job is a cost. You sacrificed the income you could have earned to go to college. Some things we think of as costs are not relevant to the decision. For instance, whether you go to college or find a full-time job, you must have a place to live and food to eat. As a result, room and board aren't relevant costs to the decision to go to college—you would have to pay these costs regardless of your choice.

Like you and other people, economies (countries) face opportunity costs. Economists use the **production possibilities curve** to represent these costs. The production possibilities curve shows the possible combinations of products that an economy can produce, given that its productive resources are fully employed and efficiently used. The production possibilities curve shows us the cost of one good in terms of the amount of the other good we must sacrifice. The bowed-out shape of the production possibilities curve reflects the fact that the opportunity cost of a good increases as we produce more of it. Look at Figure 2.1 in your text. The first few tons of wheat, moving from point a to point b, require little sacrifice of steel. This makes sense as there are some resources (fertile land) that are very suited for wheat production, but not very well suited for steel production. As we produce more and more wheat, however, we must begin to use resources that are better suited for steel production and, thus, we give an increasing amount of steel for each additional unit of wheat. You can see this as we move from point c to point d in Figure 2.1.

๛ Study Tip

The concept of opportunity cost is one of the most important concepts in microeconomics. Make sure that you can recognize all the costs of a particular decision, both the monetary costs and the opportunity costs. For an individual, the other uses of your time are an important source of opportunity cost. You also need to recognize when particular costs are not relevant to a decision.

Let's review two Applications that answer key questions we posed at the start of the chapter:

1. What is the opportunity cost of running a business?

APPLICATION 1: THE OPPORTUNITY COSTS OF TIME AND INVESTED FUNDS

When you use your own time and money in a business, you sacrifice the opportunity to use those resources in other ways. You sacrifice the opportunity to trade your time for the money you could earn working for someone else as well as the interest you could have earned investing the money you invest in your business. Even though you don't write a check for these costs, they are important costs for decision making. For example, would it be a good idea to quit a job that paid you $30,000 per year to start your own business if you could make only $22,000 per year in that business? No, the earnings from your business don't replace the income you sacrificed to start the business.

2. What are society's tradeoffs between different goods?

APPLICATION 2: THE OPPORTUNITY COST OF MILITARY SPENDING

If society has a fixed amount of money to spend on goods and services, buying one type of good or service means we sacrifice the opportunity to buy others. In this example, $100 billion can pay for the war in Iraq or 13 million children enrolled in Head Start programs. To see this idea in another way, suppose that your state legislature, in an attempt to make college more affordable, gives each full-time college student $500 to offset the cost of textbooks. The state now has less money to spend on the other goods and services the state provides, such as police patrols and highway maintenance. So, the true cost of the $500 per student may be that fewer potholes are repaired on state highways.

2.2 The Marginal Principle

Economics is concerned with making choices. We will assume that the relevant choice is whether to change a current activity level by a little bit. That is, do we hire one more worker? Produce one more unit of output? Purchase one more slice of pizza? This is what is known as a marginal change. To make a good decision, we compare the **marginal benefit**, the additional benefit resulting from a small increase in some activity, with the **marginal cost**, the additional cost resulting from a small increase in some activity. If the marginal benefit is greater than the marginal cost, we want to increase the level of the activity. Doing so will increase our total well-being by the difference between the marginal benefit and the marginal cost. If the marginal benefit is less than the marginal cost, we want to reduce the level of the activity. If they are equal, we are at the optimal amount of the activity.

☞ A marginal change refers to a small change in some activity. You can think of a marginal change as taking the next step in a logical sequence. You would never, for instance, compare the salary of someone with a Ph.D. against someone who didn't finish high school. Why not? These aren't two logical options. A person doesn't decide to either earn a Ph.D. or drop out of high school. She decides whether to drop out of high school or get a high school diploma. She next decides whether to go to college or not. Upon graduating college she decides whether to take a job or go to graduate school. These are each sequential steps, and thus we can make relevant comparisons between them. A person will continue to go to school as long as the marginal benefit of the next level of schooling exceeds the marginal cost.

Let's review an Application that answers one of the key questions we posed at the start of the chapter:

3. How do firms think at the margin?

APPLICATION 3: CONTINENTAL AIRLINES USES THE MARGINAL PRINCIPLE

In this Application, the managers of Continental Airlines recognized that some costs were not relevant—they didn't change with the number of flights. Other costs, such as fuel, food, and the crew did vary with the number of flights. Continental recognized that they should fly a plane as long as the additional benefits from flying (the money received from ticket sales) covered the additional costs of flying (crew, food, and fuel).

☞ A restaurant might use the marginal principle when deciding whether to open for breakfast in addition to lunch. Since many of the costs of the restaurant (rent, payments for equipment) are fixed, the only additional cost of opening for breakfast would be the food, labor, and utilities needed to open earlier. If the revenue from selling breakfast exceeds these costs, the restaurant should open for breakfast.

> ### ᏰᏆ Study Tip
>
> Decision making based on the marginal principle is the basis for all decisions in this book. Be sure you understand the concepts of marginal benefit and marginal cost. Recognize that people should continue to take an action as long as the marginal benefit is greater than the marginal cost.

2.3 The Principle of Voluntary Exchange

The principle of voluntary exchange states that a voluntary exchange between two people makes both people better off. Think about the last time you purchased a movie ticket. Since you were willing to pay the price of a ticket, you must have valued seeing the movie more than the ticket cost. The theater manager knows that the ticket price was higher than the theater's cost of letting you see a movie. Neither of you felt cheated in the transaction because you were both better off.

☞ Most of us recognize this principle in practice. All of us realize that we are better off trading our time for money and then spending that money on other goods and services. Many people choose to eat dinner in a restaurant, even though they could make the same food at home. This principle works for trades between individuals and, as we will see later in the book, for trades between countries as well.

Let's review an Application that answers a key question we posed at the start of the chapter:

   4.   What is the rationale for specialization and exchange?

APPLICATION 4: TIGER WOODS AND WEEDS

Tiger Woods can earn $1,000 in the time it takes him to weed his garden. Should Tiger pay someone to weed his garden, even if that person takes longer to weed the garden than Tiger Woods? Yes, if Tiger pays that person less than $1,000. If Tiger pays someone $200 to weed his garden, Tiger has a weed-free garden, and $800 (the $1,000 he earned minus the $200 he paid). If Tiger weeds his garden himself, he has only a weed-free garden. In this case, Tiger Woods is better off paying someone to weed his garden.

> 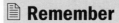 **Remember**
>
> A voluntary trade between two people will always leave both people better off.

2.4 The Principle of Diminishing Returns

The principle of diminishing returns says that if we produce output using two or more inputs and change the amount of only one input, beyond some point output will increase at a decreasing rate.

 Think of a local fast-food restaurant and imagine that they currently have only two workers on a shift. If the restaurant hired an additional person for that shift, would they be able to serve more food? Yes. That person could staff another register or cook more burgers, or take care of the drive-thru business. What if the restaurant kept hiring people? With a fixed number of registers, preparation areas or grill space, it would be harder for additional workers to add much to output because of the fixed amount of capital. In fact, at some point the workers would start to get into each other's way and output might actually fall as we hire more workers.

Let's review an Application that answers a key question we posed at the start of the chapter:

5. Do farmers experience diminishing returns?

APPLICATION 5: FERTILIZER AND CROP YIELDS

Adding fertilizer increases crop yields, but after adding the first bag, each additional bag adds less to our output than the previous bag. So, as you can see in Table 2.1, adding the first bag of fertilizer increases output by 35 bushels per acre. The second bag increases output by only 15 bushels, and each additional bag of fertilizer adds a smaller amount to output. This is the principle of diminishing returns. More fertilizer increases output, but each additional bag adds a smaller and smaller amount to total output.

> 📄 **Remember**
>
> Diminishing returns refers to the rate of change in output: Output grows at a smaller rate as we add additional units of a variable input. Diminishing returns does *not* refer to the level of output.

2.5 The Real–Nominal Principle

This principle states that what matters to people is the purchasing power of money, not its face value. Suppose that you earn $500 per month, and you spend $250 on rent, $150 on food, and $100 on entertainment. If your money income increases to $1,000, are you better off? If prices stay the same you are because you'll be able to buy more things. If, however, your rent increases to $500, food to $300, and the cost of entertainment to $200, you are no better off earning $1,000 than you were earning $500. Why? What you can purchase with your money income is the same in both cases.

> 📄 **Remember**
>
> The important concern in economics is not how many dollars you have, but what you can purchase with those dollars. This is why we distinguish between real and nominal amounts.

Let's review two Applications that answer key questions we posed at the start of the chapter:

6. How does inflation affect the real minimum wage?

APPLICATION 6: THE DECLINING REAL MINIMUM WAGE

Would you rather earn $2 per hour or $5.15 per hour? The answer depends on what you can buy with that money. Even though at $5.15 per hour the dollar amount of the minimum wage is higher in 2005 than it was in 1974, the purchasing power of the 1974 minimum wage of $2 per hour was much greater. That is, even though you earned a smaller number of dollars (the **nominal value**, or the face value of an amount of money) those fewer dollars were able to purchase more stuff (the **real value**, or the value of money in terms of the quantity of goods it can buy).

7. How does inflation affect lenders and borrowers?

APPLICATION 7: REPAYING STUDENT LOANS

Inflation reduces the purchasing power of a given sum of money. Borrowers may like inflation (as they give up fewer goods in repaying their loans) while lenders do not like inflation (the nominal dollars they receive in repayment can't buy as much as the dollars they loaned). When the nominal amount of the loan is fixed, inflation allows the loan to be repaid in less time. Deflation increases the amount of time that it takes to repay the loan.

Activity

Suppose that you earn $12 per hour. (That's the same as 20 cents per minute.) Think about the following situations and consider the opportunity cost involved.

a. At the grocery store you have the choice to spend $1.50 for a package of unsliced mushrooms or to spend $1.90 for a package of pre-sliced mushrooms. How long would you have to spend slicing mushrooms to be better off buying the presliced mushrooms?

b. There are two gas stations on opposite corners of the street. One sells gasoline for $2.35 per gallon, the other for $2.32 per gallon. Your gas tank holds 10 gallons of gas. There is a line at the gas station with the lower price, and you anticipate that you will spend five minutes waiting in that line. You could buy gas now at the gas station with the higher prices. What should you do?

Answers

a. Since you can earn 20 cents per minute, if you would spend more than 2 minutes slicing mushrooms you should buy the presliced mushrooms.

b. You will save 30 cents buying gasoline at the lower priced station since you save 3 cents per gallon on each of the 10 gallons that you purchase. In terms of time, 30 cents is only one and a half minutes. You are better off buying the higher priced gasoline.

Key Terms

Marginal benefit: The extra benefit resulting from a small increase in some activity.

Marginal cost: The additional cost resulting from a small increase in some activity.

Nominal value: The face value of an amount of money.

Opportunity cost: What you sacrifice to get something.

Production possibilities curve: A curve that shows the possible combinations of products that an economy can produce, given that its productive resources are fully employed and efficiently used.

Real value: The value of an amount of money in terms of what it can buy.

Practice Quiz

(Answers are provided at the end of the Practice Quiz.)

1. The principle of opportunity cost evolves from the concept of:
   a. consumer spending.
   b. wealth.
   c. poverty.
   d. scarcity.

2. A friend offers you a Coke, a Pepsi, or a Diet Coke. You don't like Diet Coke, so after some thought, you take the Pepsi. What is the opportunity cost of your choice?
   a. The Pepsi
   b. The Coke
   c. The Coke plus the Diet Coke
   d. The Coke plus the Diet Coke plus the Pepsi

3. Which of the following is NOT an opportunity cost of attending college?
   a. The wages that you could have earned while going to class
   b. Tuition
   c. The cost of books
   d. The cost of housing

4. This question tests your understanding of Application 1 in this chapter. From the choices A, B, and C below, choose the ones that you would include in your estimate of the opportunity cost of doing business:

   A: The expenses for fuel and other supplies
   B: The interest that the funds invested in the business could have earned at the bank or elsewhere
   C: The value of your time when used in the best alternative activity

a. A and B
b. B and C
c. A and C
d. A, B, and C

5. The table below shows the production possibilities for an economy that produces two goods: lobsters and boats. What is the opportunity cost of moving from point C to point D?

	Lobsters	Boats
A	0	10
B	100	9
C	200	7
D	300	4
E	400	0

a. 3 boats
b. 100 lobsters
c. 100 lobsters and 3 boats
d. 4 boats

6. Refer to the graph below. Which move best describes an increase in efficiency in the use of existing resources?

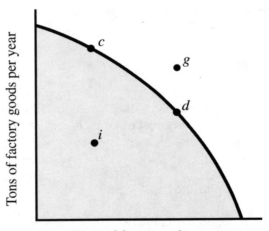

Tons of farm goods per year

a. A move from *i* to *d*
b. A move from *c* to *d*
c. A move from *d* to *g*
d. None of the above. Higher efficiency in the use of resources is not represented by a move but by a shift of the production possibilities curve.

7. Refer to the graph below. At which point, or points, are resources fully and efficiently employed?

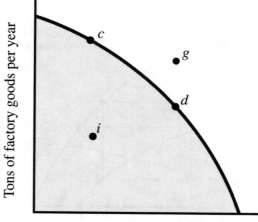

a. At points *c* and *d* only
b. At point *g* only
c. At points *c*, *d*, and *g*
d. At point *i* only

8. Refer to the graph below. Which of the following factors can cause a move from point *d* to points *g* or *h*?

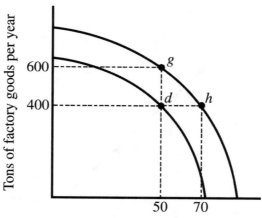

a. The economy's resources increase.
b. The opportunity cost of producing farm goods or factory goods changes.
c. The economy utilizes its resources fully.
d. Resources that used to be more suitable for producing farm goods are now perfectly adaptable to the production of either farm goods or factory goods.

9. Refer to the graph below. According to this graph, the opportunity cost of producing an additional 20 tons of wheat, from 140 to 160 tons, is:

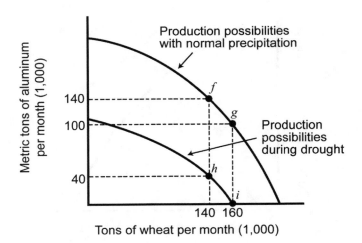

a. higher with normal precipitation than during a drought.
b. higher during a drought than with normal precipitation.
c. the same with normal precipitation or during a drought.
d. zero during a drought.

10. Refer to the graph below. What can we conclude about opportunity cost based on the shape of this production possibilities curve?

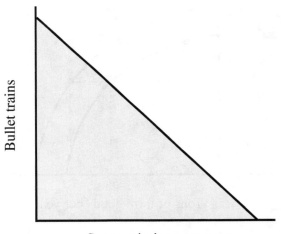

a. The curve shows that as more of a good is produced, the higher the opportunity cost of producing that good.
b. Resources appear to be perfectly substitutable, or equally adaptable to the production of either bullet trains or space missions.
c. We can conclude that as you move downward along the curve, the opportunity cost of producing bullet trains decreases.
d. The economy's resources are abundant.

11. Refer to the table below. What is the marginal benefit of the fourth slice of pizza?

Slices of Pizza	Total Cost	Total Benefit
1	$1.50	$4.00
2	$3.00	$7.00
3	$4.50	$9.00
4	$6.00	$10.50
5	$7.50	$10.75

    a. $6.00
    b. $1.50
    c. $10.50
    d. $4.50

12. The table below shows the marginal benefit that Ted earns from keeping his store open one more hour. Ted has a marginal cost of $70 per hour. How many hours should Ted stay open?

Hours	Marginal Benefit Per Hour
20	200
21	140
22	110
23	70
24	40
25	10
26	0

    a. 21
    b. 22
    c. 23
    d. 24

13. This question tests your understanding of Application 3 in this chapter: Continental Airlines uses the marginal principle. How do firms think at the margin? In the 1960s, Continental Airlines puzzled observers of the airline industry and dismayed its stockholders by running flights with up to half the seats empty. When the marginal principle is applied in the decision of whether or not to run an additional flight, which costs should the firm include in that decision?
    a. Only the costs that vary with the additional flights offered
    b. Only the fixed costs, or the costs that do not vary with the additional flights offered
    c. Both the costs that vary and the costs that do not vary with the additional flights offered
    d. The proper costs to be included, whether it is the costs that vary with additional flights or the fixed costs, depend on how many flights are not running.

14. The optimal amount of an activity is determined at the point where the activity yields:
    a. maximum marginal benefit.
    b. minimum marginal cost.
    c. equal value of marginal benefit and marginal cost.
    d. zero marginal cost.

15. Refer to the graph below. The price line indicates the additional revenue (or additional benefit) obtained from selling an additional unit of output. The marginal cost curve shows the cost of producing an additional unit. What is the optimal level of output?

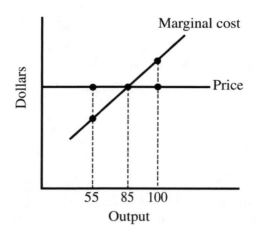

a. 55 units, where price is greater than marginal cost
b. 85 units, where price equals marginal cost
c. 100 units, where price is below marginal cost
d. Either 55 units or 100 units, or as long as price differs from marginal cost

16. This question tests your understanding of Application 5 in this chapter: Fertilizer and crop yields. Do farmers experience diminishing returns? The table below shows the relationship between the amount of fertilizer and the corn output, all else the same.

Table 2.1	FERTILIZER AND CORN YIELD
Bags of Fertilizer	**Bushels of Corn Per Acre**
0	85
1	120
2	135
3	144
4	147

What causes a farmer to experience diminishing returns?
a. The fact that he doubles up all of his inputs at once in order to increase his crop yield.
b. The fact that he changes just one of the inputs, fertilizer, in order to increase crop yield.
c. The ability of the farmer to increase his crop yield faster than the rate of increase in fertilizer.
d. The farmer experiences diminishing returns anytime this year's crop is less than last year's crop.

17. Which of the following key principles of economics is the principle of voluntary exchange?
a. If participation in a market is voluntary, both the buyer and the seller must be better off as a result of a transaction.
b. What matters to people is the real value of money or income—its purchasing power—not the face value of money or income.
c. What matters in decision making is what happens at the margin.
d. The opportunity cost of something is what you sacrifice to get it.

18. From the principle of voluntary exchange, we conclude that:
    a. often buyers are made better off and sellers are worse off when an exchange is made.
    b. often sellers are made better off and buyers are worse off when an exchange is made.
    c. both the buyer and the seller must be better off as a result of a transaction.
    d. both the buyer and the seller might be worse off as a result of a transaction.

19. According to the real-nominal principle, what matters to workers is the real wage rate (or purchasing power of wages). The real wage rate:
    a. always increases when the nominal wage rate increases.
    b. always increases when the nominal wage rate decreases.
    c. may increase or decrease when nominal wages change.
    d. will not change with a change in the nominal wage rate.

20. Which of the following is NOT an example of nominal value?
    a. A price shown on a clothing tag in a retail store
    b. The value you could sell your house for at an auction today
    c. Tuition costs that are adjusted for inflation
    d. The amount of money you receive from the bank as interest on a deposit

21. James has enough money to buy a car at the market price from fifteen years ago, but that amount of money is only half of what he would need to buy it today. Which principle does this problem represent?
    a. The principle of opportunity cost
    b. The principle of voluntary exchange
    c. The principle of diminishing returns
    d. The real-nominal principle

22. During your next job interview, you will use the marginal principle to explain why you should be hired. What will you say?

23. Think about opportunity cost. What is the opportunity cost of you attending college? Write a short essay describing what it *really* costs you to attend.

24. Which economic principles are involved in the analysis of scarcity using a production possibilities curve?

25. Among the reasons for the use of marginal analysis in economics is that there are natural and technical constraints that prevent us from achieving unlimited results. Provide five examples of situations in which additional effort yields diminishing returns.

Answers to the Practice Quiz

1. d. The concept of opportunity cost is based on the principle of scarcity. Because resources are scarce, there exists a tradeoff for every choice you make.

2. b. Opportunity cost is the value of your next best choice, which in this case, is the Coke.

3. d. Housing is not an opportunity cost because you have to live somewhere anyway. However, you are implicitly giving up the wages that you could have earned.

4. b. Opportunity costs are costs stated in terms of the alternative use, such as how the funds could have been used, or the value of your time when used in the best alternative activity.

5. a. Three boats must be sacrificed (7 - 4) in order to increase the production of lobsters by 100.

6. a. When the economy moves from a point inside to a point on the production possibilities curve, resources become fully and efficiently employed.

7. a. As long as a point lies on the curve, resources are fully and efficiently employed at that point.

8. a. An increase in the amount of resources available to the economy shifts the production possibilities curve outward.

9. c. In both instances, the economy must give up to 40 metric tons of aluminum in order to increase wheat production from 140 to 160 tons.

10. b. Since the production possibilities curve is a straight line, the opportunity cost remains constant as you move downward along the line. A linear production possibilities curve reflects perfect substitutability of resources in production.

11. b. The marginal benefit is the extra benefit provided by the 4th slice of pizza: $10.50 - $9.00 = $1.50.

12. c. The marginal benefit of the 23rd hour is $70, and at this point, marginal benefit is equal to marginal cost.

13. a. In the case of the airline, only the costs that vary with the additional flights offered, such as the cost of a flight crew, jet fuel, and food service should be included when the marginal principle is applied to the decision to run an additional flight. Fixed costs, such as airport fees and the cost of running the reservation system, should not be included in the decision to run an additional flight because these costs would be incurred whether the flight runs or not.

14. c. According to the marginal principle, we should increase the level of an activity if its marginal benefit exceeds its marginal cost; reduce the level of an activity if its marginal cost exceeds its marginal benefit. If possible, pick the level at which the activity's marginal benefit equals its marginal cost. Maximum, minimum, or zero are not the measures of optimality.

15. b. Stop the level of an activity where marginal benefit (or price in this case) equals marginal cost.

16. b. The notion of diminishing returns applies to all inputs to the production process. Because the farmer is changing just one of the inputs, fertilizer, the output will increase, but at a decreasing rate. Eventually, additional fertilizer will actually decrease output as the other nutrients in the soil are overwhelmed by the fertilizer.

17. a. According to the principle of voluntary exchange, a voluntary exchange between two people makes both people better off.

18. c. According to the principle of voluntary exchange, if participation in a market is voluntary, both the buyer and the seller must be better off as a result of a transaction.

19. c. Changes in the real wage rate depend not only on the nominal wage rate but also on the price level.

20. c. When costs are adjusted for inflation, they represent real values. An increase in prices due to inflation does not represent an actual increase in the amount of the good or service provided.

21. d. The real value of a good is a sum of money in terms of the quantity of good it can buy. The real value of this car has not changed—only its nominal value, the face value of a sum of money, has changed.

22. In accordance with the marginal principle, you should be hired because the additional cost to the company (your salary and benefits) will outweigh the contributions you will make to the firm, or the additional revenue the firm will obtain from your productive activity.

23. What is the opportunity cost of a college degree? Consider a student who spends a total of $40,000 for tuition and books. Instead of going to college, the student could have spent this money on a wide variety of goods, including housing, stereo equipment, and world travel. Part of the opportunity cost of college is the $40,000 worth of other goods the student sacrifices to pay for tuition and books. Also, instead of going to college, the student could have worked as a bank clerk for $20,000 per year and earned $80,000 over four years. That makes the total opportunity cost of this student's college degree $120,000.

24. The production possibilities curve involves two of the fundamental principles: the principle of opportunity cost, and the principle of diminishing returns. The principle of opportunity cost is described by a move from one point to another along the curve. The curve shows combinations of two goods, or sets of goods, that can be produced when resources are fully and efficiently employed.

    As we increase the production of one good, we must sacrifice some of the other good. The principle of diminishing returns explains the shape of the curve. The curve is bowed out because resources are not perfectly substitutable in production. For this reason, it takes an ever greater amount of resources to produce additional units of a good, particularly when the production of that good is already high.

25. a. Additional water into a flowerpot does not cause a flower to grow proportionally to the amount of water added.
    b. As speed rises, it becomes harder and harder to gain an extra mile of speed.
    c. As consumption rises, an extra bite does not yield as much satisfaction as the previous one.
    d. The knowledge gained from an extra hour of study is less than the knowledge gained from the previous hour, particularly when you have been studying for a long time already.
    e. In an eight-hour workday, the productivity of the last hour is smaller than the productivity of the first hour.

3

Exchange and Markets

Chapter Summary

This chapter explores specialization and exchange as well as the virtues and shortcomings of markets. Here are the main points of the chapter:

- It is sensible for a person to produce the product for which he or she has a comparative advantage, that is, a lower opportunity cost than another person.
- Specialization increases productivity through the division of labor, a result of the benefits of repetition, continuity, and innovation.
- A system of international specialization and trade is sensible because nations have different opportunity costs of producing goods, giving rise to comparative advantages.
- Under a market system, self-interested people, guided by prices, make the decisions about what products to produce, how to produce them, and who gets them.
- Government roles in a market economy include establishing the rules for exchange, reducing economic uncertainty, and responding to market failures.

Applying the Concepts

After reading this chapter, you should be able to answer these three key questions:
1. How many jobs are lost to outsourcing—the shift of production to other countries?
2. Does the protection of one domestic industry harm another?
3. Why do markets develop wherever people go?

3.1 Comparative Advantage and Exchange

The concept of comparative advantage is an application of the principle of opportunity cost from Chapter 2.

 Principle of Opportunity Cost

The opportunity cost of an item is what you must sacrifice to get the item.

To get more of one item you must sacrifice some other item. For Fred and Kate in the survivor example, the opportunity cost of a coconut is the number of fish that could have been produced in the time it takes to produce one coconut.

Trade is based on **comparative advantage**, the ability of one person or nation to produce a good at a lower opportunity cost than another person or nation. If Fred wishes to consume both fish and coconuts he can either produce both goods, or he can buy one of the goods from Kate. Since Kate can produce coconuts at a lower opportunity cost than Fred, he would prefer to buy coconuts from her. Trade encourages individuals to specialize, and in so doing, increase the total output produced by all parties.

Trade benefits both parties, even if one person can produce more of both goods. We define **absolute advantage** as the ability of one person or nation to produce a product at a lower resource cost than another person or nation. While Fred spends less time producing each coconut than does Kate, he still wants to buy coconuts from her because she gives up fewer fish to produce a coconut than does Fred. Fred gives up fewer fish buying coconuts from Kate than he would give up producing coconuts on his own. This is an example of the principle of voluntary exchange from Chapter 2. As long as Fred and Kate both agree to the trade, both will be better off as a result of the trade.

> ## 📄 Remember
>
> It is important to recognize that we are concerned with opportunity cost, the amount of one good which must be foregone to produce some other good. Comparative advantage refers to who has the lowest opportunity cost of producing a certain good. Be sure that you are comfortable not only understanding the concept of opportunity cost, but calculating opportunity costs as well.
>
> Trade is based not on who can produce the most of a good, but who can produce a good at the lowest cost. Thus, trade is based on comparative, not absolute, advantage.

3.2 Comparative Advantage and International Trade

Countries also engage in trade. An **import** is defined as a product produced in a foreign country and purchased by residents of the home country. An example of an import would be a Hyundai car, which is produced in Korea and sold in the United States. An **export** is a product produced in the home country and sold in another country. An example of an export would be agricultural products produced in the United States and sold in other countries.

Let's review two Applications that answer key questions we posed at the beginning of the chapter:

1. How many jobs are lost to outsourcing—the shift of production to other countries?

APPLICATION 1: MOVING JOBS TO DIFFERENT STATES AND DIFFERENT COUNTRIES

Firms take advantage of the principle of comparative advantage to shift production to facilities around the world. This practice is known as outsourcing or offshoring. This Application suggests that the employment effects of outsourcing are smaller than we may think. Estimates suggest that only 2 percent of layoffs in the first three months of 2004 were due to job movement overseas. In addition, lower labor costs reduce the prices that consumers have to pay and allow firms to produce more output.

☞ It is also worth remembering that while some U.S. companies are shifting production overseas, some non-U.S. companies are shifting jobs into the United States. Toyota, BMW, and Mercedes all have production plants in the United States. From Japan's perspective, Toyota jobs in Georgetown, Kentucky would be viewed as "outsourced."

☞ To see how "outsourcing" can increase the number of jobs, think about the Tiger Woods example in Chapter 2. If Tiger Woods earns $1,000 while paying his gardener $200 to weed his garden, Tiger Woods now has an additional $800 he can spend on goods and services. In fact, he might decide to spend some of the extra money hiring a personal chef. The same holds true for companies that move some jobs overseas. By lowering labor costs in one area, this provides additional resources for the firm to hire other types of labor.

📄 Remember

Principles of trade are the same whether we are examining individuals, firms, or countries. Total output increases when individuals or countries specialize in those goods for which they have a comparative advantage. Voluntary trade between individuals or countries makes both parties to the trade better off.

---

2. Does the protection of one domestic industry harm another?

APPLICATION 2: CANDY CANE MAKERS MOVE TO MEXICO FOR CHEAP SUGAR

To keep the price of sugar high, the U.S. government restricts the amount of sugar which can be imported into the United States. This restriction leads to price disparities for sugar in the U.S. relative to other countries. This Application states that sugar costs six cents per pound in Mexico, but twenty-one cents per pound in the United States. Because of this cost disparity, candy makers have relocated to Mexico to take advantage of lower sugar costs. Since 1998 about 3,000 candy making jobs have left the Chicago area in part because of the difference in sugar prices between the United States and other countries. While the trade restrictions benefit U.S. sugar producers, they harm U.S. workers involved in candy production.

3.3 Markets

A **market economy** is one in which people specialize and exchange goods and services in a market. Most of us specialize in a few things and exchange our time doing those things for money. We then trade money for the other goods and services we wish to consume. In this situation money is a medium of exchange. At the most basic level we trade our time for money, and use the money to facilitate trades for other goods.

There are a number of inventions that help markets work better:
- Contracts: Specify terms of exchange and rights and obligations of the parties to the exchange.
- Insurance: Reduces the risk from low probability, random events such as severe storms.
- Patents: Encourage innovation in new products.
- Accounting rules: Provide a common set of information on the financial status of firms.

In contrast to a market economy, a **centrally planned economy** is one in which a planning authority decides how much of each good to produce, how to produce the goods, and who gets them. In a market system these same decisions are made in a very decentralized manner with prices providing the information about relative scarcity and the incentive to provide goods by means of higher prices for goods that are relatively scarce.

To see the challenges of a centrally planned economy, suppose you were in charge of securing all the food and clothing needed in your city. Could you imagine the amount of information you would need to identify all the food products that stores should carry or trying to arrange for the production of all those products? How much should you pay the workers who produce those goods? Where will those goods be produced? What about the transportation to bring them to the stores? The market system answers these questions using prices to convey information to decentralized decision makers. The market provides incentive for farmers to grow food that people wish to eat, for truckers to transport the food from the farm to the stores and for grocery managers to stock the shelves with the food that people want to buy. As you will see later in the text, profits and losses provide incentives for firms to enter and exit markets.

📄 Remember

Prices serve an important function in markets. Prices provide information and incentives to participants in markets to provide the goods and services demanded by the market.

Let's review an Application that answers one of the key questions we posed at the start of the chapter:

3. Why do markets develop wherever people go?

APPLICATION 3: MARKETS IN A PRISONER OF WAR CAMP

Markets exist as a way to allocate goods and services to those who desire them. This Application illustrates that principle in POW camps during World War II. Prisoners all received the same goods, regardless of their desire for the goods. Prisoners would then trade for the goods they desired, using cigarettes as "money." You can see in this example how these trades improved the allocation of goods as tea-drinking British prisoners were able to trade unwanted coffee for other, more desirable goods.

3.4 Market Failure and the Role of Government

In general, markets work well and allocate resources to those who most value the resources. There are some circumstances in which markets don't do a very good job of allocating resources. These situations are known as market failure. In these cases government can intervene in the market and improve outcomes. Some examples of market failures you will study later in the book are:

- Pollution. What happens when one person's action negatively impacts someone else? Government can force polluters to consider the costs they impose on others in the economy. An example would be a tax requiring polluters to bear the cost that their actions impose on others. The tax provides a financial incentive for polluters to reduce the amount of pollution they produce.
- Public goods. What if we can't keep non-payers from consuming a good, such as a fireworks display? What if more people could use a good at no additional cost of providing the good? How do markets respond in these cases? In most cases, markets will not provide an appropriate amount of public goods, which requires the government to step in and encourage production or in many cases produce the goods itself. Police protection would be an example of a public good.
- Imperfect information. What happens in a market if the buyers of a product know less about the product's condition than the sellers? Government can take steps to provide complete information so that both sides of the market can make an informed decision. For example, the government requires that food manufacturers provide nutritional information on labels so consumers can know what is contained in the food they are eating.

- Imperfect competition. What happens when only a few firms exist in a market? Think about a utility that is the only provider of electricity in a particular area. Government will regulate the prices that the utility can charge so that it can't exploit its monopoly power.

The government plays other roles in the market economy as well, including:
- enforcing property rights.
- establishing and enforcing rules for market exchange.
- reducing economic uncertainty and providing social insurance.

Activity

Darrin Hobbes is a very skilled carpenter, though his regular career is practicing law. At the moment, Darrin is trying to put an addition on his house. He estimates that it would take him 3 weekends of work, working eight hours a day on Saturday and Sunday to complete the addition. This means it would take Darrin 48 hours of time to complete the addition.

WeBuildIt Contractors has provided Darrin an estimate to complete the addition to his house. They estimate that they would have two people spend 4 days at Darrin's house to complete the addition. This is a total of 64 hours to complete the addition. WeBuildIt charges $35 per labor hour.

a. Who has the absolute advantage in completing the addition? Why?
b. What would it cost Darrin to pay WeBuildIt to complete the addition? _____
c. Suppose Darrin earns $60 per hour in his legal practice and can work as many hours as he chooses. What would it cost Darrin to build the addition himself? _____
d. Who has the comparative advantage in completing the addition? Why?

Answers
a. Darrin, because it will take him 48 hours as opposed to 80 hours to do the same work.
b. It would cost $35(64) = $2,240 to have WeBuildIt complete the addition.
c. It would cost Darrin $60(48) = $2,880 to complete the addition himself.
d. WeBuildIt Contractors has the comparative advantage because the company can do the work at a lower cost than Darrin.

Key Terms

Absolute advantage: The ability of one person or nation to produce a product at a lower resource cost than another person or nation.

Centrally planned economy: An economy in which a government bureaucracy decides how much of each good to produce, how to produce the goods, and who gets them.

Comparative advantage: The ability of one person or nation to produce a good at a lower opportunity cost than another person or nation.

Export: A product produced in the home country and sold in another country.

Import: A product produced in a foreign country and purchased by a resident of the home country.

Market economy: An economy in which people specialize and exchange goods and services in markets.

Practice Quiz

(Answers are provided at the end of the Practice Quiz.)

1. Which of the following is NOT among the fundamental questions that every economy must solve?
   a. What goods and services will be produced?
   b. How will the goods and services be produced?
   c. At what prices will goods and services be exchanged?
   d. Who will receive the goods and services produced?

2. When people participate in markets, they are encouraged to practice:
   a. self-sufficiency.
   b. specialization.
   c. restraint in consumption.
   d. care in selecting the government officials that run the markets.

3. Which of the following key principles of economics do we use to explore the details of specialization?
   a. The nominal-real principle
   b. The principle of diminishing returns
   c. The principle of opportunity cost
   d. The marginal principle

4. Absolute advantage is the ability of an individual, firm, or country to:
   a. produce more of a good or service than competitors using the same amount of resources.
   b. produce a good or service at a lower opportunity cost than other producers.
   c. consume more goods or services than others at lower costs.
   d. reach a higher production possibilities frontier by raising opportunity costs.

5. We say that a person has a comparative advantage in producing a particular product if he or she:
   a. is self-sufficient.
   b. also has an absolute advantage.
   c. has a lower opportunity cost than another person.
   d. All of the above

6. According to the theory of comparative advantage, specialization and free trade will benefit:
   a. only the owner of a monopoly.
   b. all trading parties who specialize in the production of the good in which they have a comparative advantage.
   c. only that trading party that has an absolute advantage in the production of all goods.
   d. only the party which specializes the most.

7. The table below shows the maximum output of widgets and gadgets for two countries: Utopia and Nirvana. Which of the following is correct?

	Widgets	Gadgets
Utopia	1000	1000
Nirvana	500	250

   a. Nirvana has a comparative advantage in both goods.
   b. Utopia has a comparative advantage in both goods.
   c. Nirvana has a comparative advantage in widgets.
   d. Nirvana has a comparative advantage in gadgets.

8. Refer to the table below. Which of the following statements is correct?

	Cakes	Pies
Jorge	5	10
Rocky	4	6

   a. Rocky has the comparative advantage in pies.
   b. Jorge has the absolute and comparative advantage in pies.
   c. Jorge has a comparative advantage but not an absolute advantage in pies.
   d. Rocky has an absolute advantage but not a comparative advantage in pies.

9. The fact that specialization and exchange make people better off is an illustration of one of these principles. Which one?
   a. The principle of voluntary exchange
   b. The principle of diminishing returns
   c. The principle of opportunity cost
   d. The marginal principle

10. In his 1776 book *An Inquiry into the Nature and Causes of the Wealth of Nations*, Adam Smith noted that specialization increases productivity. Which of the following was the cause of this phenomenon?
   a. Increased slavery
   b. Combining various steps into a single job raised productivity
   c. Turning small factories into large factories
   d. The division of labor

11. A product produced in a foreign country and purchased by residents of the home country is called:
   a. an import.
   b. an export.
   c. self-sufficiency.
   d. outsourcing.

12. Which of the following is NOT a reason for the increase in productivity that comes with specialization?
   a. Repetition
   b. Continuity
   c. Innovation
   d. Absolute advantage

13. Contracts, insurance, patents, and accounting rules are:
    a. things that came naturally with the creation of markets.
    b. ideas that are unnecessary in a free-market place.
    c. inventions that make a market work better.
    d. enforced primarily in non-market economies, such as centrally planned economies.

14. In what type of economy does the government decide how economic resources will be allocated?
    a. In a market economy
    b. In a centrally planned economy
    c. In both of the above
    d. In none of the above. The government does not allocate resources in any type of economy.

15. In a market system, which of the following provides the information that individuals need to make decisions?
    a. Primarily, the government
    b. Public libraries
    c. Prices
    d. Production costs

16. Whenever markets do not produce the most efficient outcomes on their own, we call this phenomenon:
    a. the invisible hand.
    b. market failure.
    c. absolute disaster.
    d. diminishing returns.

17. Refer to the figure below. Each graph represents one country. Which country in this graph has a comparative advantage in the production of shirts?

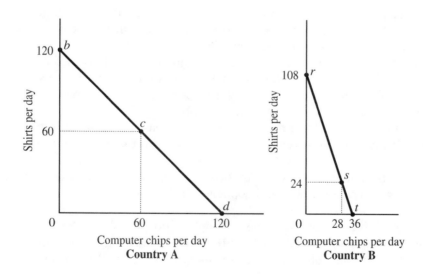

Country A

Country B

    a. Country A
    b. Country B
    c. Neither country
    d. Both countries

18. Refer to the figure below. Each graph represents one country. Which country in this graph should specialize in the production of chips?

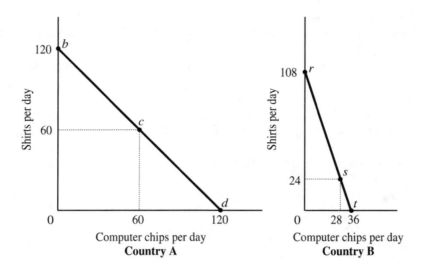

    a.   Country A
    b.   Country B
    c.   Neither country. They both should produce some chips.
    d.   Both countries should specialize in the production of chips.

19. This question tests your understanding of Application 1 in this chapter: Moving jobs to different states and different countries. How many jobs are lost to outsourcing—the shift of production to other countries?

    The impact of outsourcing on the domestic economy can be summarized as follows:
    a.   Outsourcing has resulted in a substantial loss of jobs, insignificant cost savings for outsourcing companies, higher prices for consumers, and less output for firms.
    b.   Outsourcing has resulted in a minimal loss of jobs, as well as significant cost savings for domestic companies, lower prices for consumers, and more output for firms.
    c.   The results of outsourcing have been mixed. Lower prices for consumers have been overshadowed by a substantial loss of domestic jobs.
    d.   The benefits of outsourcing have not outlasted the increases in communication costs and the costs of the standardization of software necessary to allow firms to outsource business services.

20. This question tests your understanding of Application 3 in this chapter: Markets in a prisoner of war camp. Why do markets develop wherever people go?

    To illustrate the pervasiveness of exchange, this application illustrates the emergence of markets in prisoner of war (POW) camps in World War II, as documented by economist R. A. Radford. The exchange of goods that took place among prisoners of war (POWs) during World War II is an example of how:

    a.   markets cannot work properly when severe restrictions are imposed on people.
    b.   markets in restricted places, such as prisoner camps, work poorly because product prices do not reflect the actual scarcity of goods.

c. even in prisoner camps, the market system can work because people, motivated by self-interest, rely on exchange to make themselves better off.

d. exchange that takes place through barter does not allow for the emergence of markets. Only monetary economies can support market exchange.

Answers to the Practice Quiz

1. c. The three questions are: What goods and services will be produced? How will the goods and services be produced? Who will receive the goods and services produced?

2. b. A market is an institution or arrangement that enables people to buy and sell things. The alternative to buying and selling in markets is to be self-sufficient, with each of us producing everything we need for ourselves. Rather than going it alone, most of us specialize: We produce one or two products for others and then exchange the money we earn for the products we want to consume.

3. c. A person specializes in the good for which he or she has a lower opportunity cost. We say that a person has a comparative advantage in producing a particular product if he or she has a lower opportunity cost than another person's marginal cost.

4. a.. Absolute advantage is the ability of an individual, firm, or country to produce more of a good or service than competitors using the same amount of resources.

5. c. The lesson is that those who are self-sufficient have an incentive to specialize and trade. Having an absolute advantage does not guarantee that a country also has a comparative advantage. We say that a person has a comparative advantage in producing a particular product if he or she has a lower opportunity cost than another person.

6. b. According to the theory of comparative advantage, if both nations specialize and trade in the production of goods/services in which they have a comparative advantage, both nations will be better off.

7. c. Utopia's opportunity cost is 1 for either good. Nirvana's opportunity cost of widgets is $250/500 = 1/2$. Since $1/2 < 1$, Nirvana has a comparative advantage in widgets.

8. b. Jorge can produce more pies per hour than Rocky, thus Jorge has an absolute advantage in pies. Jorge also has to give up less cake for each pie than Rocky. Thus, Jorge also has a comparative advantage.

9. a. The fact that specialization and exchange make both people better off illustrates the key principle of voluntary exchange.

10. d. Adam Smith explains how the making of a pin is divided into many operations, and then he points to the very high output that can be produced in that factory through such division of labor.

11. a. An import is a product produced in a foreign country and purchased by residents of the home country.

12. d. Repetition, continuity, and innovation are the three reasons that cause an increase in productivity that comes with specialization.

13. c. Although it appears that markets arose naturally, a number of social and government inventions have made them work better: Contracts, insurance, patents, and accounting rules are part of those inventions.

14. b. A mixed economy is an economy in which most economic decisions result from the interaction of buyers and sellers in markets, but where the government plays a significant role in the allocation of resources.

15. c. Under a market system, decisions are made by the thousands of people who already have information about consumers' desires, production technology, and resources. These decisions are guided by prices of inputs and outputs. In a market system, prices provide individuals the information they need to make decisions. Prices provide signals about the relative scarcity of a product and help an economy respond to scarcity.

16. b. "Market failure" is what happens when markets fail to produce the most efficient outcomes on their own. The role of government is to correct this problem.

17. b. The opportunity costs are as follows: The opportunity cost of shirts is: 1 chip for country A, and 1/3 chip for country B. The opportunity cost of chips is: 1 shirt for country A and 3 shirts for country B. Country B has a comparative advantage in the production of shirts because it sacrifices fewer chips to produce one shirt. Country B should therefore produce shirts.

18. a. The opportunity costs are as follows: The opportunity cost of shirts is: 1 chip for country A, and 1/3 chip for country B. The opportunity cost of chips is: 1 shirt for country A and 3 shirts for country B. Therefore, country A has a comparative advantage (or lower opportunity cost) in the production of chips because it sacrifices fewer shirts to produce one chip. Country A should therefore produce chips.

19. b. According to recent studies, the benefits of outsourcing have significantly outweighed the costs. Outsourcing has resulted in a minimal loss of jobs, substantial cost savings for domestic companies, lower prices for consumers, and more output for firms.

20. c. The prisoners used barter to exchange one good for another, and cigarettes emerged as the medium of exchange. Prisoners wandered through the camp calling out their offers of goods. In addition to food, the prisoners bought and sold clothing (80 cigarettes per shirt), laundry services (two cigarettes per garment), and hot cups of coffee (two cigarettes per cup). The prices of products reflected their scarcity.

4
Demand, Supply, and Market Equilibrium

Chapter Summary

This chapter shows how demand and supply determine prices. In addition, this chapter illustrates how to predict the effects of changes in demand or supply on market prices and quantities. Here are the main points of the chapter:

- A market demand curve shows the relationship between the quantity demanded and price, *ceteris paribus*.
- A market supply curve shows the relationship between the quantity supplied and price, *ceteris paribus*.
- Equilibrium in a market is shown by the intersection of the demand curve and the supply curve. When a market reaches equilibrium, there is no pressure to change the price.
- A change in demand changes price and quantity in the same direction: An increase in demand increases the equilibrium price and quantity; a decrease in demand decreases the equilibrium price and quantity.
- A change in supply changes price and quantity in opposite directions: An increase in supply decreases price and increases quantity; a decrease in supply increases price and decreases quantity.

✎ Study Tip

In this chapter, pay careful attention to factors that shift the position of the demand and supply curves.

Applying the Concepts

After reading this chapter, you should be able to answer these five key questions:
1. How do changes in demand affect prices?
2. What could explain a decrease in price?
3. How does the adoption of new technology affect prices?
4. How do changes in supply affect prices?
5. How do changes in one market affect other markets?

4.1 The Demand Curve

The **quantity demanded** of a particular good is the amount of a product that consumers are willing and able to buy. A number of factors affect how much of a good a consumer wants to purchase:

- the price of the product.
- the consumer's income.
- the price of substitute and complement goods.
- the consumer's preferences or tastes.
- the consumer's expectations of future prices.

To begin we examine a **demand schedule**, a table that shows the relationship between the price of a product and the quantity demanded of that product. When we talk about a demand schedule, we assume that all of the other factors listed above (tastes, income, etc.) are held constant and only the price of the good changes. Figure 4.1 of the text shows both the demand schedule and the demand curve. The **demand curve** is a graphical representation of the demand schedule. The curve shows the relationship between the price of a good and the quantity demanded of that good.

An **individual demand curve** shows the relationship between the price of a good and the quantity demanded by an individual consumer. A **market demand curve** shows the relationship between price and quantity demanded by all consumers.

☞ Think of the students in your microeconomics class. Each of you has some desired number of music downloads that you would purchase each month at a variety of prices. The relationship between price and how many downloads you purchase in a month is your individual demand curve. If your class represented the entire market for music downloads, the market demand curve would be the total number of music downloads that people in the class would buy at a particular price. This exercise gives us the market quantity demanded at that price. When we do this for a number of different prices we can find the market demand schedule or the market demand curve.

As the price of a good rises, the quantity demanded decreases. This is known as the law of demand. Formally, the **law of demand** states that there is a negative relationship between price and quantity demanded, *ceteris paribus*. The movement along a demand curve is known as a **change in quantity demanded**. This refers to how the quantity purchased changes in response to a change in the price of a good.

4.2 The Supply Curve

Much of the logic for demand also applies to the supply side of the market. The **quantity supplied** is the amount of a product that firms are willing and able to sell. A number of factors affect the decision of the sellers:

- the price of the product.
- the price of inputs such as wages, cost of materials, cost of capital.
- production technology.
- expectations about future prices.
- government taxes and subsidies.

As Figure 4.3 in the text illustrates, we define a **supply schedule** as a table that shows the relationship between the price of a product and quantity supplied (holding all the other supply factors constant), and a **supply curve** as a curve showing the relationship between price and quantity supplied. Notice that these definitions are similar to the ones you learned for the demand schedule and the demand curve.

The **law of supply** states that there is a positive relationship between price and quantity supplied. This is true of both the **individual supply curve**, which shows the relationship between price and quantity supplied by an individual firm, and the **market supply curve**, which shows the relationship between price and quantity supplied by all firms. As output increases, the cost of producing each additional unit increases. This leads to an upward sloping supply curve. This is an application of the marginal principle:

 Marginal Principle

Increase the level of an activity as long as its marginal benefit exceeds its marginal cost. Choose the level at which the marginal benefit equals the marginal cost.

☞ As a way of thinking about supply, consider the market in which you are a supplier, the labor market. An employer offers you a wage (the price of labor) and you determine how many hours you are willing to work in exchange for that wage. If an employer offers you too little money (say $3 per hour) you will choose not to work at all. The price is below your **minimum supply price**, the lowest price at which a product will be supplied. As the wage offers increase you will become willing to work and at higher prices you will be willing to offer more hours of labor. You may be willing to work five hours per week for $6 per hour but if the wage is $10 per hour, you may be willing to work 15 hours per week. The market supply curve would illustrate the number of hours that all workers in the market would be willing to supply at each wage rate.

4.3 Market Equilibrium: Bringing Demand and Supply Together

We have seen that at each price, the quantity demanded tells us how many units buyers are willing to buy and the quantity supplied tells us how many units sellers are willing to sell. **Market equilibrium** occurs at the price where the quantity demanded is equal to the quantity supplied. The price at which this occurs is called the equilibrium price because it is the price that balances the quantity demanded and the quantity supplied. At this price buyers are buying all the goods they desire, sellers are selling all the goods they desire, and there is no pressure for the market price to change.

At prices other than the equilibrium there in an imbalance between the quantity supplied and the quantity demanded. You can see this in Figure 4.6 in the text. At prices below $8, buyers want to buy more pizzas per month than sellers want to sell. This situation is known as **excess demand**, or a **shortage**, a situation where the quantity demanded exceeds the quantity supplied at the prevailing price. In a situation of excess demand the price for a good will increase causing the quantity demanded to fall and the quantity supplied to rise until they are in equilibrium. A *price ceiling* (prices capped by law below equilibrium) will create excess demand in the affected market. Rent control would be an example of a price ceiling.

At prices above $8, suppliers are willing to sell more pizzas per month than demanders wish to purchase at those prices. This is known as an **excess supply** or **surplus**, a situation in which the quantity supplied exceeds the quantity demanded at the prevailing price. A *price floor* (prices held above equilibrium by law will create excess supply in the affected market. A minimum wage is an example of a price floor.

☞ To get a picture of this situation, imagine a concert coming to your campus. Now imagine people standing in line for concert tickets, with those in the front of the line having the highest willingness to pay, and those at the back of the line the lowest willingness to pay. The face value for the tickets is $25 and we will assume, for simplicity (see chapter 2), that each person in line wants to buy one ticket. If the number of people in line exceeds the number of tickets available then the ticket window will close while people are still waiting in line to buy tickets. This is a situation of excess demand and indicates that the face value for the tickets is too low relative to equilibrium. Some buyers will be unhappy because they will not be able to buy a ticket.

If the last person in line buys a ticket and the ticket office still has tickets available to sell, we have a surplus and we can infer that the price of the tickets is too high: There are more tickets available at that price than there are buyers for the tickets. The sellers will be unhappy because they will not be able to sell all their tickets.

At the equilibrium price, the last person in line will buy the last ticket available. All buyers and sellers will be happy as they are all able to make a trade at this price.

4.4 Market Effects of Changes in Demand

A **change in demand** occurs when a variable other than the price of the product changes. When demand changes, people want to buy more or less of a product at the same price. Since the price of the good has not changed, the demand curve must have shifted.

An *increase in demand* occurs when consumers want to buy more of a good holding the price constant. An increase in demand causes the equilibrium price and quantity to increase. Here are factors that increase demand:

- Increase in income. If a good is a **normal good**, an increase in income increases demand for the good. Restaurant meals would be an example of normal goods.
- Decrease in income. If a good is an **inferior good**, a decrease in income will increase demand. Store-brand cola would be an example of an inferior good.
- Increase in the price of a substitute. A **substitute** is a good for which an increase in the price of one good increases the demand for another good. As the price of coffee increases, we expect the demand for tea to increase, holding the price of tea constant.
- Decrease in the price of a complement. A **complement** is a good for which a decrease in the price of one good increases the demand for the other good. As the price of French fries falls, people will demand more ketchup, holding the price of ketchup constant.
- Increase in population. As more people enter the market, the amount of a good demanded at any price will increase. If 1,000 new students enroll at your university, the demand for spiral bound notebooks at the campus bookstore will increase, holding the price of the notebooks constant.
- Shift in consumer preferences. When a celebrity advertises a product, more people may want that product, holding the price of the product constant.
- Expectations of higher future prices. If we anticipate that the price of a good is going to increase in the future, we will demand more of the good, at its current price.

A *decrease in demand* occurs when consumers want to buy less of a good holding the price constant. A decrease in demand lowers the equilibrium quantity and price in the market. Here are the factors that decrease demand:

- Decrease in income. Consumers will buy fewer normal goods when their incomes decrease.
- Decrease in the price of a substitute good. If the price of going to the movies falls, there will be an increase in the quantity demanded of movies. Consumers will rent fewer movies, holding the price of movie rentals constant.
- Increase in the price of a complementary good. If the price of coffee increases, leading people to decrease their quantity demanded of coffee, the demand for cream will fall. People will buy less cream, holding the price of cream constant.
- Decrease in population. If the number of people in a market decreases, there will be fewer units of a good demanded, holding the price of the good constant.
- Shift in consumer tastes. A health scare such as E. coli in fresh spinach and mad cow disease in beef will cause people to want to buy fewer units of these goods, holding the price of the good constant.

- Expectation of lower future prices. If people anticipate that the price of a good will fall in future periods, they will want to buy fewer units of that good at any price in the current period. This often happens with consumer electronics as people hold off purchasing new technology in anticipation of lower future prices.

📄 Remember

When demand changes, equilibrium price and quantity move in the same direction as demand. An increase in demand increases price and quantity. A decrease in demand decreases price and quantity.

When something changes in a market, be careful to ask yourself whether the change will cause people to want to buy a different amount of the good holding the price constant. If the answer is yes, then the demand curve will shift. If the answer is no, the demand curve remains constant.

💣 Caution!

Be very careful to understand the difference between a movement along a demand or curve and a change in demand. A movement along a demand curve is caused only by a change in the price of that good. A change in demand is caused by a change in some factor other than the price of the good changing. One way to keep the difference straight is to understand that when we move along a curve, both the price of the good and the quantity of the good are changing. When a curve shifts, people want to buy a different amount of the good, *holding the price constant.*

4.5 Market Effects of Changes in Supply

A **change in supply** is caused by a change in a variable other than the price of the product. A change in supply means that holding the price constant, suppliers now want to sell more or less of their product. Since the price has not changed, the supply curve must have shifted.

An *increase in supply* means that firms are willing to sell more units at any given price. When supply increases, the equilibrium price of the good falls, and the equilibrium quantity of the good increases. Here are the factors that increase supply:
- Decreases in input prices. When the firm can pay lower prices for its workers or materials, it is willing to sell more of a good, holding the price of the good constant.
- Technological advance. Better technology allows a firm to produce (and sell) more units of a good, holding the price constant.
- Government subsidy. If the government gives money to a firm for each unit it produces, the firm can sell its goods at a lower price in the market (the downward idea of the supply shift).
- Expected future price. If the firm anticipates that the price of its product is going to fall in the future, it will be willing to sell more units of the good now, holding the price constant.
- An increase in the number of producers. As more firms enter the market, there will be more units of the good available for sale, holding the price of the good constant.

A *decrease in supply* means that firms want to sell fewer units of a good, holding the price of the good constant. A decrease in supply lowers the equilibrium quantity of the good and raises the equilibrium price. Here are the factors that decrease supply:

- Increases in wages and prices of materials. When the costs of producing output increase, firms require a higher price to sell any given number of units.
- Tax. If the government requires the firm to pay a tax each time it sells a unit of a good, the price required to sell any number of units of the good will increase.
- Higher future prices. If the firm expects the price of the good to increase in the future, it will be willing to sell fewer units of the good in the current period, holding the price of the good constant.
- A decrease in the number of producers. As firms stop producing a good and leave the market, there will be fewer units of a good available, holding the price of the good constant.

📄 Remember

It is sometimes helpful to think of supply changes in this way: Supply increases when a firm is willing to sell the same output for a lower price. If the wages paid to a worker fall, a firm is able to sell its output for a lower price. Graphically this shifts the supply curve down—indicating that the price required to sell any quantity will decrease—and to the right—indicating that the firm will sell more holding the price constant. See Table 4.3 of the text.

In the same way, if the wages paid to a worker increase, the firm now needs to sell its product at a higher price to be willing to sell the same quantity. Graphically, the supply curve shifts up—indicating that the price required to sell any quantity has increased—and to the left—indicating that at a constant price the firm is willing to sell fewer units of the good. See Table 4.4 of the text.

When supply changes, equilibrium quantity moves in the same direction as supply and equilibrium price moves in the opposite direction. An increase in supply increases quantity and decreases price.

⌐ Study Tip

When something changes in a market, ask yourself whether the change will make suppliers want to sell a different amount of the goods holding the price constant. If the answer is yes, then the supply curve will shift. If the answer is no, the supply curve remains constant.

4.6 Predicting and Explaining Market Changes

We use our knowledge of demand and supply changes to both predict future price and quantity movements and to explain past price and quantity movements.

Examples:
- An increase in price occurs when demand increases or supply decreases.
- A decrease in price occurs when demand decreases or supply increases.
- An increase in quantity occurs when demand increases or supply increases.
- A decrease in quantity occurs when demand decreases or supply decreases.

💣 Caution!

If both curves are shifting at the same time, you will be able to predict only the movement of quantity *or* price—not both. For instance, an increase in demand combined with an increase in supply will increase the market quantity. However, the two shifts have offsetting price effects and you won't be able to forecast the price movement. After the two shifts have occurred, you will be able to determine which effect was stronger. If the price in the market increases, you know that the increase in demand was stronger than the increase in supply.

An increase in demand will cause a movement along the supply curve. Suppliers will offer more goods in the market but this is a result of a higher price being offered. A demand change can't cause the supply curve to shift. Similarly a change in supply will cause a movement along the demand curve, but won't cause the demand curve to shift.

4.7 Applications of Demand and Supply

Let's review five Applications that answer the key questions we posed at the start of the chapter:

1. How do changes in demand affect prices?

APPLICATION 1: HURRICANE KATRINA AND BATON ROUGE HOUSING PRICES

In the aftermath of Hurricane Katrina, about 250,000 residents of New Orleans relocated to Baton Rouge, LA. With the arrival of the new residents, the demand for housing in Baton Rouge increased. Note that nothing happened that would cause suppliers to want to change the amount of housing offered in the market, holding the price constant. This shift in demand led to both higher prices for housing, and a higher quantity of homes sold. Note in Figure 4 we have a change in demand, but a movement along a fixed supply curve.

2. What could explain a decrease in price?

APPLICATION 2: TED KOPPEL TRIES TO EXPLAIN LOWER DRUG PRICES

When the price of illegal drugs fell, ABC news anchor Ted Koppel suggested that lower prices indicated that attempts to control the flow of drugs into the country had failed. Why? As Koppel rightly pointed out, a decrease in price can be caused by increased supply which would suggest that efforts to control illegal drugs had failed. However, a price decrease can also occur when the demand for a good decreases. Since we have two explanations for a decrease in price, we need to see what happened to quantity in order to determine whether the drop in price was caused by a supply shift or a demand shift. Figure 4.15 indicates that the quantity of illegal drugs dropped as well as the price. This drop in quantity indicates that a decrease in demand was responsible for the lower drug prices.

3.   How does the adoption of new technology affect prices?

APPLICATION 3: ELECTRICITY FROM THE WIND

Between 2000 and 2006 new windmill technology has shifted the supply curve of wind-generated electricity to the right. As a result, the price of wind-generated electricity has fallen from 50 cents per kilowatt-hour to 4 cents per kilowatt-hour, as we would expect with an increase in supply, and the quantity produced has increased from 600 megawatt hours to 9,200 megawatt hours, again as we would expect from an increase in supply.

4.   How do changes in supply affect prices?

APPLICATION 4: THE BOUNCING PRICE OF VANILLA BEANS

What has caused the price of vanilla to change from $50 per kilo in 2000 to $500 in 2003 only to fall to $25 in 2006? In 2000, a cyclone hit Madagascar, a leading vanilla producer, and destroyed a large number of vanilla vines. The destruction reduced the amount of vanilla that suppliers could offer for sale, and as a result of the decrease in supply the price of vanilla increased. Over time, workers planted vines to replace the destroyed vines and a new variety of vanilla plants allowed other countries to grow vanilla beans for the first time. These two events increased the supply of vanilla so much that the price fell below its 2000 level.

5.   How do changes in one market affect other markets?

APPLICATION 5: PLATINUM, JEWELRY, CATALYTIC CONVERTERS

Both jewelry and catalytic converters, part of the exhaust system in automobiles, use platinum as an input. As the worldwide demand for automobiles has increased, so has the demand for platinum. This increase in the demand for platinum has increased the market price of platinum, as you would expect from an increase in demand. This price increase meant that jewelers faced higher costs for platinum jewelry, and, as a result, the supply of platinum jewelry fell. This led to higher prices for platinum jewelry, as you would expect from a decrease in supply, and a movement along the demand curve for platinum jewelry. Also, as the price of platinum increased, there was a movement along the supply curve (not a shift) for recycled platinum as sellers offered more platinum for recycling as the price increased.

Activity

Fill in the following table for music downloads. List the number of music downloads you would be willing to purchase per month at each price:

Price	Quantity	Quantity (2)
$2.00	_____	_____
$1.75	_____	_____
$1.50	_____	_____
$1.25	_____	_____
$1.00	_____	_____
$0.75	_____	_____
$0.50	_____	_____
$0.25	_____	_____
$0.00	_____	_____

a. Fill in the quantity of downloads you would want to purchase each month in the column marked Quantity.
b. Suppose that your income increased by $100 per week from its current level. In the column marked Quantity (2), indicate how many downloads you would be willing to purchase per month at each price.
c. On a graph, draw the demand curves corresponding to the Quantity and Quantity (2) columns.
d. Indicate in the table and graph a change in quantity demanded.
e. Indicate in the table and graph a change in demand.

Answers

d. This would be a move along a demand curve or within a quantity column.
e. This would be a move from one demand curve to the other, or from one quantity column to the other, holding price constant.

Key Terms

Change in demand: A shift of the demand curve caused by a change in a variable other than the price of the product.

Change in quantity demanded: A change in the quantity consumers are willing and able to buy when the price changes; represented graphically by movement along the demand curve.

Change in quantity supplied: A change in the quantity firms are willing and able to sell when the price changes; represented graphically by movement along the supply curve.

Change in supply: A shift of the supply curve caused by a change in a variable other than the price of the product.

Complements: Two goods for which a decrease in the price of one good increases the demand for the other good.

Demand schedule: A table that shows the relationship between the price of a product and the quantity demanded, *ceteris paribus*.

Excess demand (shortage): A situation in which, at the prevailing price, the quantity demanded exceeds the quantity supplied.

Excess supply (surplus): A situation in which at the prevailing price, the quantity supplied exceeds the quantity demanded.

Individual demand curve: A curve that shows the relationship between the price of a good and quantity demanded by an individual, *ceteris paribus*.

Individual supply curve: A curve showing the relationship between price and quantity supplied by a single firm, *ceteris paribus*.

Inferior good: A good for which an increase in income decreases demand.

Law of demand: There is a negative relationship between price and quantity demanded, *ceteris paribus*.

Law of supply: There is a positive relationship between price and quantity supplied, *ceteris paribus*.

Market demand curve: A curve showing the relationship between price and quantity demanded by all consumers, *ceteris paribus*.

Market equilibrium: A situation in which the quantity demanded equals the quantity supplied at the prevailing market price.

Market supply curve: A curve showing the relationship between the market price and the quantity supplied by all firms, *ceteris paribus*.

Minimum supply price: The lowest price at which a product will be supplied.

Normal good: A good for which an increase in income increases demand.

Perfectly competitive market: A market with so many buyers and sellers that no single buyer or seller can affect the market price.

Quantity demanded: The amount of a product that consumers are willing and able to buy.

Quantity supplied: The amount of a product that firms are willing and able to sell.

Substitutes: Two goods for which an increase in the price of one good increases the demand for the other good.

Supply schedule: A table that shows the relationship between the price of a product and quantity supplied, *ceteris paribus*.

Practice Quiz

(Answers are provided at the end of the Practice Quiz.)

1. The model of supply and demand explains how a perfectly competitive market operates. Which of the following is a characteristic of a perfectly competitive market?
    a. The market has a very large number of firms.
    b. The market has very few buyers so firms have to compete for them.
    c. In this market, large business firms produce large amounts of output and have a strong influence over price.
    d. All of the above

2. The *demand schedule* is:
    a. a curve that shows the relationship between price and quantity demanded, ceteris paribus.
    b. a table that shows the relationship between price and quantity demanded, ceteris paribus.
    c. a list of time periods during which the quantity of a good is demanded.
    d. the order in which individual consumers arrive to demand a good or service.

3. Refer to the figure below. Which move best illustrates a *change in quantity demanded*?

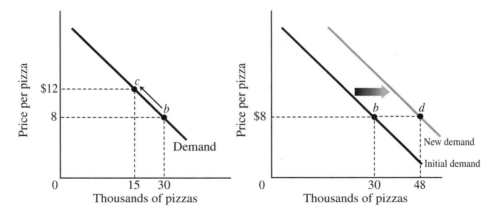

    a. The move from *b* to *c* on the graph in the left side
    b. The move from *b* to *d* on the graph in the right side
    c. A combination of the two moves above
    d. None of the above

4. Which of the following will NOT cause a shift in the demand curve for houses?
   a. A change in income
   b. A change in the price of condominiums
   c. A change in the price of houses
   d. A change in people's desire to live in houses rather than apartments

5. The change in consumption resulting from a change in the price of one good relative to the price of other goods is known as:
   a. the price effect.
   b. the income effect.
   c. the substitution effect.
   d. the real-nominal effect of a price change.

6. Which of the following variables has an effect on the decisions of sellers, using the market for pizza as an example?
   a. Producer expectations about the future price of pizza
   b. The cost of the inputs used to produce the product, for example, wages paid to workers and the cost of the pizza oven
   c. The state of production technology, such as the knowledge used in making pizza
   d. All of the above

7. Refer to the figure below. Which of the following moves best describes a change in supply?

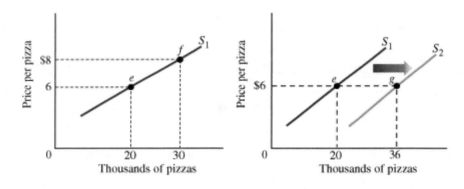

   a. The move from e to f on the graph on the left side
   b. The move from e to g on the graph on the right side
   c. Either move. Both moves above illustrate a change in supply.
   d. A change in supply is actually a combination of the moves described in each graph.

8. Refer to the figure below. If there are 100 identical pizzerias, how much is the quantity supplied when the market price equals $8?

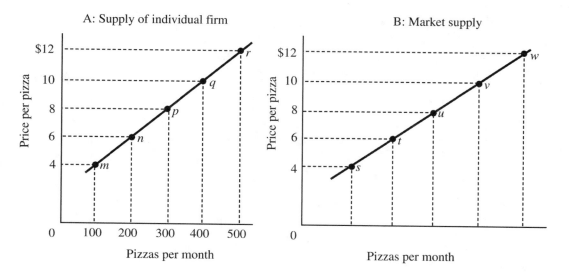

A: Supply of individual firm

B: Market supply

a. 800 pizzas
b. 100 pizzas
c. 30,000 pizzas
d. 80,000 pizzas

9. Refer to the figure below. When market price equals $12, we have a situation called:

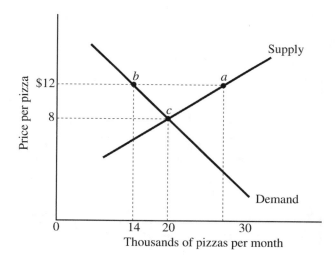

a. consumer protection.
b. market equilibrium.
c. excess demand.
d. excess supply.

10. Refer to the figure below. After the increase in demand, at the initial price of $8, there is now:

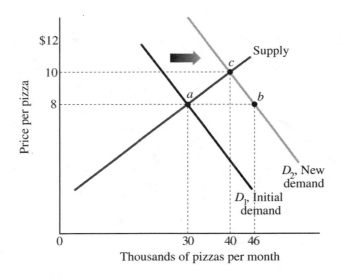

a.   equilibrium.
b.   excess quantity supplied.
c.   excess quantity demanded.
d.   a tendency for price to decrease.

11. Refer to the figure below. Which of the graphs best describes the impact of an increase in the wages and input prices that firms must pay in order to produce output?

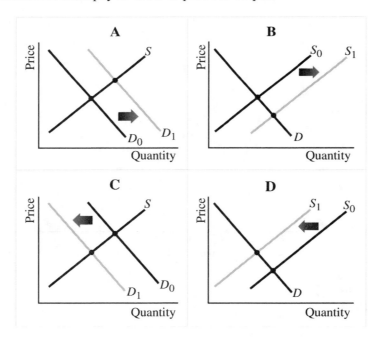

a.   A
b.   B
c.   C
d.   D

12. Refer to the figure below. Which graph shows an increase in *quantity demanded*?

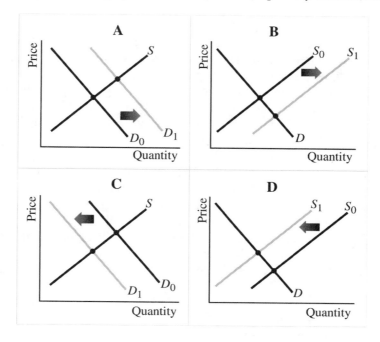

a. A
b. B
c. C
d. D

13. Refer to the figure below. This graph shows that:

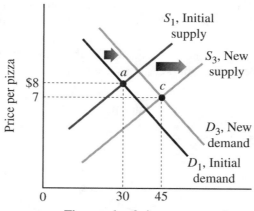

Thousands of pizzas per month

a. when the magnitude of a decrease in supply is greater than the magnitude of an increase in demand, equilibrium price will rise, and quantity will fall.
b. when the magnitude of an increase in supply is greater than the magnitude of an increase in demand, equilibrium price will fall, and quantity will rise.
c. when supply and demand both increase, price always decreases.
d. in equilibrium, quantity demanded is not always equal to quantity supplied.

14. This question tests your understanding of Application 2 in this chapter: Ted Koppel tries to explain lower drug prices. What could explain a decrease in price?

Ted Koppel, host of the ABC news program Nightline, once said, "Do you know what's happened to the price of drugs in the United States? The price of cocaine, way down, the price of marijuana, way down. You don't have to be an expert in economics to know that when the price goes down, it means more stuff is coming in. That's supply and demand." According to Koppel, the price of drugs dropped because the government's efforts to control the supply of illegal drugs had failed. However, according to the U.S. Department of Justice, the quantity of drugs consumed actually decreased during the period of dropping prices. Is Koppel's economic detective work sound?

Which of the following changes in supply and demand could explain how the quantity of drugs exchanged could increase at the same time that the price decreases?
a. An increase in demand accompanied by a decrease in supply
b. A decrease in demand accompanied by an increase in supply
c. An increase in both supply and demand, with the increase in supply being larger than the increase in demand
d. An increase in supply and a decrease in demand, with the decrease in demand being larger than the increase in supply

15. This question tests your understanding of Application 4 in this chapter: The bouncing price of vanilla beans. How do changes in supply affect prices?

The price of vanilla beans has been bouncing around a lot. Using the information below, we can explain the bouncing price of vanilla in the context of the supply and demand model.

"The 2000 cyclone that hit Madagascar, the world's leading producer, destroyed that year's crop and a large share of the vines that produce vanilla beans. But then, in the following years, the vines in Madagascar were replanted, and other countries, including India, Papua New Guinea, Uganda, and Costa Rica, entered the vanilla market. This entry was facilitated by the development of a sun-tolerant variety of the vanilla plant that allows it to be grown as a plantation crop."

Refer to the figure below. The return of Madagascar to the industry, technological advances, and the entry of other countries in the vanilla market is best represented by:

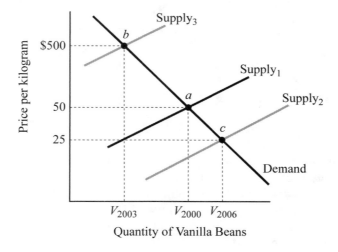

   a. The upward shift of the supply curve, from Supply$_1$ to Supply$_3$, and higher prices
   b. The rightward shift of the supply curve, from Supply$_3$ to Supply$_2$, and lower prices
   c. The move along the demand curve, from point *a* to point *b*
   d. The move of the supply curve, from Supply$_1$ to Supply$_2$, then over to Supply$_3$

16. Markets have a natural tendency to arrive at equilibrium. Expand.

17. A movement along the demand curve is decomposed into a substitution effect and an income effect. Describe these effects, assuming that the good in question is a normal good.

18. Use the model of supply and demand to explain why ticket scalpers exist.

19. If supply and demand both increase, equilibrium price may increase or decrease. Explain.

20. Describe the role of expectations in the model of supply and demand

Answers to the Practice Quiz

1. a. The model of supply and demand explains how a perfectly competitive market operates. A perfectly competitive market is a market that has a very large number of firms, each of which produces the same standardized product in amounts so small that no individual firm can affect the market price.

2. b. The demand schedule is a table that shows the relationship between price and quantity demanded by an individual consumer, *ceteris paribus* (everything else held fixed).

3. a. A *change in quantity demanded* is a change in the amount of a good demanded resulting from a change in the price of the good. Such a move is illustrated by a move along the demand curve, from one point to another.

4. c. A change in the price of houses will result in movement along the demand curve, NOT a shift in the demand curve.

5. c. The substitution effect is the change in consumption resulting from a change in the price of one good relative to the price of other goods. The lower the price of a good, the smaller the sacrifice associated with the consumption of that good.

6. d. All of the above are known as the main determinants of supply.

7. b. A change in supply (movement of the supply curve) is different from a change in quantity supplied (movement along a supply curve). A change in quantity supplied is a change in the amount of a good supplied resulting from a change in the price of the good; represented graphically by a movement along the supply curve in the graph on the left side. A change in supply is caused by changes in determinants of supply other than price; represented by a shift of the entire supply curve on the right-side graph.

8. c. Market supply equals 100 times the quantity supplied by a single firm at each price level.

9. d. Excess supply is a situation in which, at the prevailing price, producers are willing to sell more than consumers are willing to buy.

10. c. At the initial price of $8, there is now excess quantity demanded.   Equilibrium is restored at point *n*, with a higher equilibrium price and a larger equilibrium quantity.

11. d. Higher input prices will decrease supply, that is, will shift the supply curve to the left, resulting in a lower equilibrium quantity and higher equilibrium price for the good produced by the firms.

12. b. In this graph, there is an increase in supply and an increase in quantity demanded.

13. b. The price decreases because the increase in supply is greater than the increase in demand.

14. c. The increase in supply and demand results in a definite increase in the quantity exchange. Whether the price increases or decreases depends on the magnitudes of change in supply and demand. If the increase in supply outweighs the increase in demand, equilibrium price will fall.

15. b. The price was $50 per kilo (2.2 pounds) in 2000, then rose to $500 in 2003, then dropped to $25 in 2006. The changes in the supply of vanilla between 2003 and 2006 are shown by a shift of the supply curve downward and to the right. The entry of additional producers in the vanilla market causes the supply curve to shift to the right.

16. Only in equilibrium, quantity supplied equals quantity demanded, and the wishes of buyers coincide with the wishes of sellers; buyers and sellers agree on a single price at which the good is exchanged. When a market is not in equilibrium, price is either too high or too low. When price is too high, quantity supplied is greater than quantity demanded, resulting in a surplus of output. This surplus, or excess supply, will put downward pressure on price. When the price is too low, quantity demanded will exceed quantity supplied. Excess demand will put upward pressure on price. In either case, the market has a natural tendency to move toward equilibrium.

17. The substitution and income effects explain why a demand curve is downward sloping. The substitution effect states that when the price of a good decreases, for example, consumers are induced to substitute from alternative goods into the good in question. The income effect states that a decrease in price results in greater real income, or higher purchasing power. The substitution and income effects of a price change work in the same direction. In the case of a price decrease, for example, both effects contribute to an increase in quantity demanded.

18. When a stadium sells tickets for a popular event, it issues a number of tickets equal to the number of seats available. The stadium assumes that quantity supplied will equal quantity demanded once the tickets are sold out. Ticket scalpers, however, have a hunch that the quantity demanded greatly exceeds the quantity supplied at the price determined by the stadium. In other words, they assume that equilibrium price is higher than the price determined by the stadium. The excess of quantity demanded over quantity supplied means that someone must be willing to pay a higher price than the official price. Scalpers are first in line to buy the tickets at the official price, then, they go out in the streets to look for those who are willing to pay a price closer to the equilibrium market price.

19. In order to establish the impact on price from a change in supply and demand, we must examine the magnitudes of the change in each. By itself an increase in supply pushes price down while an increase in demand by itself pushes price up. If supply increases more than demand does, equilibrium price

will fall. If demand increases more than supply does, equilibrium price will rise. And, if the magnitudes of change are the same, price will remain the same; only equilibrium quantity will change.

20. Expectations are an important component of both supply and demand. On the demand side, expectations determine whether buyers will buy more of a good today, or wait until tomorrow. Expectations are built into all rational household decisions. Decisions about how much to buy, how much to save, and how much labor to supply take into account both the present and the future. If households feel optimistic about the future, they may increase their present consumption. Pessimism, on the other hand, will cause households to hold back on their consumption expenditures. On the supply side, expectations also play a major role in decision making. Business firms decide what and how much output to produce based on a plan. This plan includes a forecast of future expected input and output prices. If producers are optimistic about the future, they will plan to expand capacity and increase production in future periods. If they feel pessimistic, they may plan to reduce capacity and output in the future. It is important to understand that the expectations of producers and consumers are independent. This means that producers do not have complete control of production and investment decisions.

5

Measuring a Nation's Production and Income

Chapter Summary

You've probably read or heard headline news stories like "GDP growth is at 3%" or "GDP growth expected to slow." In this chapter, you'll learn what these numbers mean, who generates the numbers, and why they're important to countries and their citizens. Here are the main points of the chapter:

- The primary measurement of a country's output is called gross domestic product, or GDP. GDP is one of several acronyms you'll learn in this chapter.
- GDP serves an important purpose, but has limitations because it doesn't measure all of a country's activities.
- Price changes from one year to the next affect GDP calculations.
- Economies experience business cycles in which an economy grows rapidly, followed by slowing growth, and then the economy grows rapidly again.

Applying the Concepts

After reading this chapter, you should be able to answer these three key questions:

1. How can we use economic analysis to compare the size of a major corporation to a country?
2. How do we determine when a recession has occurred in the United States?
3. Do increases in gross domestic product necessarily translate into improvements in the welfare of citizens?

5.1 The "Flip" Sides of Macroeconomic Activity: Production and Income

Simply stated, production generates income. Workers go to work and produce goods and services. In exchange for their work they receive income. Firms take the goods and services produced by workers and sell them. Workers then take some of their income and spend it on newly produced goods and services. Production leads to income and income leads to production.

Figure 5.1 illustrates this simple relationship between households and firms called the circular flow diagram. Households and firms participate in two markets: product markets, where final products and services are sold, and factor markets, where factors of production (such as labor and capital) are traded. Household income is created from the sale of factors of production. Revenue from the sale of goods and services generates income for the firms. Firms incur costs to pay for the factors they demand. Households have to pay for the goods they purchase. The green arrows show how income flows. The red arrows in Figure 5.1 show how goods and services flow.

ᎪᎠ **Study Tip**

A good way to understand the circular flow diagram is to look at the diagram from a transactions view. In other words, look at the transactions between income and goods. For example, look at the relationship between households and the factor market. You go to work and supply your time or labor to your employer. The employer in turn pays you income. Remember that markets are arrangements bringing buyers and sellers together. The market facilitates the transaction between the firms and households.

5.2 The Production Approach: Measuring a Nation's Macroeconomic Activity Using Gross Domestic Product

---

ᎪᎠ **Study Tip**

Memorize the definition of GDP. It is the easiest way to know what it does and does not measure. You will see this definition used to measure output throughout the remainder of the text.

Gross domestic product, or GDP, is the total market value of all final goods and services produced in an economy in a given year. This definition is very specific. Think about the following phrases:

- Total market value
- Final goods and services
- Produced in an economy
- In a given year

💣 **Caution!**

Don't count intermediate goods in GDP. **Intermediate goods** are goods used in the production process that are not final goods and services. Count only final goods and services. For example, if you are an artist commissioned to paint a mural for your student center, you would not count the paint or the canvas in GDP, but you would count the market value of the final artwork you produced.

To calculate GDP, we take the quantity of each good produced, multiply the quantity by the price of that good, and then add up the totals. This is called **nominal GDP** since the GDP was valued with current prices (current dollars). Nominal GDP can change due to either changes in prices or changes in quantities. To measure the **real GDP**, a measure of GDP that controls for changes in prices, we hold the price of each product constant. These GDP calculations are shown on page 103 of your textbook. The calculation of nominal GDP and real GDP is a direct application of the Real-Nominal Principle you learned in Chapter 2.

Real-Nominal Principle

What matters to people is the real value of money or income—its purchasing power—not the face value of money or income.

Sustained increases in real GDP over a long period of time are called **economic growth.** Figure 5.2 shows real GDP in the U.S. from 1930 to 2005. Notice how major events, such as the Great Depression and World War II, affect economic growth in Figure 5.2.

Another way to look at GDP is to understand who demands the GDP that is produced. The following equation explains who purchases our GDP.

☑ Key Equation

$GDP = C + I + G + NX$,
where
C = consumption expenditures – purchases by consumers
I = private investment – purchases by firms
G = government spending – purchases by federal, state, and local governments
NX = net exports – net purchases by foreign sector (domestic exports minus domestic imports)

Consumption expenditures are purchases of newly produced goods and services by households. Consumption expenditures include durables such as refrigerators and cars, nondurables such as food and clothing, and services such as advice from doctors and lawyers. **Intermediate goods** are goods used in the production process that are not final goods and services.

Private investment expenditures are purchases of newly produced goods and services by firms. Investment expenditures include new plants and equipment, newly produced housing, and new inventories.

 Caution!

When talking about private investment, we are not talking about purchasing stocks and bonds, which are financial instruments. Private investment expenditures are purchases of real capital, such as new buildings for a company or new computers for a call center. Remember new housing construction is included in private investment expenditures and not consumption expenditures.

Government expenditures include purchases of newly produced goods and services by local, state, and federal governments. **Transfer payments** are payments from governments to individuals that do not correspond to the production of goods and services. Examples of transfer payments include Social Security, Medicare, and Medicaid. Transfer payments are not included in government expenditures because the person receiving the payments is not producing a good or service in return.

Lastly, **imports** are goods produced in a foreign country and purchased by residents of the home country. For example, if you live in the United States and bought a Nintendo Playstation3 from Japan, you have purchased an import. **Exports** are goods produced in the home country and sold in another country. For example, if you live in the United States and sell wheat produced in the United States to Russia, you have sold an export. **Net exports** are exports minus imports. In Table 5.1, we see that net exports in the third quarter of 2005 were −$730 billion. Net exports were negative because our imports exceeded our exports. When a country has an excess of imports over exports, we have a **trade deficit**. A **trade surplus** occurs when there is an excess of exports over imports. Figure 5.3 shows the U.S. trade surplus as a share of GDP from 1960 to 2005.

5.3 The Income Approach: Measuring a Nation's Macroeconomic Activity Using National Income

Another way to look at GDP information is using national income accounts to add up GDP. Table 5.2 shows an example of National Income Accounts. The authors used the following equations to reach the figures in Table 5.2.

☑ Key Equations

Gross National Product = GNP = GDP + Net Income earned abroad

GNP − Depreciation = NNP or Net National Product

National Income = NNP − Indirect Taxes

National Income = Total Compensation of Employees + Corporate Profits + Rental Income + Proprietor's Income + Net Interest

Personal Income = National Income + Transfer Payments − Retained Profits

Personal Income = Labor Income + Transfer Payments + Capital Income Paid to Individuals

Personal Disposable Income = Personal Income − Personal Income Taxes

---

Another way to measure national income is using value added. **Value added** is the sum of all the income—wages, interest, profits, and rent—generated by an organization. For a firm, we can measure value added by the dollar value of the firm's sales minus the dollar value of the goods and services purchased from other firms. This income would include wages, profits, rents, and interest. Adding up all the value added by firms, nonprofit organizations, and government organizations equals national income. Refer to Table 5.3 for an example of a value added calculation.

Let's review an Application that answers one of the key questions we posed at the start of the chapter:

1. How can we use economic analysis to compare the size of a major corporation to a country?

APPLICATION 1: USING VALUE ADDED TO MEASURE THE TRUE SIZE OF WAL-MART

This Application uses value added analysis to make comparisons to a nation's GDP. In 2004, Wal-Mart's total sales were $285 billion. Wal-Mart's value added was substantially less than its total sales. Based on Wal-Mart's annual reports, its cost of sales was $219 billion, leaving approximately $66 billion in value added. Using the measure of value added, Wal-Mart's value added is close to the Ukraine's value added, which is ranked 53rd in the world.

Figure 5.4 expands the circular flow diagram to include the government and net exports. Both households and firms pay taxes to the government. The government, in turn, supplies goods and services in the product market and also purchases inputs—labor and capital—in the factor markets, just like private-sector firms do. Net exports, positive or negative, interact with the product market.

5.4 A Closer Examination of Nominal and Real GDP

After reviewing how GDP is calculated, we can explore how prices change the measurement of GDP. This is where we measure nominal GDP and real GDP.

The following equations will help you understand the calculations in the text and complete your homework assignments.

☑ Key Equations

Growth Rate of GDP $= \dfrac{GDP_{cy} - GDP_{py}}{GDP_{py}}$, where "cy" is the current year and "py" is the previous year.

GDP Deflator $= \dfrac{\text{Nominal GDP}}{\text{Real GDP}} \times 100$

The **GDP Deflator** is an index that measures how the prices of goods and services included in GDP change over time. As you study the equation that follows, notice how the GDP Deflator index is based on a given base year from which the real GDP calculation is computed.

📄 Remember

Real GDP calculations are related to some base year's prices, and nominal GDP calculations are related to prices during the year the GDP was produced.

💣 Caution!

The GDP deflator, like most price indexes, is multiplied by 100. When using a price index to deflate a nominal value, be sure to divide the price index by 100 first!

5.5 Fluctuations in GDP

Business cycles are fluctuations in the growth rate of real GDP. Look at Figure 5.6 to learn the anatomy of an economic cycle, specifically, the 1990 recession. Every economic cycle has the following phases:

- **Peak**: the date at which a recession starts.
- Recession: the period of time when real GDP is decreasing. A **recession** is commonly defined as six consecutive months of declining real GDP.
- **Trough**: the date at which output stops falling in a recession.
- **Expansion**: the period after a trough in the business cycle during which the economy recovers.

Let's review an Application that answers one of the key questions we posed at the start of the chapter:

2. How do we determine when a recession has occurred in the United States?

APPLICATION 2: THE NBER AND THE 2001 RECESSION

The National Bureau of Economic Research (NBER) is the organization that declares when a recession starts and ends. The NBER looks at a variety of data before it declares a recession. The NBER defines a recession as a "significant decline in activity spread across the economy, lasting more than a few months, visible in industrial production, employment, real income, and wholesale-retail trade."

5.6 GDP as a Measure of Welfare

GDP is a measure of how much output an economy produces within a given year. From our discussions of the circular flow diagram, we also noted that the market value of output generates income. Since income creation contributes to a nation's standard of living, GDP can be used as a measure of welfare. The greater the output produced, the greater the income for people to spend on goods and services.

However, GDP by its own definition doesn't count all aspects of a nation's welfare. The following are examples of areas not included in GDP:

- Housework and childcare
- Leisure
- Underground economy
- Pollution

☞ Many simple household activities are never counted in GDP. Think about when you clean your room, wash your dishes, or mow your lawn. Those activities, while productive, won't get counted in GDP since they never make it to the market. Reading a good book or re-watching a favorite DVD is not counted in GDP because no new production happens. The underground economy includes illegal activities such as drug trafficking that create production that is not legally reported and does not show up in GDP accounting. Tax avoidance, such as cash payments for services such as waitress/waiter tips, cab tips, or other cash payments under the table are parts of the underground economy.

Let's review an Application that answers one of the key questions we posed at the start of the chapter:

3. Do increases in gross domestic product necessarily translate into improvements in the welfare of citizens?

APPLICATION 3: THE LINKS BETWEEN SELF-REPORTED HAPPINESS AND GDP

GDP is used as a measure of welfare, but does increasing income generate greater happiness? Over the last 30 years, reported levels of happiness have actually declined in the United States and remained relatively flat in the United Kingdom despite very large increases in per capita income in both countries. While increases in income have increased happiness, it differs based on race, gender, and age. Other variables influence happiness levels other than income.

☞ This may seem like a keen sense of the obvious, but college students find happiness without large incomes. Good friends, good health, and family offer happiness that income can't buy.

Activity

The following activity will give you practice in computing GDP and other National Income Account data. Just fill in the blanks of the table where information is missing. The left side of the table will have the title of the account. The right side of the table will have the numerical information relating to the account. The answer is listed at the end of the Activity.

Gross Domestic Product	$9,000
Net Income Earned Abroad	
Gross National Product	$9,600
Net National Product	$7,600
National Income	$6,500

Answers

Using the key equations in section 5.3, you should come up with the following answers based on the table above (the answers are bold and italicized):

Gross Domestic Product	$9,000
Net Income Earned Abroad	***+$600***
Gross National Product	$9,600
Depreciation	***-$2,000***
Net National Product	$7,600
Indirect Taxes	***-$1,100***
National Income	$6,500

Key Terms

Chain-weighted index: A method for calculating changes in prices that uses an average of base years from neighboring years.

Consumption expenditures: Purchases of newly produced goods and services by households.

Depreciation: Reduction in the value of capital goods over a one-year period due to physical wear and tear and also to obsolescence; also called *capital consumption allowance.*

Depression: The common name for a severe recession.

Economic growth: Sustained increases in the real GDP of an economy over a long period of time.

Expansion: The period after a trough in the business cycle during which the economy recovers.

Export: A good produced in the home country (for example, the United States) and sold in another country.

GDP deflator: An index that measures how the prices of goods and services included in GDP change over time.

Government purchases: Purchases of newly produced goods and services by local, state, and federal governments.

Gross domestic product (GDP): The total market value of final goods and services produced within an economy in a given year.

Gross investment: Total new investment expenditures.

Gross national product (GNP): GDP plus net income earned abroad.

Import: A good produced in a foreign country and purchased by residents of the home country (for example, the United States).

Inflation: Sustained increases in the average prices of all goods and services.

Intermediate goods: Goods used in the production process that are not final goods and services.

Macroeconomics: The study of the nation's economy as a whole; focuses on the issues of inflation, unemployment, and economic growth.

National income: The total income earned by a nation's residents both domestically and abroad in the production of goods and services.

Net exports: Exports minus imports.

Net investment: Gross investment minus depreciation.

Nominal GDP: The value of GDP in current dollars.

Peak: The date at which a recession starts.

Personal income: Income, including transfer payments, received by households.

Personal disposable income: Personal income that households retain after paying taxes.

Private investment expenditures: Purchases of newly produced goods and services by firms.

Real GDP: A measure of GDP that controls for changes in prices.

Recession: Commonly defined as six consecutive months of declining real GDP.

Trade deficit: The excess of imports over exports

Trade surplus: The excess of exports over imports.

Transfer payments: Payments from governments to individuals that do not correspond to the production of goods and services.

Trough: The date at which output stops falling in a recession.

Value added: The sum of all the income—wages, interest, profits, and rent—generated by an organization. For a firm, we can measure value added by the dollar value of the firm's sales minus the dollar value of the goods and services purchased from other firms.

Practice Quiz

(Answers are provided at the end of the Practice Quiz.)

1. Macroeconomics focuses on which of the following topics?
    a. Unemployment, inflation, growth, and trade
    b. Individual firms, government, and the structure of society as a whole
    c. Households, industries, and the distribution of income
    d. All of the above are topics in macroeconomics.

2. Which of the following terms are the "flip" sides of macroeconomic activity?
    a. Unemployment and inflation
    b. Production and income
    c. Growth and trade
    d. Exchange rates and interest rates

3. In the circular flow of income, markets in which households supply labor and capital used to produce output are called:
    a. factor markets.
    b. output markets.
    c. free markets.
    d. product markets.

4. Refer to the figure below. Which letter best represents the supply of factors of production?

    a. A
    b. B
    c. C
    d. D

5. Which of the following is NOT an intermediate good?
    a. Corn sold by the farmer to a miller to be made into cornmeal
    b. Corn sold by the farmer to a wholesaler to be sold to grocery stores
    c. Corn sold by the farmer to a consumer at a roadside stand
    d. Corn used by the farmer to feed a hog to be sold to a meat-processing plant

6. Only one answer below is entirely correct. When we use current prices to measure GDP, we give GDP the name:
   a. nominal GDP, which can increase as a result of higher production but not because of higher prices.
   b. nominal GDP, which can increase as a result of higher production or higher prices.
   c. real GDP, which can increase as a result of higher production or higher prices.
   d. real GDP, which cannot increase as a result of higher production or higher prices.

7. The value of GDP (in billions of dollars) in 2005 was:
   a. $12,605.
   b. $8,844.
   c. $2,099.
   d. $2,392.

8. In GDP accounting, purchases of durable goods, nondurable goods, and services are categories of purchases more closely related to:
   a. the household sector.
   b. the business sector.
   c. the government.
   d. All of the above

9. The true addition to the stock of capital of the economy in a given period is called:
   a. gross investment.
   b. net investment.
   c. depreciation.
   d. inventories.

10. Which of the following statements about the federal government's budget is correct?
    a. A small part of the federal government budget is not part of GDP.
    b. A large part of the federal government budget is not part of GDP.
    c. All of the federal government budget is part of GDP.
    d. None of the federal government budget is part of GDP.

11. A *trade deficit* occurs when:
    a. exports are greater than imports.
    b. imports are greater than exports.
    c. net exports are greater than imports.
    d. net exports are less than imports.

12. To arrive at *net national product* (NNP), we must:
    a. add depreciation to GDP.
    b. subtract depreciation from GNP.
    c. add the income of individuals to national income.
    d. count the output produced by U.S. firms within the United States only.

13. The largest component of national income is:
    a. corporate profits.
    b. compensation of employees.
    c. proprietor's income.
    d. net interest.

14. The *value added* of a firm is:
    a. the value of the firm's products after production costs have been subtracted.
    b. the payments the firm has made that are not directly associated with the production process.
    c. the sum of all the income—wages, profits, rents, and interest—that it generates.
    d. the value of all its assets—plant and equipment—that are used in each subsequent production period.

15. The cycle of short-term ups and downs in the economy is called:
    a. deflation.
    b. recession.
    c. depression.
    d. the business cycle.

16. The value of the GDP deflator in 2007 equals:
    a. [(nominal GDP in 2007)/(real GDP in 2007)] x 100
    b. [(real GDP in 2007) x (real GDP in 2007)]/100
    c. [(real GDP in 2007)/(nominal GDP in 2007)] x 100
    d. [(nominal GDP in 2007) x (real GDP in 2007)] x 100

17. Refer to the figure below. When does the economy begin a period of expansion?

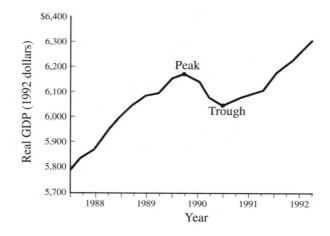

    a. After the peak
    b. After the trough
    c. All along this curve the economy has been expanding.
    d. It is difficult to determine precisely when the economy began expanding.

18. Refer to the figure below. During which period of time is the economy generally considered to be in a recession in this business cycle?

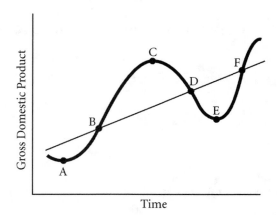

a. The period from A to B
b. The period from C to D
c. The period from C to E
d. The period from D to F

19. GDP is a better measure of:
    a. the value of output produced in the formal or official economy.
    b. the welfare or well-being of people in an economy.
    c. all the transactions that take place in an economy.
    d. All of the above

20. This question tests your understanding of Application 1 in this chapter: using value added to measure the true size of Wal-Mart. How can we use economic analysis to compare the size of a major corporation to a country?

    "During 2004, Wal-Mart's sales were approximately $285 billion, nearly 2.4 percent of U.S. GDP. But to produce those sales, Wal-Mart had to buy goods from many other companies."

    Which of the following is the smallest value?
    a. The cost of sales
    b. Total sales
    c. Value added in the final stage of production and distribution, or when goods are finally sold to the consumer
    d. Nominal GDP

21. Explain the difference between gross national product and net national product.

22. Explain the difference between GDP and GNP. Why do you think the United States switched from GNP to GDP in 1991?

23. Describe some of the shortcomings of the GDP measure.

24. Suppose that the cost of a given market basket in 1993 was $100, and the cost of the same market basket in 1996 was $142. What is the price index in 1996? Now, suppose that nominal spending in 1993 was $100, and nominal spending in 1996 was $130. Has real spending increased or decreased?

25. Average hourly earnings in 1983 were $8.02. Average hourly earnings in 1995 were $11.46. The CPI in 1995 was 152.4 (in 1983 dollars). Did the real wage rate increase or decrease between 1983 and 1995? By how much?

Answers to the Practice Quiz

1. a. Macroeconomics focuses on the economic issues—unemployment, inflation, growth, trade, and the gross domestic product—that are most often discussed in the media and in political debates.

2. b. The terms production and income are the "flip" sides of the macroeconomic "coin." Every day, men and women go off to work, where they produce or sell merchandise or provide services. At the end of the week or month, they return home with their paychecks or "income."

3. a. Households and firms make transactions in two markets known as factor markets and product markets. In factor, or input, markets, households supply labor to firms. Households are also the ultimate owners of firms, as well as all the resources that firms use in their production, which we call capital. Consequently, we can think of households as providing capital to firms—land, buildings, and equipment—to produce output. Product, or output, markets are markets in which firms sell goods and services to consumers.

4. d. Households supply factors of production to the factor market and in return receive income.

5. c. The corn was sold to the "ultimate" user.

6. b. Real GDP is a measure of GDP that takes into account price changes. This measure of total output does not increase just because prices increase. When we use current prices to measure GDP, that is what we call nominal GDP, which can increase as a result of higher production or higher prices.

7. a. Refer to the "Composition of U.S. GDP, Third Quarter 2005 (billions of dollars expressed at annual rates)."

8. a. Economists divide GDP into four broad expenditure categories: Consumption expenditures: purchases by consumers; Private investment expenditures: purchases by firms; Government purchases: purchases by federal, state, and local governments; and Net exports: net purchases by the foreign sector (domestic exports minus domestic imports).

9. b. What was built minus what deteriorated equals what's left.

10. b. Transfer payments are funds paid to individuals but not associated with the production of goods and services. A large part of the federal government budget is not part of GDP.

11. b. When we buy more goods from abroad than we sell, we have a trade deficit.

12. b. When we subtract depreciation from GNP, we reach net national product (NNP).

13. b. Refer to the "Composition of U.S. National Income, Third Quarter of 2005 (billions of dollars)."

14. c. The value added of a firm is the sum of all the income—wages, profits, rents, and interest—that it generates.

15. d. Instead of growing at an even rate at all times, economies tend to experience short-term ups and downs in their performance. The technical name for these ups and downs is the business cycle.

16. a. The GDP deflator measures the change in prices over time using index numbers.

17. b. After a trough, the economy enters a recovery period or period of expansion.

18. c. It is possible for the level of output to be high, yet the economy is in a recession. A recession is a period of time from peak to trough.

19. a. GDP is our best measure of the value of output produced by an economy, but as a measure of welfare, it has several recognized flaws that you need to be wary of.

20. c. This application shows that Wal-Mart's value added was substantially less than its total sales. Based on Wal-Mart's annual reports, its cost of sales was $219 billion, leaving approximately $66 billion in value added.

21. The difference between gross product and net product comes from the difference between gross investment and net investment. Gross private domestic investment minus depreciation equals net private domestic investment. This adjustment takes into account both gains in terms of the new additions to the nation's stock of capital, such as new plants, equipment, and infrastructure, and losses in terms of the deterioration of the existing capital. The stock of capital at the end of this year equals the stock of capital at the end of last year plus net investment this year.

22. GDP measures output produced by factors of production, both foreign and domestic within the United States. GNP measures output produced by U.S. firms in both the United States and abroad. The United States switched to the GDP measure because more and more foreign firms now operate in the United States. As the foreign ownership of productive resources in the United States increases, the output produced by these firms within the United States becomes a more significant portion of total output. This output would not be accounted for in GNP.

23. GDP ignores the underground economy, where transactions are not reported to official authorities. GDP does not value changes in the environment that arise from the production of output. GDP ignores the value of unpaid home production. GDP ignores leisure time, along with other non-market activities. GDP fails to accurately reflect the quality improvements of some goods and services. Finally, GDP does not account for the social and psychological impact of output growth, such as crime or suicide.

24. If the cost of a market basket was $100 in 1993 and $142 in 1996, then it takes $1.42 to buy the same goods that $1 purchased in 1993. The price index is 142. To determine if real spending has increased or decreased, divide $130 by 1.42 = $91.55. Therefore, $100 of real expenditures in 1993 correspond to $91.55 of real expenditures in 1996. Although nominal spending ($130) has increased, real spending ($91.55) has decreased.

25. Divide the wage in 1995 by the CPI of 152.4. Then, the real wage rate in 1995, expressed in 1983 was $7.52. Therefore, the real wage rate decreased by 6.2% or [(1 − (7.52/8.02)] x 100 = 6.2%.

6
Unemployment and Inflation

Chapter Summary

Does fighting the war in Iraq affect the unemployment rate? This is just one of the questions this chapter will help you answer. This chapter deals with unemployment and inflation, both of which affect the quality of our lives. We'll study ways to measure unemployment and inflation and how each affects society. Here are the main points of the chapter:

- The unemployed are individuals who do not have jobs but who are actively seeking employment. The labor force comprises both the employed and the unemployed. The unemployment rate is the percentage of the labor force that is unemployed.
- Economists distinguish among different types of unemployment. Seasonal patterns of economic activity lead to seasonal unemployment. There are three other types of unemployment. Frictional unemployment occurs through the normal dynamics of the economy as workers change jobs and industries expand and contract. Structural unemployment is due to a mismatch of workers' skills with job opportunities. Cyclical unemployment occurs with the fluctuations in economic activity.
- Unemployment rates vary across demographic groups. Alternative measures of unemployment take into account individuals who would like to work full time, but who are no longer in the labor force or are holding part-time jobs.
- Economists measure changes in the cost of living through the Consumer Price Index (CPI), which is based on the cost of purchasing a standard basket of goods and services by consumers.
- We measure inflation as the percentage change in the price level.
- Economists believe that most price indexes, including the CPI and the chain-weighted index for GDP, overstate true inflation because they fail to capture quality improvements in goods and services.
- Unemployment imposes both financial and psychological costs on workers.
- Both anticipated and unanticipated inflation imposes costs on society.

Applying the Concepts

After reading this chapter, you should be able to answer these four key questions:
1. What do the recent data show about trends in the percentage of women who are working?
2. Who are the new discouraged workers in Japan?
3. What are the costs of either too high or too low levels of unemployment insurance?
4. Are Social Security payments properly adjusted for changes in the cost of living?

6.1 Examining Unemployment

Understanding the following key terms related to unemployment measurement is critical to computing unemployment statistics:
- Employed: People who have jobs
- Unemployed: People who don't have jobs, but are seeking work
- Labor Force: The employed plus the unemployed

Within these definitions, we can compute the following unemployment statistics:

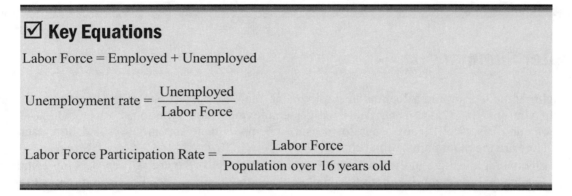

☑ Key Equations

Labor Force = Employed + Unemployed

$$\text{Unemployment rate} = \frac{\text{Unemployed}}{\text{Labor Force}}$$

$$\text{Labor Force Participation Rate} = \frac{\text{Labor Force}}{\text{Population over 16 years old}}$$

The labor force participation rate measures the percentage of the civilian population over age 16 who are participating in the labor force. To understand these measurement relationships, consider Figure 6.1. In February 2004, approximately 66 percent of the working population participated in the labor force. The unemployment rate was 4.8 percent, equal to the 7,193,000 unemployed divided by the 150,450,000 in the labor force.

In Figure 6.2, we can see other developed nation's unemployment rates. You can see among those nations that the U.S. is second lowest in unemployment rate to Japan.

💣 Caution!

The unemployment rate measures the percentage of the labor force that is unemployed, not the percentage of the civilian population over 16 years old.

☞ Remember the question posed at the beginning of this chapter? Since full-time military personnel are not considered civilians, they would not be counted in either the civilian population over 16 years old or the labor force. So, sending full-time military soldiers to fight in Iraq would not change the unemployment statistics since those soldiers are not counted in the first place.

〰 Study Tip

The best way to understand unemployment statistics is to practice problems using the equations above. Now would be a good time to try some practice problems, either those at the end of this chapter or from myeconlab.com.

Let's review an Application that answers one of the key questions we posed at the start of the chapter:

1. What do the recent data show about trends in the percentage of women who are working?

APPLICATION 1: AFTER GROWING SHARPLY, WOMEN'S LABOR FORCE PARTICIPATION HAS LEVELED OFF

In 1948, the labor force participation rate for women 20 years and older was 32 percent. By 1970, it had grown to 43 percent, and by 1997 it had reached 60 percent. But since 1997, the figure has remained virtually constant at 60 percent. While technology has made it possible for women to participate in the workforce, they are still running out of available time.

☞ Other forces may be playing into the flattening of the labor force participation for women. Even with time-saving technology such as computers, cell phones, and microwave ovens, women are still primary caregivers. Devoting time to household activities means less time for careers for women than men.

We need to look beyond the statistics to understand why people choose not to participate in the work force. Remember, these individuals are not counted in the unemployment rate since they are neither working nor seeking work. Examples include discouraged workers and marginally attached workers. **Discouraged workers** are workers who left the labor force because they could not find jobs. Marginally attached workers are individuals who would like to work, have searched for work in the recent past, but have stopped looking for work for a variety of reasons. Some workers may be employed but are settling for part-time work when they really want full-time work. We can see from Figure 6.3, the official statistics for unemployment do not include the full range of individuals who would like to participate fully in the labor market. The statistics provide us information about unemployment, but we need to look beyond the numbers to understand what is happening in the labor force and the working population.

Let's review an Application that answers one of the key questions we posed at the start of the chapter:

2. Who are the new discouraged workers in Japan?

APPLICATION 2: NEETs ARE THE NEW DISCOURAGED WORKERS IN JAPAN

Young workers who have given up looking for work and often receive support from their parents are known as *NEETs*—"not in education, employment, or training." Because Japan has an aging population and does not encourage immigration, it is concerned about labor shortages and has focused attention on the NEETs.

6.2 Categories of Unemployment

Cyclical unemployment is unemployment that occurs during fluctuations in real GDP. People fired during a recession become cyclically unemployed. As real GDP decreases, cyclical unemployment increases. **Frictional unemployment** is unemployment that occurs with the normal workings of the economy, such as workers taking time to search for suitable jobs and firms taking time to search for qualified employees. For example, when you finish college, you may not take the first job that you are offered. You may look for something better. You would be considered frictionally unemployed. **Structural unemployment** occurs when there is a mismatch of skills and jobs. There may be plenty of biotechnology jobs in the job market, but unfortunately you got your degree in an unrelated field. This would be a mismatch with the existing jobs and the skills of the workers.

☞   Another type of unemployment was discussed in the previous section. This would be seasonal unemployment. Seasonal unemployment is attributed to seasonal factors. Examples of seasonal employment include golf courses, ski resorts, professional sports, and big game hunting, to name a few.

The **natural rate of unemployment** is the unemployment rate that exists when there is no cyclical unemployment. Frictional and structural unemployment still exist, so the natural rate of unemployment is not zero. An economy is considered at **full employment** when the unemployment rate is at the natural rate of unemployment. We explore this concept further in Chapter 7.

6.3 The Costs of Unemployment

The main cost of unemployment is lowered output and income. When the economy produces less than potential GDP during a year, that output is lost forever. Similarly, the income workers would have earned producing that output is also lost. Full employment means the labor force has no cyclical unemployment *and* actual real GDP equals potential real GDP. Over time, unemployed workers may lose skills making jobs harder to find. Table 6.1 shows the duration of unemployment in February, 2006. Lastly, there are psychological costs to being unemployed. People may experience depression, divorce, and criminal activity due to a loss of work. At the most extreme, economists have noted the suicide rate tends to rise and fall with the unemployment rate. **Unemployment insurance** is payments unemployed people receive from the government. Such payments are designed to alleviate hardships caused by unemployment.

Let's review an Application that answers one of the key questions we posed at the start of the chapter:

   3.   What are the costs of either too high or too low levels of unemployment insurance?

APPLICATION 3: FINDING THE OPTIMAL LEVEL OF UNEMPLOYMENT INSURANCE

Economist Jonathan Gruber of MIT explored both the benefits and costs of unemployment insurance and attempted to calculate the optimal amount of unemployment insurance. Looking at both the costs and the benefits of unemployment insurance, Gruber found that the optimal level of insurance was probably somewhat lower (closer to 30 percent) than the current 40 percent provided by the states.

6.4 The Consumer Price Index and the Cost of Living

The study of prices and price indices such as the Consumer Price Index is an extension of the real-nominal principle.

Real-Nominal Principle

What matters to people is the real value of money or income—its purchasing power—not the face value of money or income.

The **Consumer Price Index** or CPI is a price index measuring prices of a fixed basket of goods chosen to represent the consumption pattern of a typical consumer. Figure 6.5 shows the basket of goods used to calculate the CPI. The equation for the CPI is:

☑ Key Equation

$$\text{CPI in year } K = \frac{\text{cost of basket in year } K}{\text{cost of basket in base year}} \times 100$$

Other price indices use the same basic formula as the CPI except for the GDP deflator. Since 1996, the Commerce Department has used a chain-weighted index replacing the GDP deflator to measure changes in prices for goods and services included in GDP. The chain-weighted index for GDP and the CPI are both measures of average prices for the economy, yet they differ in two ways:

1. The CPI measures consumer prices, while the chain-weighted index measures the average price of output (not just consumption spending). The chain-weighted price index for GDP does not measure price changes from either used goods or imports. However the CPI measures the average price of spending on consumer goods, including imported goods purchased by consumers.

2. Unlike the chain-weighted price index for GDP, the CPI asks how much a *fixed* basket of goods costs in the current year compared to the cost of those same goods in a base year.

𝓖𝓼 Study Tip

Notice that whatever base year you choose for your index, it is 100 on your index. To start your index, your year K is the same as the base year. Since the numerator and the denominator are the same, they equal one. This value is multiplied by 100 to equal 100.

💣 Caution!

Price indices are based on a base year, while inflation rates are computed by comparing prices to the previous year. Inflation rates are annual percentage rates of increases in price levels, thus are based on what happened in the previous year.

☞ For more information about the CPI, go to the Bureau of Labor Statistics Web site at http://stats.bls.gov/cpi/home.htm.

Most economists believe that in reality all the indexes, including the chain-weighted index for GDP and the CPI, overstate actual changes in prices. In other words, the increase in prices is probably less than the reported indexes tell us. Changes in price indices are usually overstated due to difficulty in measuring quality improvements and introducing new products.

☞ Quality improvements, such as high plasma televisions or incorporating GPS systems in cars, may inflate the price of the goods in the basket. For example, a new car today costs around $20,000. About ten years ago, a new car probably cost around $10,000. The CPI indicates the price of a new car has doubled in only ten years, but that price increase *does not* take into account that today's cars have better safety features, better gas mileage, and better computerized equipment than they did ten years ago. Therefore, the CPI overstates the price increase in cars and similar products that have had significant quality improvements. New products such as cell phones, E-mail, iPods, and DVD players were not in the CPI back in the 1970s. When these products were introduced, their costs would abnormally inflate the

CPI. On the other hand, removal of goods, such as 8-track stereos, CB radios, and Beta video recorders, that consumers no longer purchase, may affect the CPI. (Ask your parents what these items are if you have questions.)

Since many government payments and union contracts adjust for inflation, they use the CPI to approximate the cost of living. **Cost-of-living adjustments** or **COLAs** are automatic increases in wages or other payments that are tied to the CPI. Cost-of-living adjustments are often overestimated since they use the CPI. This results in higher government payments and labor costs.

Let's review an Application that answers one of the key questions we posed at the start of the chapter:

4.   Are Social Security payments properly adjusted for changes in the cost of living?

APPLICATION 4: USING THE CPI TO ADJUST SOCIAL SECURITY BENEFITS

Each year, the federal government increases Social Security payments to the elderly by the rate of increase of prices as measured by the Consumer Price Index. The reason for this adjustment is to make sure that the elderly, whose other income tends to be fixed, do not suffer from cost-of-living increases. Economists believe that the CPI overstates actual price increases by between 0.5 and 1.5 percent a year. Assume that the figure is 1 percent. According to the Congressional Budget Office, if we reduced this adjustment for Social Security by 1 percent, it would save $42 billion over a five-year period! However, although the CPI may overstate price increases in general, it probably understates the rate of price increases facing the elderly. The elderly consume more medical care than do average citizens in the United States, and prices for medical care have increased faster than other prices in the economy.

6.5 Inflation

The **inflation rate** is the percentage change in the price level. As such, inflation rates are always measured in relation to the prior years. The inflation rate is computed as shown in the following key equation:

☑ **Key Equation**

Inflation Rate = % change in the price level = $\dfrac{\text{CPI}_{cy} - \text{CPI}_{py}}{\text{CPI}_{py}}$ where "cy" is the current year and "py" is the previous year.

For example, suppose that the CPI for 2005 was 110 and the CPI for 2006 is 120. Using the key equation above:

$$\frac{\text{CPI}_{2006} - \text{CPI}_{2005}}{\text{CPI}_{2005}} = \frac{120 - 110}{110} = \frac{10}{110} = 0.0909 \text{ or } 9.09\%$$

☞ Figure 6.6 shows historical U.S. inflation rates. Notice what happened after 1975. During this period of time, inflation grew dramatically due to the increase in oil prices as OPEC cut production of oil. Another reason for the increases in the price level is the excessively large increase in the growth rate of the money supply.

💣☀ **Caution!**

Price indices are based on a base year, while inflation rates are the year-to-year percentage change in the price index.

Deflation happens when there is negative inflation or falling prices of goods and services. At first this may not sound like a bad thing, but it may produce adverse effects. Consider the Great Depression. Prices fell 33 percent on average, and wages fell along with prices. The biggest problem caused by a deflation is that people cannot repay their debts.

☞ Suppose you bought a car for $12,000. You take out a loan to pay off your car in 5 years. With deflation your wages and prices drop. But the financing of the loan is still fixed and doesn't adjust with the price drop. Your wages come down and now your car may be repossessed as you can't make the payments due to your lower income. People with fixed debts are especially at risk with a price deflation. Yet some debt is set up to account for inflation. Adjustable rate mortgages, or ARMs, take into account inflation or deflation and adjust according to what is happening with prices.

6.6 The Costs of Inflation

The costs of inflation can be broken into two types of costs, anticipated and unanticipated. Let's explore what costs are associated with anticipated inflation and unanticipated inflation.

Anticipated inflation costs include menu costs, shoe-leather costs, and distortions to the financial and tax system. **Menu costs** are costs associated with changing prices and printing new price lists when there is inflation. Firms take on additional costs to change menus or advertising their goods and services when prices change. Another anticipated cost of inflation happens when people hold less money due to inflation. These costs are called **shoe-leather costs**. The cost of holding money is the loss of purchasing power as inflation increases. In order to prevent losing wealth, they put their money into something that earns a rate of return so they don't lose their wealth. There may be transaction costs associated with decreasing money balances.

☞ The term shoe-leather cost is an old term describing how people went about reducing or increasing their money balances. Before the use of online banking and computerized banking transactions, people had to physically go to the bank and withdraw money or deposit checks. They wore out the leather on their shoes going to the bank to get more money. Hence the term shoe-leather cost.

Lastly, the tax system is distorted due to inflation. In practice, our tax and financial systems do not fully adjust even to anticipated inflation. It is difficult for the government and businesses to change their normal rules of operation every time inflation changes. Our tax system is typically based on nominal income, not real income. Suppose you own a stock in a corporation that increases by 5 percent during the year. If the inflation rate is also 5 percent a year, your stock did not increase in real terms—it just kept up with inflation. Nonetheless, if you sold your stock at the end of the year, you would be taxed on the full 5 percent gain, despite the fact that the real value of your stock did not increase. Inflation distorts the operation of our tax and financial system.

Unanticipated costs cause arbitrary income redistributions. The textbook example is excellent in understanding these types of redistribution costs.   Suppose you live in a very safe neighborhood where no one locks the doors. If a rash of burglaries (transfers between you and the crooks) starts to occur, people will invest in locks, alarms, and more police. You and your community will incur real costs to prevent these arbitrary redistributions. The same is true for unanticipated inflation. If a society experiences unanticipated inflation, individuals and institutions will change their behavior. Some people will gain from the redistribution and some will lose from the redistribution.

What about the loans made prior to the unanticipated inflation? In this case, debtors will gain at the expense of creditors. Creditors, on the one hand, will lose because inflation will erode the amount of money they planned to earn on the loans. But since the loans have already been made, there's nothing they can do about it. Debtors, on the other hand, will get a deal. It will be easier for them to repay their loans with inflated dollars. If unanticipated inflation becomes extreme, individuals will spend more of their time trying to profit from inflation rather than working at productive jobs. Speculation starts to overtake production of goods and services, causing an economic slowdown.

An extreme form of inflation is called hyperinflation. **Hyperinflation** happens when the inflation rate exceeds 50 percent per month. The cost of hyperinflation is that prices increase so much that markets become ineffective in allocating goods and resources. Money loses its value and markets fail. Trading goods for goods may still occur, but the economy loses efficiency. We will discuss hyperinflation in more detail in Chapter 16.

Let's try an activity that gives you practice in creating a CPI and inflation rates.

Activity

The table below gives information on the cost of a fixed basket of goods for the years 2002–2006. From the price information, compute the CPI and the inflation rates for each of the years. Assume the base year is 2002.

Year	Cost of Bundle of Consumer Goods	CPI	Inflation Rate
2002	$1000		
2003	$1200		
2004	$1400		
2005	$1300		
2006	$1500		

Answers

Calculating the CPI

Remember the base year is 2002, so all prices will be compared to 2002 prices. Using the following equation:

$$\text{CPI in year } K = \frac{\text{cost of basket in year } K}{\text{cost of basket in base year}} \times 100. \text{ We can compute the following CPI:}$$

2002: CPI in year 2002 = $\dfrac{\text{cost of basket in year 2002}}{\text{cost of basket in base year, 2002}}$ x 100 = $\dfrac{\$1000}{\$1000}$ x 100 = 100

2003: CPI in year 2003 = $\dfrac{\text{cost of basket in year 2003}}{\text{cost of basket in base year, 2002}}$ x 100 = $\dfrac{\$1200}{\$1000}$ x 100 = 120

2004: CPI in year 2004 = $\dfrac{\text{cost of basket in year 2004}}{\text{cost of basket in base year, 2002}}$ x 100 = $\dfrac{\$1400}{\$1000}$ x 100 = 140

2005: CPI in year 2005 = $\dfrac{\text{cost of basket in year 2005}}{\text{cost of basket in base year, 2002}}$ x 100 = $\dfrac{\$1300}{\$1000}$ x 100 = 130

2006: CPI in year 2006 = $\dfrac{\text{cost of basket in year 2006}}{\text{cost of basket in base year, 2002}}$ x 100 = $\dfrac{\$1500}{\$1000}$ x 100 = 150

To calculate the inflation rates, use the following equation:

Inflation Rate = % change in the price level = $\dfrac{CPI_{cy} - CPI_{py}}{CPI_{py}}$ where "cy" is the current year and "py" is the previous year.

Based on our information, there is no change in 2002. The inflation rate would be zero. Inflation rates for the other years are calculated as follows:

Inflation rate for 2003: $\dfrac{CPI_{2003} - CPI_{2002}}{CPI_{2002}} = \dfrac{120 - 100}{100} = \dfrac{20}{100} = 0.20$ or 20%

Inflation rate for 2004: $\dfrac{CPI_{2004} - CPI_{2003}}{CPI_{2003}} = \dfrac{140 - 120}{120} = \dfrac{20}{120} = 0.167$ or 16.7%

Inflation rate for 2005: $\dfrac{CPI_{2005} - CPI_{2004}}{CPI_{2004}} = \dfrac{130 - 140}{140} = \dfrac{-10}{140} = -0.0714$ or -7.14%

Inflation rate for 2006: $\dfrac{CPI_{2006} - CPI_{2005}}{CPI_{2005}} = \dfrac{150 - 130}{130} = \dfrac{20}{130} = 0.154$ or 15.4%

Year	Cost of Bundle of Consumer Goods	CPI	Inflation Rate
2002	$1000	100	0
2003	$1200	120	20%
2004	$1400	140	16.7%
2005	$1300	130	-7.14%
2006	$1500	150	15.4%

Key Terms

Anticipated inflation: Inflation that is expected.

Consumer Price Index (CPI): A price index that measures the cost of a fixed basket of goods chosen to represent the consumption pattern of a typical consumer.

Cost-of-living adjustments (COLAs): Automatic increases in wages or other payments that are tied to the CPI.

Cyclical unemployment: Unemployment that occurs during fluctuations in real GDP.

Deflation: Negative inflation or falling prices of goods and services.

Discouraged workers: Workers who left the labor force because they could not find jobs.

Frictional unemployment: Unemployment that occurs with the normal workings of the economy, such as workers taking time to search for suitable jobs and firms taking time to search for qualified employees.

Full employment: The level of unemployment that occurs when the unemployment rate is at the natural rate.

Hyperinflation: An inflation rate exceeding 50 percent per month.

Inflation rate: The percentage rate of change in the price level.

Labor force: The total number of workers, both the employed and the unemployed.

Labor force participation rate: The percentage of the population over 16 years of age that is in the labor force.

Menu costs: The costs associated with changing prices and printing new price lists when there is inflation.

Natural rate of unemployment: The level of unemployment at which there is no cyclical unemployment. It consists of only frictional and structural unemployment.

Seasonal unemployment: The component of unemployment attributed to seasonal factors.

Shoe-leather costs: Costs of inflation that arise from trying to reduce holdings of cash.

Structural unemployment: Unemployment that occurs when there is a mismatch of skills and jobs.

Unanticipated inflation: Inflation that is not expected.

Unemployment insurance: Payments unemployed people receive from the government.

Unemployment rate: The percentage of the labor force that is unemployed.

Practice Quiz

(Answers are provided at the end of the Practice Quiz.)

1. Which of the following individuals are included in the labor force?
    a. Anyone who is 16 years of age or older and capable of working
    b. Those who are employed and those who are unemployed
    c. The employed and anyone who could potentially fill a job but may not be currently interested in working
    d. Anyone who is employed, unemployed workers, and discouraged workers—those who are not looking for work

2. The ratio of the labor force to the adult population is known as:
    a. the employment rate.
    b. the unemployment rate.
    c. the labor force participation rate.
    d. the population rate.

3. This question tests your understanding of Application 1 in this chapter: After growing sharply, women's labor force participation has leveled off. What do the recent data show about trends in the percentage of women who are working?

    "In 1948, the labor force participation rate for women 20 years and older was 32 percent. By 1970, it had grown to 43 percent, and by 1997 it had reached 60 percent. But since 1997, the figure has remained virtually constant at 60 percent."

    What is a possible explanation as to why the women's labor force participation has reached a peak in the United States?
    a. It appears that advances in technology have displaced many workers, in particular women, who are less and less able to find jobs.
    b. It appears that women simply have run out of time available to increase their hours of work.
    c. The reason is that a new trend is evolving, where more and more women are choosing once again to exit the labor force and become the primary caretakers of their households.
    d. It appears that men and women today are competing for similar jobs and, as the labor force participation rate of men increases, the labor force participation rate of women decreases.

4. Refer to the figure below. The chart below shows employment data for February 2006. Group 5 equals:

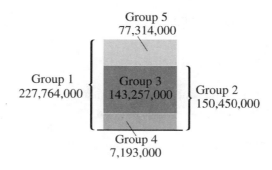

a.   the adult population.
b.   the unemployed.
c.   adults not in the labor force.
d.   the employed.

5.   Refer to the figure below. As a result of a severe and prolonged recession, the number of discouraged workers increases. Which groups below are affected?

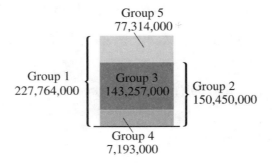

a.   Group 4 only
b.   Groups 2, 3, 4, and 5
c.   Groups 3 and 5 only
d.   Groups 3 and 4 only

6.   In 2006, unemployment rates in developed countries around the world:
a.   showed substantial variations.
b.   were quite similar.
c.   were the lowest they have been in 25 years.
d.   revealed that lack of government support for the unemployed leads to higher unemployment rates.

7.   When you add discouraged workers, other marginally attached workers, and individuals working part-time for economic reasons, measured unemployment:
a.   increases but only slightly.
b.   increases substantially.
c.   actually decreases slightly.
d.   remains the same.

8.   The unemployment that is created when different sectors give way to other sectors or certain jobs are eliminated while new types of jobs are created is called:
a.   cyclical unemployment.
b.   frictional unemployment.
c.   structural unemployment.
d.   seasonal unemployment.

9.   Which of the following is true about unemployment insurance?
a.   Unemployment insurance is typically only temporary.
b.   Unemployment insurance often replaces a worker's full earnings.
c.   Unemployment insurance actually helps to reduce the time spent unemployed.
d.   All of the above

10. This question tests your understanding of Application 3 in this chapter: finding the optimal level of unemployment insurance. What are the costs of either too high or too low levels of unemployment insurance?

"How do we balance the benefits and costs of unemployment insurance? Suppose that the government provided all unemployed workers a payment that was equal to their previous salary as long as they remained unemployed. While this would prevent unemployed workers from suffering any financial hardship, very few workers would return to work if the government were paying them their full salaries. This, of course, would lead to excessive unemployment. States recognize this and replace only a fraction of a worker's prior salary—typically about 40 percent."

"Economist Jonathan Gruber of MIT explored both the benefits and costs of unemployment insurance and attempted to calculate the optimal amount of unemployment insurance. In his research, Gruber found that the amount necessary to just offset the resulting decrease in consumption from being unemployed is":
   a.   an amount slightly greater than the actual benefits provided by the government.
   b.   an amount significantly greater than the actual benefits provided by the government.
   c.   an amount slightly smaller than the actual benefits provided by the government.
   d.   an amount significantly smaller than the actual benefits provided by the government.

11. If the cost of a market basket in 1992, the base year, is $200, and the cost of the same market basket in 2004 is $250, what is the CPI in 2004?
   a.   .25
   b.   25%
   c.   125
   d.   80%

12. Both the CPI and the chain index for GDP are measures of the average prices for the economy, yet they differ in several ways. Which of the following statements is correct?
   a.   The CPI includes goods produced in prior years, as well as imported goods, while the chain price index does not.
   b.   Both the chain price index for GDP and the CPI ask how much a fixed basket of goods costs in the current year compared to the base year.
   c.   Both assertions above are correct.
   d.   Neither assertion above is correct.

13. Which of the following is the best definition of inflation?
   a.   The percentage rate of change of a price index
   b.   An increase in the stated prices of goods and services
   c.   A decrease in the purchasing power of consumers
   d.   A decrease in the Consumer Price Index over time

14. Which of the following is true about the history of U.S. inflation rates?
   a.   The price level has increased at a relatively constant rate ever since 1875.
   b.   The price level grew steadily before World War II, then it stabilized and has grown at a constant rate ever since.
   c.   After remaining relatively flat for 60 years, the price level began to steadily increase after World War II.
   d.   Between 1875 and World War II, the price level was highly volatile. After World War II, the price level began to decline steadily.

15. A sustained decrease in the average level of prices and wages in the economy:
    a. is considered desirable.
    b. is thought to be impossible.
    c. is called disinflation.
    d. is called deflation.

16. What is the impact of unanticipated inflation?
    a. None. If inflation is unanticipated, it has no impact on the economy.
    b. Unanticipated inflation makes everyone in the economy worse off.
    c. Unanticipated inflation makes everyone in the economy better off.
    d. Unanticipated inflation creates arbitrary redistributions of income.

17. Describe the problem of underemployment. How is underemployment related to frictional, cyclical, and structural unemployment? Explain.

18. Unanticipated inflation is worse than anticipated inflation. Explain.

19. Explain the meaning of full employment.

20. Beyond the loss of income, what are the costs of unemployment to the individual and to society as a whole?

Answers to the Practice Quiz

1. b. The unemployed are those individuals who do not currently have a job but who are actively looking for work. The employed are individuals who currently have jobs. The employed plus the unemployed comprise the labor force.

2. c. This ratio shows the number of adults in the population who choose to participate in the labor force.

3. b. It appears that women's labor force participation has reached a peak in the United States. One explanation for this trend is that women may simply have run out of available time. With the advent of new technologies, women could increase their labor force participation yet still take primary care of their households. But even with new technology, housework and childcare do take time. Because women provide more household services than men, it is understandable why their labor force participation may have reached a peak.

4. c. This group comprises the people who are institutionalized, retired, full-time students, discouraged workers, and those who work at home without pay.

5. b. Group 3 will decrease, group 4 will increase, and a severe and prolonged recession will also increase the number of discouraged workers who fall out of the labor force, thereby increasing group 5. As the number of people in group 5 increases, there are fewer people in group 2.

6. a. There are substantial variations in unemployment around the world.

7. b. Measured unemployment increases substantially. Depending on the statistic you want to emphasize, the unemployment rate could vary from the official 5.8% to as much as 9.4%.

8. c. Structural unemployment occurs when the economy evolves. It occurs when different sectors give way to other sectors or certain jobs are eliminated while new types of jobs are created.

9. a. Unemployment insurance is typically only temporary and does not replace a worker's full earnings. Unemployment insurance may actually lead to additional time spent unemployed.

10. c. Unemployment insurance can offset part of the sharp decrease in consumption. Economist Jonathan Gruber of MIT found that the optimal level of insurance was probably somewhat lower (closer to 30 percent) than the current 40 percent provided by the states.

11. c. CPI04= (250/200) x 100 = 125

12. a. The CPI includes goods produced in prior years, as well as imported goods, while the chain price index does not. Also, unlike the chain price index for GDP, the CPI asks how much a fixed basket of goods costs in the current year compared to the base year.

13. a. The percentage rate of change of a price index is the inflation rate.

14. c. The Price Index for U.S. GDP, 1875–2005, shows that after remaining relatively flat for 60 years, the price level began to steadily increase after World War II.

15. d. Deflation refers to a sustained decrease in the average level of prices and wages in the economy. Deflation is undesirable. The biggest problem caused by decreasing prices and wages is that people cannot repay their debts, which do not fall with deflation.

16. d. The cost of unexpected or unanticipated inflation is arbitrary redistributions of income. Inflation creates winners and losers. These redistributions impose real costs on the economy. If a society experiences unanticipated inflation, individuals and institutions will change their behavior.

17. The underemployed are workers who hold a part-time job but prefer to work full time or hold jobs that are far below their capabilities. Underemployment may occur during recessions, when jobs are hard to find and people may decide to take whatever they can find. But more importantly, underemployment is a structural phenomenon. The economy may have many jobs available, but the skills of the underemployed don't match the skills required to fill those vacancies. Engineers who can't find engineering jobs, for example, may have to take jobs as teachers or taxi drivers.

18. When banks do not anticipate inflation correctly, for example, and inflation turns out to be higher than anticipated, they will issue loans at nominal interest rates that are too low. If nominal interest rates did not anticipate the higher inflation rate, then borrowers pay back loans in "cheaper dollars." Therefore, unanticipated inflation hurts lenders and benefits borrowers. In general, any decision involving an expectation of inflation that is incorrect will throw the model of information off. If economic agents use all information available to make their decisions, an unexpected increase in the rate of inflation will cause them to make incorrect decisions.

19. Full employment is the level of employment that occurs when the unemployment rate is at the natural rate. The natural rate of unemployment is the level of unemployment at which there is no cyclical unemployment. When the economy operates at full employment, it produces the natural or potential level of output, or the output that can be produced when resources are fully employed. Full employment is associated with a normal (not a maximum) rate of capacity utilization. In addition, full employment does not mean that the unemployment rate equals zero. In the United States, economists estimate that the natural rate of unemployment is between 5.0% and 6.5%. The natural rate of

unemployment consists of only frictional and structural unemployment. Some frictional unemployment is needed for the economy to operate efficiently.

20. The loss of income is not the only important consequence of unemployment. Unemployed individuals also lose their self-esteem and have a greater tendency for social deviance. Crime, drug abuse, suicide, and mental illness tend to increase during periods of high unemployment. The social cost of unemployment is not only the cost of the output lost as a result of it, but also the cost of psychological damage to unemployed workers.

7

The Economy at Full Employment

Chapter Summary

Classical models are economic models that assume wages and prices adjust freely to changes in demand and supply. Classical models were the primary means of explaining economic behavior until the Great Depression. Yet during the Great Depression, unemployment was rampant—nearly 25 percent of the labor force was unemployed. Economists subsequently began to develop models that explained persistent unemployment. We will discuss alternative models to the classical model later.

Classical models were based on the premise that labor markets determined the output level of an economy. In other words, real factors of production such as labor and capital produce output for an economy. From there, we will look at how a given labor force produces goods and services. Here are the main points of the chapter:

- Models that assume wages and prices adjust freely to changes in demand and supply are called classical models. They are useful to understand how the economy operates at full employment.
- Full-employment output, or potential output, is the level of GDP produced from a given supply of capital when the labor market is in equilibrium. Potential output is fully determined by the supply of factors of production in the economy.
- Increases in the stock of capital raise the level of full-employment output and real wages.
- Increases in the supply of labor will raise the level of full-employment output but lower the level of real wages.
- The full-employment model has many applications. Many economists use it to study the effects of taxes on potential output. Others have found the model useful in understanding economic fluctuations in models of real business cycles.
- At full employment, increases in government spending must come at the expense of other components of GDP. In a closed economy, either consumption or investment must be crowded out. In an open economy, net exports can be crowded out as well. Decreases in government spending will crowd in other types of spending.

Applying the Concepts

After reading this chapter, you should be able to answer these three key questions:
1. Although we normally think that increased immigration will reduce wages, what factors could cause increased immigration to raise wages?
2. Why are differences in the amount of labor supply across countries an important determinant of economic performance?

3. Do differences in taxes and government benefits explain why Europeans work substantially fewer hours per year than do Americans or the Japanese?

⌒ Study Tip

Starting in this chapter, you learn about macroeconomic theory. Theories are based on models that attempt to depict reality. A model is a descriptive representation of the reality under study. Think of building a model car. You have an idea of how the car should look from the picture on the box. You then build the car from the parts included in the box until you complete the model. The model car is still not exactly the same as a real car, but it does help you understand how the car works. In the same way, we will be building economic models. We will simplify how the world works by making basic assumptions. The assumptions are like the picture on the box. Based on those assumptions, we will try to create a model of how the economy works with those assumptions. The assumptions for the classical model are the picture on the box. The parts of the model will be the production function and the labor market. So let's start building.

7.1 Wage and Price Flexibility and Full Employment

⌒ Study Tip

Study the assumptions in this section carefully. They will help you understand what economists were thinking when they put the classical model together. In other words, the assumptions describe how they believed the economic world worked.

The classical model operates on two basic assumptions:
1. The price mechanism coordinates economic activity since prices and wages are flexible and adjust quickly.
2. The economy will produce at full employment due to flexible wages and prices because the labor market will be at equilibrium.

✹ Caution!

Full employment does not mean that the unemployment rate is zero. Frictional and structural unemployment may exist.

To understand what is meant by producing at full employment, we must look at the labor market. Full employment means that there is no cyclical unemployment in the economy. Unemployment may still exist, but it exists in the form of frictional and/or structural unemployment. The unemployment rate is at the natural rate of unemployment. No booms or busts exist in conditions of full employment. In other words there is no business cycle in the long run.

☞ Consider what happens when you get out of high school. You are an adult and need to find a job. There are jobs available, but you may not like the pay so you keep looking for a job with higher pay. You would be frictionally unemployed. Or you may want to be a genetic engineer, but you don't have the knowledge and expertise to take the job even if the paycheck is right. You would be structurally unemployed in that case. In conclusion, full employment implies that there are jobs for everyone who accepts the wage rate determined by the market.

7.2 The Production Function

> ### 𝒢𝒶 Study Tip
>
> Building on our concept of models, this is the first piece of the classical model. Study how the model works so you can understand how it fits with the labor market. As you review the text, try to understand the variables that make up the production function and how it influences the shape of the curves.

The **production function** shows the relationship between the level of output and the factors of production that are inputs to production. A simple equation depicts the production function as follows:

> ### ☑ Key Equation
>
> $Y = F(K, L)$, where
> Y is output
> K is the capital stock
> L is the labor force

The production function has two primary inputs, capital and labor. The stock of capital or capital stock represents the total of all machines, equipment, and buildings in an entire economy. Labor is the human effort, both physical and mental, used to produce output. The capital stock is assumed constant since current investment changes the amount of capital in existence very little. Since the capital stock is relatively constant, the production function exhibits the principle of diminishing returns. In other words, you can add more inputs, such as labor, and add to your total output produced. However, you will add output at a diminishing rate.

 Principle of Diminishing Returns

Suppose that output is produced with two or more inputs and that we increase one input while holding the other inputs fixed. Beyond some point—called the *point of diminishing returns*—output will increase at a decreasing rate.

Figure 7.1 illustrates a basic production function. The numerical values are in Table 7.1. Note that the shape of the production function demonstrates diminishing returns. As the labor increases, we move along the given production function, but this results in less total output per labor input.

⌒ **Study Tip**

You should take a moment to draw the production function. Take as many times as you need until you feel comfortable with this part of the model. Figure 7.1 gives you a picture of what the production function should look like. Label your graph correctly so you can see the relationship between the labor force and output.

What happens if the capital stock isn't fixed any longer? Since labor inputs and output define our production function, changes in the capital stock will change the position of the production function. Capital stock increases shift the production function upward, as shown in Figure 7.2. The logic behind this upward shift is that workers have more capital to use in production. The capital increase allows for greater labor productivity, leading to increases in output with a given labor force. We will see how this occurs in Chapter 8.

7.3 Wages and the Demand and Supply for Labor

⌒ **Study Tip**

The labor market is the final piece of the classical model that we explore in this chapter. You will need to understand how the demand and supply for labor affect the size of the labor force. Later you will put the production function together with the labor market to create our classical model. You will see how changes in the labor market affect output levels.

As seen from our production function, the labor force is the prime variable in producing output. We must understand how the labor market behaves in order to understand production. As in any market, there is demand and supply. It is no different in the labor market. In the labor market, firms demand labor and workers supply labor. The **real wage** is the wage rate paid to employees adjusted for changes in the price level. The real wage acts as the price of labor in labor markets.

Firms behave according to the law of demand. As the real wage is a cost to firms, the higher the real wage, the less quantity of labor the firms demand. On the other hand, with lower real wages, firms demand higher quantities of labor as shown in panel A of Figure 7.3.

Workers behave according to the law of supply. Workers will work more as the real wage increases. This explains why workers face an upward-sloping labor supply curve shown in panel B of Figure 7.3.

Bringing together the demand and supply for labor creates labor market equilibrium. Labor market equilibrium occurs where the labor supply curve intersects the labor demand curve. The equilibrium determines the quantity of the labor force and the real wage. This intersection also depicts a full employment condition in the labor market according to the classical model as shown in Panel C of Figure 7.3.

💣 **Caution!**

Before going further, if you had difficulty understanding what causes changes or shifts of demand and supply curves, review Chapter 4.

You have noticed that the labor market is critical in the classical model. Remember, changes in demand or supply will change the level of employment and the real wage.

The labor decision is another example of the marginal principle. Workers will supply an additional hour if the wages are greater than the cost of leisure time. Workers will continue to add additional hours until the wages and the cost of leisure is equal.

 Marginal Principle

Increase the level of an activity as long as its marginal benefit exceeds its marginal cost. Choose the level at which the marginal benefit equals the marginal cost.

At the same time, firms are making decisions on how many hours workers should work. They will demand more hours so long as the production value gained exceeds the cost of real wages paid to workers. Firms will demand more hours until the production value is equal to the real wage.

> **Study Tips**
>
> Changes in supply shift the supply curve; changes in demand shift the demand curve. Increases in supply shift the curve to the right; decreases in demand shift the curve to the left.

Let's review an Application that answers one of the key questions we posed at the start of the chapter:

1. Although we normally think that increased immigration will reduce wages, what factors could cause increased immigration to raise wages?

APPLICATION 1: IMMIGRATION AFFECTS BOTH THE DEMAND AND SUPPLY FOR LABOR

A recent study by Gianmarco Ottaviano and Giovanni Peri estimated that during the 1990s immigration, on average, increased the average wage of American-born workers by 2.7 percent. In their analysis, they took into account that increased immigration not only led to increases in the supply of labor, but also led to additional investment. As new workers became available to the U.S. economy, firms were able to add new plant and equipment to profitably employ these workers. Ottoviano and Peri also found that the wages of high-school dropouts fell while the wages of workers with at least a high-school education increased. The reason for this difference was that high-school dropouts compete most directly with the new immigrants, whereas those workers with more education do not. Their study reinforces the importance of value of education for workers in the global economy.

7.4 Labor Market Equilibrium and Full Employment

> **Study Tip**
>
> Now we have the pieces of the model, the production function, and the labor market. It is time to put the pieces of the model together.

You can see we are building the model one piece at a time. First, we started with the production function. Then, we built an understanding of the importance of the labor market in determining real wages and the quantity of the labor force. Now, we are going to bring those tools together to complete the basic classical model. If you look at Figure 7.5, you will notice that the production function is drawn above the labor market. Figuratively (no pun intended), the labor market supports directly the production function like a foundation. If you draw the labor market first at equilibrium then draw the production function above it, you will notice that the connecting variable is the labor force. You should get used to drawing these two graphs when asked to analyze an economy using a classical model.

᧒ Study Tip

Draw the graphs of the basic classical model. The more you draw them, the more comfortable you will be in using them. Draw the graphs together, as in Figure 7.5. It is easier to see the relationships that way.

᧒ Study Tip

Now that our classical model is complete, we can use it to analyze other economic situations. The classical model will also be used in other chapters in the book. Be sure and review it so it stays fresh in your mind.

Let's review an Application that answers one of the key questions we posed at the start of the chapter:

2. Why are differences in the amount of labor supply across countries an important determinant of economic performance?

APPLICATION 2: LABOR SUPPLY VARIES ACROSS COUNTRIES AND TIME

Although work may be universal, the amount of work done varies substantially and consequently affects output. Consider vacation time. Apart from national holidays, a typical worker in the United States has 12 days of vacation. The United Kingdom has 28 vacation days, Germany has 35 days, and Italy has 42 days of vacation. Per capita GDP would be comparable if these countries worked as many hours as the United States. Women have contributed greatly to potential output based on labor force participation rates.

7.5 Using the Full-Employment Model

᧒ Study Tip

This is a good opportunity to apply the classical model. Using the graphs you learned on page 150, see if you can show what happens in when employment taxes are levied in the economy.

Employment taxes are a good example of a variable that affects the labor market. Consider the example in the book where employment taxes increase. You can see what would happen in the labor market depending on the shape of the labor supply curve. The upward-sloping supply curve would combine with a decrease in demand for labor, causing a decrease in the labor force and the real wage. If this is combined to the production function, then you can see that this would also decrease output as well. In the case of a vertical labor supply, the real wage decreased, but the labor force stayed constant, resulting in no change in the output level.

☞ Many people ask themselves, "Should I work overtime hours? It will just be taken in taxes anyway." This is another example of the marginal principle. Workers assess whether the cost of time is worth the overtime pay less taxes taken for higher income. They will work overtime if the incomes they earn after taxes are taken are greater than the opportunity cost doing something else during those hours.

Let's review an Application that answers one of the key questions we posed at the start of the chapter:

3. Do differences in taxes and government benefits explain why Europeans work substantially fewer hours per year than do Americans or the Japanese?

APPLICATION 3: A NOBEL LAUREATE EXPLAINS WHY EUROPEANS WORK LESS THAN AMERICANS OR THE JAPANESE

On average, today the French (and other Europeans) work one-third fewer hours than do Americans. However, in the early 1970s Europeans actually worked slightly more hours than did Americans. Nobel laureate Edward Prescott attributes the decreases in hours of work in Europe to increases in the tax burden that ultimately falls on workers. Government spending and transfers play a larger role in European economies than in the United States.

A theory explaining how the technology affects output is called the real business cycle theory. This theory is based on the work of Edward Prescott. The basic premise of the theory is that technological shocks, positive or negative, will have impacts on real output. The impact of these shocks can result in permanent changes in the economy. Figure 7.7 shows how an adverse technological shock could impact labor markets and thus output.

7.6 Dividing Output among Competing Demands for GDP at Full Employment

As seen in our classical model, full employment output is determined by the labor force. Full employment output is a fixed amount, causing a phenomenon called "crowding out."

Table 7.2 presents data on the percent of GDP in alternative uses for five countries in 2003. Recall that consumption (C), investment (I), and government purchases (G) refer to total spending by residents of that country. Net exports (NX) is the difference between exports (sales of goods to foreign residents) and imports (purchases of goods abroad).

💣 Caution!

These data in Table 7.2 are from the *World Development Indicators*, which the World Bank publishes. In these data, government purchases include only government consumption, such as military spending or wages for government employees. Government investment, such as spending on bridges or roads, is included in the investment category (I). This shouldn't keep you up at night, but to read the data correctly, it is important to make this distinction.

Each country has its own spending patterns when it comes to GDP. This wide diversity challenges economists to explain these differences. Some economists have suggested that China's high savings rate (low share of consumption) can be explained by its one-child-per-family policy. They argue that this policy leads workers to save more for retirement, because they cannot depend on their children to support them. There are a variety of reasons why countries spend the way they do. In general, differences across countries are hard to explain.

Crowding out happens when there is a reduction in investment (or other component of GDP) caused by an increase in government spending. The underlying premise is that under full employment conditions, you have a fixed amount of output.

Principle of Opportunity Cost
The opportunity cost of something is what you sacrifice to get it.

To increase government expenditures, something has to be traded off. The opportunity cost of the increased government spending is private investment and/or consumption. In other words, government spending "crowds out" private investment and/or consumption. See Figures 7.8 and 7.9 for examples of crowding out. Crowding out occurs when we are in a closed economy or without an international sector.

☞ Suppose you have a car lot of 20 cars. Ten cars go to consumers, 5 cars go to businesses, and the other 5 cars go the government. Since there are only 20 cars, if the government comes and buys 10 cars, then there are only 10 cars left for businesses and consumers when there were originally 15. That is the essence of crowding out.

The concept of crowding out works in an open economy. However, the variable that is crowded out is some combination of net exports and private investment.

Another possibility can happen when government expenditures decrease. This is called "crowding in." This may create the opportunity for private investment and/or consumption to increase. The equation below summarizes the concepts of "crowding out" and "crowding in":

☑ Key Equation

$Y = C + I + G$, where
Y is full employment output.
As $G \uparrow$, I and/or $C \downarrow$ (Crowding out with a closed economy)
As $G \uparrow$, NX, and/or $I \downarrow$ (Crowding out with an open economy)
As $G \downarrow$, NX, and/or $I \uparrow$ (Crowding in with an open economy)

Activity

Draw the graphs at equilibrium as shown on page 150 to show what would happen in the following situation: Suppose the economy suffers from a pandemic that wipes out half the population. Show what happens using the graphs and tell what happens to the real wage, the labor force, and output.

Remember also from our assumptions that the equilibrium labor force is at full employment. The corresponding labor force L^* from the labor market to the production function maps out the full employment output level Y^*. This economy has fully realized its potential output level. Full employment output is also called potential output.

Answer

The pandemic would wipe out half the population. The supply of workers would decrease, shifting the supply curve to the left. This would cause an increase in real wages, a decrease in the labor force, and a decrease in output. The graph should look like this:

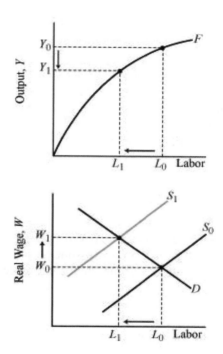

Key Terms

Classical models: Economic models that assume wages and prices adjust freely to changes in demand and supply.

Closed economy: An economy without international trade.

Crowding in: The increase of investment (or other component of GDP) caused by a decrease in government spending.

Crowding out: The reduction in investment (or other component of GDP) caused by an increase in government spending.

Full-employment output: The level of output that results when the labor market is in equilibrium and the economy is producing at full employment.

Labor: Human effort, including both physical and mental effort, used to produce goods and services.

Open economy: An economy with international trade.

Production function: The relationship between the level of output of a good and the factors of production that are inputs to production.

Real business cycle theory: The economic theory that emphasizes how shocks to technology can cause fluctuations in economic activity.

Real wage: The wage rate paid to employees adjusted for changes in the price level.

Stock of capital: The total of all machines, equipment, and buildings in an entire economy.

Practice Quiz

(Answers are provided at the end of the Practice Quiz.)

1. Models that assume that wages and prices adjust freely to changes in demand and supply are called:
   a. free-market models.
   b. classical models.
   c. Keynesian models.
   d. neo-Keynesian models.

2. The classical school of thought that dominated economics until the mid-1930s sustained that, after changes in supply and demand that throw the economy out of full employment:
   a. wages and prices adjust slowly, but over time, the economy returns, ever so slowly, back to full employment.
   b. wages and prices adjust freely, but the economy does not return to full employment unless the government intervenes.
   c. wages and prices will adjust quickly and naturally, over a relatively short period of time, to bring the economy back to full employment.
   d. for all practical purposes, wages and prices are fixed, which results in shortages and surpluses any time supply and demand change.

3. What types of unemployment exist when the economy is at full employment?
   a. Frictional and cyclical
   b. Frictional and structural
   c. Structural and cyclical
   d. None. When the economy is at full employment, there is no unemployment.

4. What name is given to all the machines, equipment, and buildings that exist in the entire economy?
   a. Productive capacity
   b. The stock of capital
   c. Investment
   d. None of the above. There is no name for such an aggregation.

5. The stock of capital that a society has at any point in time is determined by:
   a. investments it has made in new buildings, machines, and equipment in the past.
   b. current consumer expenditures that affect the demand for output.
   c. the demand and supply of labor.
   d. the amount of stocks, bonds, and government securities purchased by households.

6. Which of the following principles of economics is more closely associated with the economy's production function?
   a. The principle of opportunity cost
   b. The real-nominal principle
   c. The principle of diminishing returns
   d. The marginal principle

7. Refer to the figure below. Which of the following could have caused the move from point *a* to point *b*?

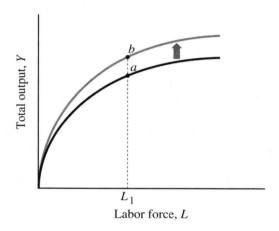

   a. An increase in the amount of labor
   b. A decrease in the amount of labor
   c. An increase in the amount of capital
   d. A decrease in the amount of capital

8. In deciding how many workers to hire, which of the following economic principles does a firm use?
   a. The principle of crowding out
   b. The real-nominal principle
   c. The principle of diminishing returns
   d. The marginal principle

9. Using the model of supply and demand to study the labor market, what is the likely impact of an increase in immigration?
   a. Immigration will likely cause real wages to fall, and the quantity of labor employed also to fall.
   b. Immigration will likely cause real wages to fall, and the quantity of labor employed to increase.
   c. Immigration will likely cause both real wages and employment to rise.
   d. Immigration will likely cause real wages to rise and the quantity of labor employed to fall.

10. This question tests your understanding of Application 1 in this chapter: Immigration affects both the demand and supply for labor. Although we normally think that increased immigration will reduce wages, what factors could cause increased immigration to actually raise wages?

A recent study about the impact of immigration on wages conducted by Gianmarco Ottaviano of the University of Bologna and Giovanni Peri of the University of California, Davis, found that during the 1990s:
   a. immigration, on average, increased the average wage of American-born workers.
   b. immigration increased both the demand and the supply for labor, with the shift in supply slightly outpacing the shift in demand, leading to a decrease in wages.
   c. only the wages of high-school dropouts increased as a result of immigration. The wages of workers with at least a high-school education decreased.
   d. immigration diminishes the value of education for workers in the global economy.

11. Which of the following is *full-employment output*?
   a. The level of output that is produced when the labor market is in equilibrium
   b. The level of output produced when the economy is producing at full employment
   c. A level of output also known as potential output
   d. All of the above

12. How do economists determine the level of full-employment output?
   a. They first estimate potential output, then estimate the amount of unemployment due to frictional and cyclical factors.
   b. They estimate the amount of cyclical unemployment, then subtract it from the amount of frictional and structural unemployment to determine potential output.
   c. They first estimate unemployment due to frictional and cyclical factors, then estimate how many workers will be employed if cyclical unemployment is 0, then determine the potential output those workers can make.
   d. They first look at how many workers are employed, then estimate how much output those workers can produce.

13. In the United States, estimates of the natural rate of unemployment in recent years have varied between:
   a. 3% and 10%.
   b. 5% and 6.5%.
   c. 3% and 4.5%.
   d. 10% and 25%.

14. Refer to the graph below. Which graph best describes the impact of a tax that business firms have to pay when they hire additional labor?

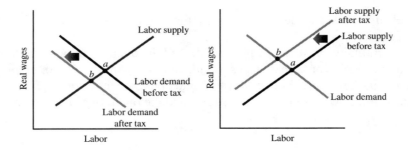

a. The graph on the left
b. The graph on the right
c. Both graphs shift simultaneously with the tax.
d. Neither graph is affected by the tax.

15. When the supply curve for labor is vertical, a tax paid by employers for hiring labor will have the following effect:
    a. Wages will fall and employment will rise.
    b. Both wages and employment will rise.
    c. Both wages and employment will fall.
    d. Wages will fall, but employment will not change.

16. An adverse technological shock would:
    a. shift labor supply to the right.
    b. shift labor demand to the left.
    c. shift labor supply to the left.
    d. shift labor demand to the right.

17. Which of the following is correct? When government spending increases:
    a. investment automatically increases.
    b. all the remaining shares of GDP are crowded in.
    c. other demands for GDP may be crowded out.
    d. both consumption and investment will rise.

18. In a closed economy, full-employment output is divided among how many uses?
    a. Only one
    b. Two
    c. Three
    d. Four

19. In an open economy, increases in government spending:
    a. could crowd out either consumption or investment, but never net exports.
    b. would probably lead to higher exports and lower imports.
    c. does not possibly result in any kind of crowding out of consumption, investment, or net exports.
    d. could, theoretically, lead to a reduction in net exports without a change in consumption or investment.

20. A decrease in government spending results in:
    a. crowding out.
    b. crowding in.
    c. a real business cycle.
    d. a beneficial demand shock.

21. Describe the premises of the economic theory known as the *real business cycle*.

22. Differentiate how output is divided among competing demands in a close economy versus in an open economy, and describe the impact of higher government spending in each of these economies.

Answers to the Practice Quiz

1. b. Models that assume that wages and prices adjust freely to changes in demand and supply are called classical models.

2. c. The term classical refers to a school of economics that believed that over a relatively short period of time wages and prices will adjust quickly and naturally to bring the economy back to full employment.

3. b. When the economy is at full employment, the only types of unemployment are frictional and structural. There is zero cyclical unemployment.

4. b. The stock of capital comprises all the machines, equipment, and buildings in the entire economy.

5. a. The stock of capital that a society has at any point in time is determined by investments it has made in new buildings, machines, and equipment in the past.

6. c. With capital fixed, the relationship between output and labor shown here reflects the principle of diminishing returns. PRINCIPLE OF DIMINISHING RETURNS: Suppose output is produced with two or more inputs and we increase one input while holding the other input or inputs fixed. Beyond some point—called the point of diminishing returns—output will increase at a decreasing rate.

7. c. When capital increases, the production function shifts up. At any level of labor input, more output can be produced than before the stock of capital was increased.

8. d. Applied to the demand for labor, the marginal principle states that a firm should increase the level number of workers it hires if the marginal benefit exceeds the marginal cost of an extra worker; reduce the number of workers if the marginal cost exceeds the marginal benefit. If possible, pick the number of workers for which the marginal benefit equals the marginal cost.

9. b. An increase in immigration causes an increase in the supply of labor. This shifts the supply of labor to the right, resulting in lower real wages and more workers employed.

10. a. Immigration, on average, increased the average wage of American-born workers by 2.7 percent. In their analysis, they took into account that increased immigration not only led to increases in the supply of labor, but also led to additional investment. As new workers became available to the U.S. economy, firms were able to add new plant and equipment to profitably employ these workers.

11. d. Full-employment output is the level of output that is produced when the labor market is in equilibrium and the economy is producing at full employment. It is also known as potential output.

12. c. Economists start with an estimate of what the unemployment rate would be if cyclical unemployment were zero—that is, if the only unemployment were due to frictional or structural factors. In the United States, estimates of the natural rate in recent years have varied between 5.0 to 6.5 percent. Economists then estimate how many workers will be employed and use the production function to determine potential output.

13. b. In the United States, estimates of the natural rate in recent years have varied between 5.0 to 6.5 percent.

14. a. A tax on labor will make labor more expensive and raise the marginal cost of hiring workers. The demand for labor shifts leftward. The tax reduces both wages and employment.

15. d. A vertical labor-supply curve means that workers will supply the same amount of labor regardless of the wage. For example, a single parent might work a full 40 hours a week regardless of the wage, so the supply curve will be vertical. If, say, other workers in the economy also put in the same hours regardless of the wage, the supply curve for labor in the entire economy will be vertical. With a vertical supply curve, the tax will reduce wages but have no effect on employment and therefore no effect on output.

16. b. An adverse shock to the economy shifts the labor demand curve to the left. The result is lower wages, reduced employment, and reduced output.

17. c. Increased government spending "crowds out" other demands for GDP. This is called crowding out.

18. c. In a closed economy, full-employment output is divided among three different demands: $C + I + G$.

19. d. In an open economy, increases in government spending need not crowd out either consumption or investment. Increased government spending could lead to reduced exports and increased imports. In practice, however, increases in government spending in an open economy would crowd out consumption, investment, and net exports.

20. b. Governments do not always increase spending. Sometimes, they decrease spending. When the government cuts spending and the level of output is fixed, some other type of spending will increase. We call this *crowding in*.

21. The real business cycle is a school of economic thought that emphasizes how shocks to technology can cause fluctuations in economic activity. Changes in technology will usually change the level of full employment or potential output. An adverse shock to the economy shifts the labor demand curve to the left. The result is lower wages, reduced employment, and reduced output. The key lesson from real business cycle theory is that potential output itself will vary over time.

22. An economy without international trade is called a closed economy. In this economy, full-employment output is divided among three different demands: $Y = C + I + G$. The supply of output (Y) is fixed, therefore, increases in government spending reduce, or crowd out, either consumption or investment. In general, both are affected. In an open economy, an economy with international trade, full-employment output is divided among four uses: $Y = C + I + G + (X - M)$. In an open economy, increases in government spending need not crowd out either consumption or investment. Increased government spending could lead to reduced exports and increased imports.

8

Why Do Economies Grow?

Chapter Summary

Economic growth is a fundamental goal for an economy because increasing real GDP increases income for the economy, leading to a higher standard of living. The chapter shows how economic growth over time affects how we live our lives differently today than we did 200 years ago. Economic growth is measured to see if real GDP is growing or not. This chapter will explore how growth is measured and the policies that the government uses to promote growth. Capital deepening and technological progress will be discussed in detail. The appendix describes the basic growth model put forth by Nobel laureate Robert Solow. Here are the main points of the chapter:

- Per capita GDP varies greatly throughout the world. There is debate about whether poorer countries in the world are converging in per capita incomes to richer countries.
- Economies grow through two basic mechanisms: capital deepening and technological progress. Capital deepening is an increase in capital per worker. Technological progress is an increase in output with no additional increases in inputs.
- Ongoing technological progress will lead to sustained economic growth.
- Various theories try to explain the origins of technological progress and determine how we can promote it. These theories include spending on research and development, creative destruction, the scale of the market, induced inventions, and education and the accumulation of knowledge, including investments in human capital.
- Governments can play a key role in designing institutions that promote economic growth, including providing secure property rights.

Applying the Concepts

After reading this chapter, you should be able to answer these seven key questions:
1. How does economic growth affect social indicators such as child labor?
2. Does economic growth necessarily cause more inequality?
3. How can we use economic analysis to understand the sources of growth in different countries?
4. Why did labor productivity in the United States fall sharply during the 1970s and 1980s?
5. How did the emergence of the Internet affect economic growth in the United States?
6. How are economic growth and health related to one another?
7. Why are clear property rights important for economic growth in developing countries?

8.1 Economic Growth Rates

In Chapter 5, **economic growth** was defined as sustained increases in the real GDP of an economy over a long period of time. Economic growth can be illustrated with the use of the production possibility curve, as shown in Figure 8.1. To see if economic growth has occurred, we need a means of measurement. There are three forms of measurement, which we discuss next:

- GDP
- Real GDP per capita
- Rule of 70

Since real GDP is the indicator of economic growth, real GDP is a starting point for measuring such growth. A country's economic growth can be measured from one year to the next using real GDP. If we want to measure how real GDP affects the population, then we need a different measurement. The measurement we use for this purpose is called real GDP per capita. **Real GDP per capita** is gross domestic product per person adjusted for changes in constant prices. It is the usual measure of living standards across time and between countries.

☞ The beginning of the chapter shows a woman living in 1783, and the next page shows a family living today. If we compare these people, we can see they have different economic conditions. The woman in the 1700s is using the fireplace as a place for cooking meals and keeping warm. The family shown on the other page is using the fireplace for warmth and decoration. As income increases, standards of living tend to improve. The more income you have in a country, the more its people can afford. A reason to measure economic growth and understand how to make economic growth happen is to improve standards of living. Comparing countries allows economists and policy makers to decide what policy would improve standards of living.

Another way to measure economic growth over time is to use growth rates. A **growth rate** is the percentage rate of change of a variable from one period to another. You already used growth rates when you calculated inflation rates. This time you will use real GDP as your measure of growth.

If you wish to know how long it takes for a country to double its real GDP, you can use the rule of 70. The following are the formulas useful for understanding economic growth:

> 𝓰𝓼 **Study Tip**
>
> The best way to get better at calculations is to practice them. Take a moment to practice using the equations below on a few problems at the end of the chapter or on myeconlab.com.

☑ Key Equations

$$\text{Real GDP per capita} = \frac{\text{Real GDP}}{\text{Population}}$$

$$\text{Growth rate} = g = \frac{\text{Real GDP}_{cy} - \text{Real GDP}_{py}}{\text{Real GDP}_{py}} \quad \text{where "cy" is the current year and "py" is}$$

the previous year.

$$\text{Rule of 70} = \frac{70}{\text{Percentage growth rate}}$$

Economists use growth rates and real GDP per capita to compare countries' economic growth. Table 8.1 shows real GDP per capita and growth rate data for various countries. Some people might believe that higher growth rates guarantee higher real GDP per capita. Yet notice in the table that even though some countries have a higher growth rate, their real GDP per capita may be lower than other countries. Comparing both growth rates and real GDP per capita allows economists and policy makers to make better policy decisions.

☀ Caution!

As you calculate growth rates, the percentage change is always calculated relative to the previous year.

Let's review an Application that answers one of the key questions we posed at the start of the chapter:

1. How does economic growth affect social indicators such as child labor?

APPLICATION 1: INCREASED GROWTH LEADS TO LESS CHILD LABOR IN DEVELOPING COUNTRIES

Contrary to what many people might think, most child labor occurs in agriculture, with parents as employers, rather than in manufacturing plants. As the incomes of the parents increase, they tend to rely less on their children and more on substitutes for child labor, such as fertilizer and new machinery. Careful studies in Vietnam revealed a significant drop in child labor during the 1990s, with the bulk of that decrease accounted for by higher family incomes.

Convergence is the process by which poorer countries close the gap with richer countries in terms of real GDP per capita. Figure 8.2 demonstrates the relationship between average growth rates from 1870–1979 and real GDP per capita in 1870. The line is plotted through 16 developed nations. Obstfeld and Rogoff found that the higher the average growth rate, the lower the real GDP per capita. This showed the possibility of convergence of lesser developed nations with developed nations. However, modern convergence analysis shows that this may not be the case in modern times.

Let's review an Application that answers one of the key questions we posed at the start of the chapter:

2.   Does economic growth necessarily cause more inequality?

APPLICATION 2: GROWTH NEED NOT CAUSE INCREASED INEQUALITY

Nobel laureate Simon Kuznets showed a relationship between economic growth and inequality. As a country develops, inequality within a country followed an inverted "U" pattern—it initially increased as a country developed and then narrowed over time. However, Piketty and Saez conclude that inequality is not based solely on growth. Inequality—as measured by the income share of the top 10 percent of families—increased from 40 percent at the beginning of the 1920s to 45 percent through the end of the Great Depression. During World War II, the share fell to 32 percent by 1944 and remained at that level until the early 1970s, at which time inequality began to again increase.   Economists Piketty and Saez indicate that other forces besides economic growth may cause inequality. Social norms and other factors, such as perceived fairness of compensation and the nature of the tax system, also play a role. Moreover, the United States experience suggests that these norms can change over time, even within the same country, regardless of growth rates.

8.2 Capital Deepening

Figure 8.3 demonstrates the classical model you learned about in Chapter 7. In the model, it was assumed that the capital stock (K) was fixed and the labor force (L) could change. Figure 8.3 demonstrates what happens when you have fixed labor force and the capital stock varies. An increase in capital with a fixed labor force will cause the production function to change its position, generating more output, moving from Y_1 to Y_2. To increase the capital stock, we need to increase investment.

To understand the relationship between investment and saving, we assume a simple domestic economy where only households and firms exist. The output generated in the economy creates the income the economy can spend. Income can either be spent on consumption goods or saved. The two types of goods that can be produced are consumption goods (C) and investment goods (I). Since the amount of consumption spending equals the amount of income spent on consumption goods, savings equals investment. Hence the equations below:

☑ Key Equations

$C + S = Y$ (Income)
$C + I = Y$ (Output)
$S = I$

Simply stated, saving funds investment spending. How does investment then affect the capital stock? Consider the stock of capital in a country at the beginning of the year. Additional investment during the year will add to the capital stock. At the same time, the capital stock will decrease due to depreciation. The net effect of investment and depreciation determines the amount of the capital stock at the end of the year. The difference between investment and depreciation is called *net investment*. In other words, net investment equals gross investment minus depreciation.

🔗 Study Tip

To increase the capital stock, net investment must be greater than zero. In other words, investment must be greater than the amount of worn out capital to increase the capital stock.

☞ Suppose you own a call center and you have 8 computers. Five of the computers stop working due to use and wear. The other 3 still work. If you wanted to increase the capital stock of your company, you would have to purchase more than 5 computers. The capital stock of an economy works basically the same way. The amount of investment must be larger than the replacement capital to increase the capital stock.

💣 Caution!

When talking about investment, we are not talking about purchasing financial instruments like stocks and bonds. Investment in economics means purchasing real capital.

Other forces can influence capital deepening such as population growth, government, and trade. Population growth allows the labor force to increase. This means more people are working and producing more output. Yet if the capital stock is constant, then the economy experiences diminishing returns.

Principle of Diminishing Returns

Suppose that output is produced with two or more inputs and that we increase one input while holding the other inputs fixed. Beyond some point—called the *point of diminishing returns*—output will increase at a decreasing rate.

Diminishing returns occur because there is less capital relative to the growing labor force. This decreases output per worker leading to less output produced.

☞ Recall the previous call center example. Suppose we have 8 computers, but hire 2 more workers than we have computers. The 2 additional workers can take calls but would have to share the computers with the other 8 workers. We would be able to take more calls in total, but we will do so at a diminishing rate because we have to share the 8 computers.

Government expenditures and taxes affect capital deepening in an economy. On the one hand, tax increases take away from income and thus reduce saving. Reduced savings reduce investment used for capital deepening. On the other hand, tax decreases have the opposite effect on income and can actually contribute to capital deepening. In reality, gross investment does not have to come solely from the private sector. Government expenditures in infrastructure such as roads, sewer treatment plants, or computers increase the capital stock of an economy and contribute to capital deepening.

Foreign trade can have a positive effect on capital deepening. Foreign investment in a domestic economy adds to the capital stock even if it generates a trade deficit. However, trade deficits produced by purchasing consumption goods does not contribute to capital deepening.

☞ When foreign companies create plants in the United States, it has a positive effect on capital deepening. When Toyota and Nintendo start operations in the United States, they increase United States capital stock as they build plants and equipment.

While capital deepening promotes economic growth, it has its limits. The limits to capital deepening are due to the following:
1. Diminishing returns due to a given labor force.
2. Net investment is zero or less than zero. This means that depreciation exceeds the investment. The capital stock stays the same or decreases.
3. You can't save all your income. You have to have some consumption goods to live.

8.3 The Key Role of Technological Progress

Technological progress happens when more efficient ways of organizing economic affairs allow an economy to increase output without increasing inputs. Technological progress can take different forms. New inventions, innovations, and new ways of doing things are forms of technological progress.

Nobel laureate Robert Solow created a method to measure technological progress called **growth accounting.** Using a basic production function, Solow measured the growth of output, labor, and capital in terms of growth rates in percentage terms. Solow added one more variable to the production function, growth rate of technological progress.

☑ Key Equation: Growth Accounting Equation (See Table 8.2)

Total output growth = growth due to capital growth + growth due to labor growth + technological progress

---

In Table 8.2, Edward Denison used growth accounting to show sources of real GDP growth from 1929–1982. Notice that growth due to technological advance accounts for about 1.02 percent annually.

Growth accounting can be used in another way. Growth accounting can be used to measure growth and sources of growth between two countries.

Let's review three Applications that answer the key questions we posed at the start of the chapter:

3. How can we use economic analysis to understand the sources of growth in different countries?

APPLICATION 3: HOW GROWTH IN SINGAPORE AND HONG KONG DIFFERED

Singapore and Hong Kong grew approximately 6 percent from 1980–1985. In Singapore, nearly all the growth was accounted for by increases in labor and capital. Investment levels were extremely high in Singapore, reaching 43 percent as a share of GDP in 1983. Hong Kong had a much lower investment rate than Singapore—approximately a 20 percent share of GDP—and technological progress made an important contribution. These source differences may have impacts on future growth.

4. Why did labor productivity in the United States fall sharply during the 1970s and 1980s?

APPLICATION 4: WORLDWIDE FACTORS SLOWED U.S. PRODUCTIVITY GROWTH

Labor productivity is defined as output per hour of work. Since 1973, the growth of labor productivity has slowed in the United States and other countries in the world. U.S. productivity growth since 1959 is shown in Table 8.3. The slowdown in productivity growth has also meant slower growth in real wages and in GDP in the United States since 1973. Figure 8.4 plots real hourly earnings and total compensation for U.S. workers. Labor productivity is decreased for many reasons. Those reasons include:
- declines in the education and skills of the workforce
- lower levels of investment, and thus a lower level of capital
- less spending on infrastructure, such as highways and bridges
- increased spending on pollution-control equipment that improves the environment but does not lead to increased output
- the belief that managers are more concerned with producing short-term profits than long-term profits

In addition to these reasons, productivity has become more difficult to measure as the U.S. economy has become more service-oriented during this period, and productivity improvements in services are hard to measure.

Using growth accounting methods, economists typically find that the slowdown in labor productivity, in the United States and abroad, cannot be explained by reduced rates of capital deepening. Nor can they be explained by changes in the quality or experience of the labor force. Either a slowdown in technological progress or other factors that are not directly included in the analysis, such as higher worldwide energy prices, must be responsible for the slowdown. Moreover, because the slowdown has been worldwide, it's possible that factors that affect all countries (such as higher energy prices) are responsible rather than factors specific to a single country.

5. How did the emergence of the Internet affect economic growth in the United States?

APPLICATION 5: THE INTERNET AND INFORMATION TECHNOLOGY RAISED PRODUCTIVITY THROUGHOUT THE ECONOMY

"New economy" proponents believe the computer and Internet revolution are responsible for the increase in productivity growth. Skeptics wonder, however, whether this increase in productivity growth is truly permanent or just temporary. Robert Gordon of Northwestern University used growth accounting to study the impact of technological progress. Initially he found technological progress in the durable manufacturing sector, particularly in the computer industry itself. Later he found technological progress in other sectors. Other economists have confirmed these findings and think that such progress may be permanent and not temporary.

8.4 What Causes Technological Progress?

Now that we have discussed how technological progress is measured, we have to ask what causes technological progress. There are a variety of causes:
- Research and Development Funding – Governments and large firms play a role in funding research and development. Such funding creates the means for new ideas and innovations. Figure 8.5 shows research and development funding by country.

- Monopolies That Spur Innovation – Monopolies are often created by patents. Patent protection gives incentives for firms to create new ideas and products. This can generate what Joseph Schumpeter called creative destruction. **Creative destruction** is the view that a firm will try to come up with new products and more efficient ways to produce products to earn monopoly profits. Intellectual property rights protection is required to ensure ongoing invention and innovation.
- The Scale of the Market – Larger markets promote the creation of greater amounts and varieties of goods in an economy. Larger markets promote free trade and technological progress.
- Induced Innovations – Innovations that are designed to reduce costs.
- Education, Human Capital, and the Accumulation of Knowledge – There are two basic ways education contributes to technological advance:
  1. Increased knowledge and skills complement our current investments in physical capital
  2. Education enables people to produce new ideas, copy ideas, or import them from abroad.

  Human capital theory has two implications for economic growth:
  1. Not all labor is the same. People differentiate themselves by their education, knowledge, and experience.
  2. Health and fitness affects productivity.

Let's review an Application that answers one of the key questions we posed at the start of the chapter:

6. How are economic growth and health related to one another?

APPLICATION 6: A VIRTUOUS CIRCLE: GDP AND HEALTH

Economic growth produced a "virtuous" circle. It increased food supplies, enabling workers to become more productive and increase GDP even more. According to Nobel laureate Robert Fogel of the University of Chicago, the average weight of English males in their thirties was about 134 pounds in 1790—20 percent below today's average. Fogel has argued that these lower weights and heights were due to inadequate food supplies and chronic malnutrition. As health conditions improved, workers became more productive.

Another theory describing how economic growth occurs is new growth theory. **New growth theories** are modern theories of growth that try to explain the origins of technological progress. Economists such as Robert Lucas and Paul Romer developed models that contained technological advance as essential to economic growth. The impacts of research and development funding to basic education are current areas of research in new growth theory.

8.5 A Key Governmental Role: Providing the Correct Incentives and Property Rights

As discussed in Chapter 3 and earlier in this chapter (see "Monopolies That Spur Innovation" in section 8.4), protection of property rights is essential to economic growth. Without property right protection, there are no incentives to invest in the future. This is a common problem in the developing world. Governments have a key role in providing property right protection, creating the environment for economic growth. International institutions such as the World Bank have attempted to assist developing nations to grow economically. Yet there have to be incentives for governments to want to provide such protection.

Let's review an Application that answers one of the key questions we posed at the start of the chapter:

7. Why are clear property rights important for economic growth in developing countries?

APPLICATION 7: LACK OF PROPERTY RIGHTS HINDERS GROWTH IN PERU

Hernando DeSoto has studied the consequences of "informal ownership" in detail. He argues that throughout the developing world, property is often not held with clear titles. Without clear evidence of ownership, these owners are not willing to make long term investments to improve their lives. But there are other important consequences as well. Economists recognize that strong credit systems—the ability to borrow and lend easily—are critical to the health of developing economies. But without clear title, property cannot be used as collateral (or security) for loans. As a consequence, the poor may in fact be living on very valuable land, but be unable to borrow against that land to start a new business.

Activity

Use the equations presented earlier in this chapter and the following data to compute the missing data:

Country	Real GDP, 2005	Real GDP, 2006	Population	Real GDP per Capita, 2006	Growth Rate
Zerotia	$10 trillion	$12 trillion	1 billion		
Tukuland	$8 trillion	$7 trillion	500 million		

Answers

Country	Real GDP, 2005	Real GDP, 2006	Population	Real GDP per Capita, 2006	Growth Rate
Zerotia	$10 trillion	$12 trillion	1 billion	$12,000	20%
Tukuland	$8 trillion	$7 trillion	500 million	$14,000	-12.5%

Key Terms

Capital deepening: Increases in the stock of capital per worker.

Convergence: The process by which poorer countries close the gap with richer countries in terms of real GDP per capita.

Creative destruction: The view that a firm will try to come up with new products and more efficient ways to produce products to earn monopoly profits.

Growth accounting: A method to determine the contribution to economic growth from increased capital, labor, and technological progress.

Growth rate: The percentage rate of change of a variable from one period to another.

Human capital: The knowledge and skills acquired by a worker through education and experience and used to produce goods and services.

Labor productivity: Output produced per hour of work.

New growth theory: Modern theories of growth that try to explain the origins of technological progress.

Real GDP per capita: Gross domestic product per person adjusted for changes in constant prices. It is the usual measure of living standards across time and between countries.

Rule of 70: A rule of thumb that says output will double in $70/x$ years, where x is the percentage rate of growth.

Saving: Income that is not consumed.

Technological progress: More efficient ways of organizing economic affairs that allow an economy to increase output without increasing inputs.

Appendix – A Model of Capital Deepening

✐ Study Tip

We are building models again. The parts of the model are the production function, the savings function and depreciation. Put these parts together by drawing each as you review this appendix.

The model of capital deepening discussed in the appendix is a simple growth model developed by Robert Solow. The model provides a graphical framework to understand capital deepening and technological progress. We will assume constant population and no government or foreign sector. We will look at savings, depreciation, and capital deepening.

The first step of the model is to develop a production function between capital and output. Remember that population growth is constant, thus causing the production function to show diminishing returns.

 Principle of Diminishing Returns

Suppose output is produced with two or more inputs and we increase on input while holding the other inputs fixed. Beyond some point—called the point of diminishing returns—output will increase at a decreasing rate.

Figure 8A.1 shows the production function with diminishing returns to capital. What causes this production function to increase? Gross investment must exceed depreciation.

Remember

To increase the capital stock, net investment must be greater than zero.

For this to happen, saving must be greater than depreciation. A fraction of our income (Y) can be saved.

☀ Caution!

The saving function should always be below the production function. You can't save more than your income earned.

Figure 8A.2, panel A, shows the relationship between the production function and savings. Saving will always be under the production function since a nation can't save all its income. The last item we need to complete the model is depreciation. Figure 8A.2, panel B, shows depreciation as a function of the capital stock. Larger capital stock, given a constant rate of depreciation, will cause depreciation to increase. With saving and depreciation defined, we can see how changes in the capital stock occur.

☑ Key Equations

Savings = $S = sY$
Where
S = total savings
s = savings rate
Y = total income

Depreciation = dK
Where
d = depreciation rate
K = capital stock

Change in Capital Stock = Savings – Depreciation = $sY - dK$

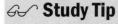 Study Tip

To increase the capital stock, net investment must be greater than zero. With that in mind, $sY - dK > 0$.

Figure 8A.3 shows the basic Solow Growth Model. By combining the features we just described—A and B—we can see graphically how an economy would grow through capital deepening to its long-run equilibrium. As long as saving is greater than depreciation, you will grow your capital stock, or in other words, experience capital deepening. Capital deepening allows more capital per worker, leading to greater output per worker, increasing output. This leads to higher real wages.

The economy will continue to capital deepen until savings equals depreciation and the economy reaches its long-run equilibrium. It may take some time for a nation to reach this point. Can the economy change its long-run equilibrium? Yes, by increasing the savings rate.

By increasing the savings rate, you increase investment. This will cause savings to be greater than depreciation and thus you can increase your capital stock to a new long-run equilibrium. This concept is demonstrated in Figure 8A.4. By increasing the savings rate, the saving curve increased, shifting upwards from s_1Y to s_2Y. Depreciation stayed in its position since there was no variable change in depreciation. Point e_1, the original long-run equilibrium, is no longer the long-run equilibrium since savings is greater than depreciation. Capital deepening will continue along s_2Y until it reaches the new long-run equilibrium, e_2. The capital stock increased from K_1 to K_2.

Another way to increase capital deepening is technological progress. Technological progress increases output without changing inputs to production. Savings increases as income increases as shown in Figure 8A.5, shifting the saving rate upward, allowing for more capital deepening.

ᏬᏒ Study Tip

The only way to get better at graphs is to draw them. You should draw and label this graph in Figure 8A.5 enough times that it becomes comfortable to you.

Basic Points of the Solow Growth Model

1. Capital deepening, an increase in the stock of capital per worker, will occur as long as total saving exceeds depreciation. As capital deepening occurs, there will be economic growth and increased real wages.
2. Eventually, the process of capital deepening will come to a halt as depreciation catches up with total saving.
3. A higher saving rate will promote capital deepening. If a country saves more, it will have higher output. But eventually, the process of economic growth through capital deepening alone comes to an end, even though this may take decades to occur.
4. Technological progress not only directly raises output, but it also allows capital deepening to occur.

Practice Quiz

(Answers are provided at the end of the Practice Quiz.)

1. The ability to produce more output without using any more inputs is called:
    a. capital deepening.
    b. technological progress.
    c. human capital.
    d. investment.

2. If the economy started at 100 and grew at a rate of 3% for 20 years, then real GDP after 20 years would roughly equal:
    a. 180.
    b. 148.
    c. 127.
    d. 190.

3. GDP per capita in 2004, and the per capita growth rate from 1960 until 2004 for the United States were, respectively:
    a. $39,170 and 2.19%.
    b. $30,040 and 4.10%.
    c. $27,860 and 3.00%.
    d. $31,460 and 2.46%.

4. This question tests your understanding of Application 1 in this chapter: Increased growth leads to less child labor in developing countries. How does economic growth affect social indicators such as child labor?

    Dartmouth economists Eric V. Edmonds and Nina Pavcnik have studied the factors that lead to changes in child labor in developing countries.

    Which of the following assertions is consistent with their findings?
    a. Most child labor occurs in manufacturing plants, not in agriculture.
    b. Child labor is commonly found across the social strata in developing countries. Changes in the income of the parents do not seem to influence the use of child labor.
    c. Child labor is a phenomenon closely associated with extreme poverty.
    d. Over time, as developing economies grow, child labor tends to be widespread.

5. Refer to the figure below. Each dot represents one country. The conclusion drawn from the study associated with this graph is that:

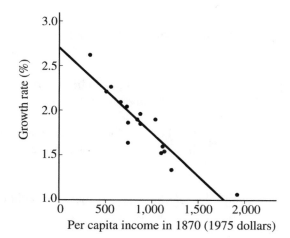

a. Lower growth rates of output result in lower per capita income.
b. Since 1870, we have been unable to establish a relationship between growth rates and per capita income.
c. Countries with higher levels of GDP in 1870 grew more slowly than countries with lower levels of GDP.
d. The income of persons who earned 2,000 in 1870 grew at a slower rate than the income of persons who earned less income.

6. How does an economy increase its stock of capital?
a. The economy's savings must be greater than its total depreciation.
b. The economy must consume more so businesses have a profit incentive to invest.
c. The economy must develop better technology.
d. All of the above

7. Which of the following statements is entirely correct?
a. The stock of capital increases with any gross investment or depreciation.
b. As capital grows, depreciation also grows, eventually catching up to the level of gross investment, and putting a stop to the growth of capital deepening.
c. In order for the stock of capital to increase, gross investment must exceed savings.
d. All of the above

8. The impact of population growth on capital deepening is an illustration of a key principle of economics. Which one?
a. The principle of creative destruction
b. The principle of the new growth model
c. The real-nominal principle
d. The principle of human capital

9. When a country experiences a trade deficit, which of the following helps in the process of capital deepening?
   a. Trade deficits that fund current consumption
   b. The export of investment goods
   c. Borrowing in order to finance the import of investment goods
   d. All of the above

10. The role of technological progress in economic growth can be described as follows:
    a. Technological progress does not cause real GDP to rise, rather it shifts what goods the economy makes.
    b. Technological progress will be beneficial only if the population also grows as real GDP grows.
    c. Per capita output will rise when we discover new and more effective uses of capital and labor.
    d. All of the above

11. Consider the following relationship: $Y = f(K, L, A)$. To measure technological progress, we do the following:
    a. We observe increases in K, L, and Y.
    b. We observe the impact of changes in A on K and L.
    c. We observe changes in Y by studying changes in K, L, and A.
    d. We observe changes in K and L to establish the magnitude of the ratio K/L.

12. This question tests your understanding of Application 3 in this chapter: How growth in Singapore and Hong Kong differed. How can we use economic analysis to understand the sources of growth in different countries?

    "Singapore and Hong Kong have both had phenomenal post–World War II economic growth. From 1980 to 1985, each grew at a rate of approximately 6 percent a year. But a closer examination by Alwyn Young of the University of Chicago revealed that the sources of growth in each country were very different. In Singapore, nearly all the growth was accounted for by increases in labor and capital. Investment levels were extremely high in Singapore, reaching 43 percent as a share of GDP in 1983. Hong Kong had a much lower investment rate than Singapore—approximately a 20 percent share of GDP—and technological progress made an important contribution."

    Which of the following were the main concerns arising from the different type of growth that each country was experiencing?
    a. The residents of Hong Kong were worried that the type of growth they were experiencing would allow them to save but not consume a higher fraction of their GDP.
    b. Singapore realized that simply increasing inputs to production might not be sufficient in order to maintain healthy long-term prospects for economic growth.
    c. After Hong Kong became a part of China, Hong Kong's residents became more optimistic about the prospects for sustaining a system that produced technological innovation.
    d. Both Hong Kong and Singapore realized that unless they imposed significant barriers to trade, their prospects for growth would be poor.

13. From 1980 to 1985, the economies of Hong Kong and Singapore both grew at impressive rates of about 6%, yet the causes and results of growth in each country were very different. Which of the statements below is correct?
    a. Both Hong Kong and Singapore's growth was attributed to increases in labor and capital, not technological progress.
    b. Both Hong Kong and Singapore's growth was attributed strictly to increases in the labor force. Neither capital nor technological progress was the key to growth.
    c. Singapore's growth was attributed to increases in labor and capital, while in Hong Kong technological progress was the key to growth.
    d. Singapore's growth was attributed to increases in technological progress, while in Hong Kong the key to growth was increases in labor and capital.

14. Refer to the figure below. Which of the following statements is correct?

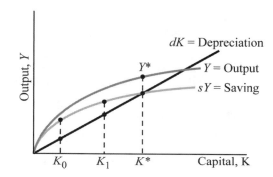

    a. At the capital usage point K_0, the capital stock of the country is falling.
    b. At the capital usage point K_1, the capital stock of the country is rising at a faster rate than at K_0.
    c. At the capital usage point K_1, the capital stock of the country is rising, but at a slower rate than at K_0.
    d. At the capital usage point K^*, the capital stock of the country is rising, but at a faster rate than at K_0 or K_1.

15. Which of the following endeavors results in technological progress in the long run?
    a. Scientists attempting to make progress in the field of chemistry.
    b. Scientists attempting to make progress in the field of biology.
    c. "High tech," or the development of super fast, small computer chips.
    d. All of the above

16. This question tests your understanding of Application 5 in this chapter: The Internet and information technology. How did the emergence of the Internet affect economic growth in the United States?

"U.S. productivity growth climbed in the last half of the 1990s. 'New economy' proponents believe the computer and Internet revolution are responsible for the increase in productivity growth. Skeptics wonder, however, whether this increase in productivity growth is truly permanent or just temporary. Higher investment in computer technology began in the mid-1980s, but until recently there was little sign of increased productivity growth. Had the investment in information technology finally paid off?"

The studies conducted by Robert J. Gordon of Northwestern University, and those of other economists using growth accounting methods to shed light on this issue, found that:

a. Increases in technological progress are largely confined to the durable goods manufacturing industry, including the production of computers itself.

b. Productivity growth was rapid in the late 1990s, but it began to slow down during the recessionary period at the beginning of this century.

c. Technological progress has been more widespread throughout the economy than originally suspected, suggesting that the increase is likely to be permanent.

d. If productivity growth continues at its current rate, we will likely suffer from less rapid economic growth in the United States and across the globe.

17. The process by which competition for monopoly profits leads to technological progress is called:
   a. creative destruction.
   b. monopolistic creativity.
   c. destructive creation.
   d. creative monopolization.

18. In terms of understanding the role of human capital investment in economic growth, which of the following is correct?
   a. All labor should be treated as equal.
   b. Health and fitness affect productivity. If workers are frail and ill, they can't contribute much to national output.
   c. Human capital is an investment in the machines that make humans more productive.
   d. All of the above

19. Explain how government spending and taxation affect the process of capital deepening.

20. Explain how the foreign sector affects the process of capital deepening.

21. List the sources of output growth, and describe how growth accounting explains where growth comes from.

22. Different sources of economic growth have different implications for future growth. Which source allows households to consume more now and in the future?

23. An increase in real wages occurs when output per worker increases. Then, what causes an increase in output per worker?

24. Specifically, how does education contribute to economic growth?

Answers to the Practice Quiz

1. b. Economists believe that there are two basic mechanisms that increase GDP per capita over the long term. One is capital deepening: an increase in the economy's stock of capital—plant and equipment—relative to its workforce. The other is technological progress: the ability to produce more output without using any more inputs—capital or labor.

2. a. The growth rate is g = 3%. The number of years is n = 20. The formula is $(1 + g)^n (100)$. Then $(100 + 5\%)20 = 180.6$.

3. a. The United States has the largest GDP per capita among the countries listed.

4. c. Child labor is a phenomenon closely associated with extreme poverty. Over time, as economies grow, child labor will tend to disappear.

5. c. The relationship between growth rates and per capita income in 1870 is downward-sloping. Countries with higher levels of GDP in 1870 grew more slowly than countries with lower levels of GDP.

6. a. The economy must save and invest in new capital faster than the existing capital is being used up in order to increase the total amount of capital.

7. b. This is how the process of capital deepening occurs.

8. b. With less capital per worker, output per worker will also tend to be less because each worker has fewer machines to use. This is an illustration of the principle of diminishing returns.

9. c. An economy can run a trade deficit and import investment goods to aid capital deepening. It can finance the purchase of those goods by borrowing, and as investment rises, GDP and economic wealth rises and the country can afford to pay back the borrowed funds. Trade deficits that fund current consumption do not aid in the process of capital deepening.

10. c. Technological progress, or the birth of new ideas, is what makes us more productive. Per capita output will rise when we discover new and more effective uses of capital and labor.

11. a. Increases in A represent technological progress, or more output produced from the same level of inputs, K and L. We can measure technological progress indirectly by observing increases in capital, labor, and output.

12. b. Economic leaders became concerned that increasing its inputs to production would not lead to growth unless they managed to also increase their rate of technological progress.

13. c. Singapore's growth was attributed to increases in labor and capital, while in Hong Kong technological progress was the key to growth.

14. c. The difference between sY and dK is smaller at K_1 than at K_0, so the increase in the capital stock will be smaller.

15. d. Not all technological progress is "high tech."

16. c. It took a substantial period of time before businesses began to harness the use of modern computer technology and the Internet. Today, however, the growth of productivity is high, and if it does continue at its current high rate, we will enjoy more rapid economic growth in the United States and across the globe.

17. a. The process by which competition for monopoly profits leads to technological progress is called creative destruction by Schumpeter. By allowing firms to compete to be monopolies, society benefits from increased innovation.

18. b. Human capital is an investment in human beings—in their knowledge, skills, and health. In terms of understanding economic growth, human capital investment has two implications: Not all labor is equal. Individuals with more education will, on average, be more productive. Health and fitness affect productivity. If workers are frail and ill, they can't contribute much to national output.

19. When the government taxes the private sector to engage in consumption spending, it takes away some of the household saving which could have been used for capital deepening. Therefore, taxation destined for government consumption reduces total investment in the economy and capital deepening. When the government taxes the private sector to engage in government investment expenditures, such as roads, buildings, and airports, the government is directly contributing to the process of capital deepening. Since people finance part of their taxes by reducing consumption and part by reducing savings, when the government uses the tax revenue for investment purposes it actually diverts more of national income to investment than was invested by the private sector.

20. If a country runs a trade deficit (or buys more than it sells abroad) to acquire consumer goods, the country would be borrowing from abroad, but there would be no additional capital deepening, therefore, no additional future output growth to help pay the funds back. On the other hand, if the country runs a trade deficit to import investment goods, the deficit is valuable to the economy because it contributes to the process of capital deepening. The country will be able to pay the funds borrowed once economic growth raises GDP.

21. The sources of economic growth are labor growth, capital growth, and technological growth. Growth accounting explains the contributions to economic growth from each of these sources by observing increases in capital, labor, and output over a given period. Using these, we can measure technological progress indirectly. We first ask how much of the change in output can be explained by contributions from the changes in capital and labor, then, whatever growth cannot be explained must have been caused by increases in technological progress.

22. When growth comes from increases in investment in capital and labor, growth must be supported by a high rate of saving. In contrast, when growth comes from technological progress, consumers can consume, not save, a higher fraction of GDP. Therefore, contributions by technological progress allow a higher level of consumption today. This is also true in the future. There are natural limits to growth through the process of capital deepening. Technological progress has better growth prospects than capital deepening.

23. Output per worker will rise when workers acquire better skills and knowledge (human capital). Output per worker also rises with an increase in private investment. Additions of physical capital result in an increase in the productivity of labor. Government investment, in roads, bridges, and public works (social capital) also raises the productivity of labor in the same manner as private investment in physical plant and equipment does.

24. Education contributes to economic growth in two ways. First, investment in human beings complements investment in physical capital. New growth theory is a field of economics that studies how incentives for research and development, for example, interact with the accumulation of physical capital. Second, education enables the workforce to use its skills and knowledge to develop new ideas, or to import ideas from abroad. The adoption of ideas requires an educated workforce to tap into this knowledge.

9

Aggregate Demand and Aggregate Supply

Chapter Summary

Aggregate demand and aggregate supply analysis helps explain relationships between price levels and output. Here are the main points of the chapter:

- Because prices are sticky in the short run, economists think of GDP as being determined primarily by demand factors in the short run.

- The aggregate demand curve depicts the relationship between the price level and total demand for real output in the economy. The aggregate demand curve is downward sloping because of the wealth effect, the interest rate effect, and the international trade effect.

- Decreases in taxes, increases in government spending, and increases in the supply of money all increase aggregate demand and shift the aggregate demand curve to the right. Increases in taxes, decreases in government spending, and decreases in the supply of money all decrease aggregate demand and shift the aggregate demand curve to the left. In general, anything (other than price movements) that increases the demand for total goods and services will increase aggregate demand.

- The total shift in the aggregate demand curve is greater than the initial shift. The ratio of the total shift in aggregate demand to the initial shift in aggregate demand is known as the multiplier.

- The aggregate supply curve depicts the relationship between the price level and the level of output firms supply in the economy. Output and prices are determined at the intersection of the aggregate demand and aggregate supply curves.

- The long-run aggregate supply curve is vertical because, in the long run, output is determined by the supply of factors of production. The short-run aggregate supply curve is fairly flat because, in the short run, prices are largely fixed, and output is determined by demand.

- Supply shocks can shift the short-run aggregate supply curve.

- The short-run aggregate supply curve shifts in the long run, restoring the economy to the full-employment equilibrium.

Applying the Concepts

After reading this chapter, you should be able to answer these three key questions:

1. What does the behavior of prices in retail catalogs demonstrate about how quickly prices adjust in the U.S. economy?

2. How can changes in demand cause a recession? In particular, what factors do economists think caused the 2001 recession?
3. Do changes in oil prices always hurt the U.S. economy?

9.1 Sticky Prices and Their Macroeconomic Consequences

What causes economic fluctuations? The price system serves as a coordinating mechanism in the economy. When prices and wages are flexible and adjust quickly, prices signal to markets what should and should not be produced. Equilibrium is restored and resources are efficiently allocated to their best use. But what if prices are not flexible and don't adjust quickly? That is the issue with sticky prices.

Sticky prices happen when prices don't immediately adjust to changing market conditions. If prices are not flexible and stick, then market coordination doesn't work efficiently, causing economic fluctuations. Economic fluctuations are adjustments the economy makes as it returns to equilibrium. The fluctuation may be an abnormal increase in production like an economic boom or an abnormal decrease in production such as a recession.

☞ Some of you drive a car with a manual transmission or a stick shift. Have you ever had a time when you get stuck in a gear or can't find a gear to shift into? The gears grind. You can't change speeds and, if prolonged, start to slow down. The price system is like the gear mechanism in a car. When it moves fluidly and without sticking, then the car runs smoothly. The price system operates in a similar fashion. When it works, prices coordinate economic activity precisely. However, when prices stick like the gears, then the economy doesn't allocate resources to their best use.

Wages are often sticky as they don't adjust immediately. Wage stickiness may be caused by union contracts or occupations that don't change wages except once a year. Wage stickiness can be found in the wages of college professors and government workers, because their wages are set once a year regardless of market conditions. Suppose that an automobile firm hires union workers under a contract that fixes their wages for a specific period. If the economy suddenly thrives at some point during that period, the automobile company will employ all the workers and perhaps require some to work overtime. If the economy stagnates at some point during that period, the firm will lay off some workers, using only part of the union labor force. Notice that demand for labor becomes the coordinating factor instead of the wages. Since a firm's major input cost is wages, output prices may also remain sticky. In the short run, supply and demand are hampered and may not reach equilibrium.

💣 **Caution!**

Demand—not prices—drives the production of inputs and products in the short run.

If the demand for inputs, such as labor or machines, is sustained over a long period of time, then prices may adjust to the new level of sustained demand.

To summarize, the **short run in macroeconomics** is the period in which prices do not change or do not change very much. In the macroeconomic short run, both formal and informal contracts between firms mean that changes in demand will be reflected primarily in changes in output, not prices.

Let's review an Application that answers one of the key questions we posed at the start of the chapter:

1. What does the behavior of prices in retail catalogs demonstrate about how quickly prices adjust in the U.S. economy?

APPLICATION 1: PRICE STICKINESS IN RETAIL CATALOGS

University of Chicago economist Amil Kashyap investigated prices of various outdoor products. He found considerable price stickiness. Prices of the goods that he tracked such as shoes, blankets, chamois shirts, binoculars, and a fishing rod and fly were typically fixed for a year or more.

☞ Another place where prices are sticky is at restaurants. Prices of restaurant meals don't change too often when economic changes occur. There are costs associated with changing menus. Those prices are sticky and don't change when there is a change in the market. In that case, people demand what is on the menu and prices are not negotiated. Yet, not all prices are sticky. Sometimes there is some price flexibility. Seafood such as lobster or crab have "market price" listed on the menu. The price of lobster or crab may vary from day to day due to market conditions, but the menu cost didn't change.

9.2 Understanding Aggregate Demand

In this section, we will put together the aggregate demand and aggregate supply curves. The model of aggregate demand and aggregate supply is a tool that helps us analyze macroeconomic behavior and the effect of macroeconomic policies.

Aggregate demand is the total demand for goods and services in an entire economy. In other words, it is the demand for currently produced GDP by consumers, firms, the government, and the foreign sector. The **aggregate demand curve (AD)** shows the relationship between the level of prices and the quantity of real GDP demanded. Figure 9.1 shows an aggregate demand curve. The curve plots the total demand for GDP as a function of the price level.

> 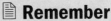 **Remember**
>
> The price level is the average price in the economy, as measured by a price index.

The aggregate demand curve is downward sloping. As the price level falls, the total quantity demanded for goods and services increases. As you studied in Chapter 5, consumption spending (*C*), investment spending (*I*), government purchases (*G*), and net exports (*NX*) are the four parts of aggregate demand The aggregate demand curve describes the demand for total GDP at different price levels.

Price level changes cause changes in purchasing power throughout the economy. Recall the key principle from the book:

 Real-Nominal Principle

What matters to people is the real value of money or income—its purchasing power—not the face value of money or income.

There are three basic reasons for such purchasing power changes leading to changes in aggregate demand:

- **The Wealth Effect**: The **wealth effect** is an increase in spending that occurs because the real value of money increases when the price level falls. Lower prices lead to higher levels of wealth, and higher levels of wealth increase spending on total goods and services. When the price level rises, consumers can't simply substitute one good for another that's cheaper, because at a higher price level everything is more expensive.
- **The Interest Rate Effect:** With a given supply of money in the economy, a lower price level will lead to lower interest rates. With lower interest rates, both consumers and firms will find it cheaper to borrow money to make purchases. As a consequence, the demand for goods in the economy will increase.
- **The International Trade Effect:** Price level decreases will make domestic goods cheaper relative to foreign goods. If domestic goods become cheaper than foreign goods, exports will increase and imports will decrease. Thus, net exports—a component of aggregate demand—will increase.

What happens to the aggregate demand curve if a variable *other* than the price level changes? An increase in aggregate demand means that total demand for all the goods and services contained in real GDP has increased—even though the price level hasn't changed. In other words, increases in aggregate demand shift the curve to the right.

Conversely, factors that decrease aggregate demand shift the curve to the left—even though the price level hasn't changed.

> 💣 **Caution!**
>
> Anything affecting C, I, G, or NX other than the price level will cause shifts of the aggregate demand curve. Price level changes will cause movement along the aggregate demand curve.

The following are factors that cause changes in aggregate demand:

- **Changes in the Money Supply:** At any given price level, a higher supply of money will mean more consumer wealth and an increased demand for goods and services. A decrease in the supply of money will decrease aggregate demand and shift the aggregate demand curve to the left.
- **Changes in Taxes:** A decrease in taxes will increase aggregate demand and shift the aggregate demand curve to the right. An increase in taxes will decrease aggregate demand and shift the aggregate demand curve to the left. Higher taxes will decrease the income available to households and decrease their spending.
- **Changes in Government Spending:** At any given price level, an increase in government spending will increase aggregate demand and shift the aggregate demand curve to the right. Similarly, decreases in government spending will decrease aggregate demand and shift the curve to the left.
- **Other Changes in Demand:** Increases in net exports will increase aggregate demand, shifting the curve to the right. Decreases in net exports will decrease aggregate demand, shifting to the left. Other variables may increase or decrease aggregate demand. For example, expectations of the future will cause changes in aggregate demand. If the future looks bleak, then firms may not want to expand and thus decrease private investment expenditures. Aggregate demand would decrease, shifting the curve to the left. On the other hand, optimistic expectations may cause firms to expand and thus increase private investment expenditures. Aggregate demand would increase, shifting the curve to the right.

Figure 9.2 shows how aggregate demand curves shift and what causes changes in aggregate demand.

✍ Study Tip

Take some time to study Table 9.1 to know how different variables cause aggregate demand changes.

Take a look at Figure 9.3. Notice the total shift in the aggregate demand curve from *a* to *c* in Figure 9.3 is greater than the initial shift in the curve from *a* to *b*. This is the multiplier in action. So what is the multiplier? The **multiplier** is the ratio of the total shift in aggregate demand to the initial shift in aggregate demand. In other words, an initial expenditure will generate additional spending. For example, suppose the government increases spending for government services such as education. Those services will generate income for households. Households will wish to spend, or consume, part of that income, which will further increase aggregate demand. It is this additional spending by consumers, over and above what the government has already spent, that causes the further shift in the aggregate demand curve. Figure 9.3 shows how the multiplier shifts aggregate demand.

Knowing the value of the multiplier is important for two reasons:
- First, it tells us how much shocks to aggregate demand are amplified.
- Second, to design effective economic policies to shift the aggregate demand curve, we need to know the value of the multiplier to measure the proper "dose" for policy.

To understand how the multiplier works in detail, you need to understand the following equations:

☑ Key Equations

Consumption Function: $C = C_a + by$, where C_a is autonomous consumption expenditures, b is the marginal propensity (MPC) to consume, and y is income.

$$MPC = \frac{\text{additional consumption}}{\text{additional income}}$$

$$MPS = \frac{\text{additional saving}}{\text{additional income}}$$

$$MPC + MPS = 1$$

$$\text{Multiplier} = \frac{1}{1 - MPC}$$

As stated in the Key Equation box, consumption expenditures can be broken into two pieces. **Autonomous consumption spending** is the part of consumption expenditures that does not depend on income. The other term in the consumption function is spending that changes when income changes. The **marginal propensity to consume**, or MPC, is the fraction of additional income spent on consumption goods. The remaining fraction of additional income is saved, and is called the **marginal propensity to save**, or MPS.

The multiplier is mainly a function of the MPC. The greater the MPC, the larger the multiplier. The smaller the MPC, the smaller the multiplier. Page 199 gives a good example of how to compute the MPC and MPS.

ᡬ Study Tip

Read carefully the example on pages 199–200 to understand how the multiplier works with an initial expenditure of $10 million.

Table 9.2 illustrates how the multiplier impacts aggregate demand with an initial government expenditure of $10 million. This analysis is carried out until all income is spent. There is an easier way to calculate the size of the multiplier. The last equation of the previous Key Equation box computes the size of the multiplier.

9.3 Understanding Aggregate Supply

The **aggregate supply curve (AS)** shows the relationship between the level of prices and the total quantity of final goods and services that firms are willing and able to supply. To determine both the price level and real GDP, we need to combine both aggregate demand and aggregate supply. Since prices are sticky in the short run but can be flexible in the long run, we will be deriving two different AS curves to represent those conditions.

There are two aggregate supply curves that we need to understand, the long-run aggregate supply curve and the short-run aggregate supply curve. They will both be used to analyze macroeconomic activity. The **long-run aggregate supply curve** is a vertical aggregate supply curve that represents the idea that in the long run, output is determined solely by the factors of production. The reason the curve is vertical is based on the premise that a fully employed economy will produce a fixed amount of output regardless of prices as shown in Figure 9.4.

We combine the aggregate demand curve and the long-run aggregate supply curve in Figure 9.5. The intersection of an aggregate demand curve and an aggregate supply curve determines the price level and equilibrium level of output. At that intersection point, the total amount of output demanded will just equal the total amount supplied by producers—the economy will be in macroeconomic equilibrium.

ᡬ Study Hint

In the long run, aggregate demand only determines the price level. The level of output is completely determined by the quantities of factors of production and the production technology available in the economy.

In the long run, an increase in aggregate demand will raise prices but leave the level of output unchanged. In general, shifts in the aggregate demand curve in the long run do not change the level of output in the economy, but only change the level of prices.

📄 Remember

In the long run, output is determined solely by the supply of human and physical capital and the supply of labor, not by the price level.

Figure 9.6 shows the short-run aggregate supply curve (AS). The **short-run aggregate supply curve** is a relatively flat aggregate supply curve that represents the idea that prices do not change very much in the short run and that firms adjust production to meet demand. The short-run aggregate supply curve has a small upward slope. As firms supply more output, they increase prices only slightly due to sticky prices. We previously discussed that with formal and informal contracts firms will supply all the output that is demanded with only relatively small changes in prices.

The intersection of the AD and AS curves at point a_0 determines the price level and the level of output. Because the aggregate supply curve is flat, aggregate demand primarily determines the level of output. In Figure 9.6, as aggregate demand increases, the new equilibrium will be at a slightly higher price, and output will increase from y_0 to y_1.

Let's review an Application that answers one of the key questions we posed at the start of the chapter:

2. How can changes in demand cause a recession? In particular, what factors do economists think caused the 2001 recession?

APPLICATION 2: BUSINESS INVESTMENT, NET EXPORTS, AND THE 2001 RECESSION

Kevin Kliesen of the Federal Reserve Bank of St. Louis compared data for recessions over time. Kliesen found that during earlier recessions, spending on consumer durables decreased, as did new residential housing production. However, during the 2001 recession, spending on consumer durables and new housing production *both* grew throughout the recession. Business investment and net exports, however, dropped. Prior to the recession, there had been large increases in business investment. But following the sharp fall in the stock market in 2000, both investors and firms realized that the economic boom times of the late 1990s were over. As expectations were dashed, firms cut back sharply on their planned investment spending. Net exports fell during the recession for two reasons. First, world economic growth slowed, decreasing the demand for U.S. goods. Second, the value of the dollar increased relative to foreign currencies, making U.S. goods more expensive.

Supply shocks are external events that shift the aggregate supply curve. Figure 9.7 illustrates an adverse supply shock that raises prices. The short-run aggregate supply curve shifts up with the supply shock because firms will supply their output only at a higher price. The AS curve shifts up, raising the price level and lowering the level of output from y_0 to y_1. Adverse supply shocks can therefore cause a fall in real output with increasing prices. This phenomenon is known as **stagflation**.

Let's review an Application that answers one of the key questions we posed at the start of the chapter:

3.   Do changes in oil prices always hurt the U.S. economy?

APPLICATION 3: HOW THE U.S. ECONOMY HAS COPED WITH OIL PRICE FLUCTUATIONS

Between 1997 and 1998, the price of oil on the world market fell from $22 a barrel to less than $13 a barrel. The result was that gasoline prices, adjusted for inflation, were lower than they had ever been in over 50 years. In 2005, oil prices shot up to $60 a barrel, largely because of increased demand throughout the world, particularly in fast-growing countries such as China and India. Gasoline prices exceeded $3 a gallon. Despite these increases, the economy appeared to absorb the price increases without too much difficulty, and the price increases did not have the adverse effects on aggregate demand as in prior years. Perhaps many years of coping with oil price changes combined with a strong economy made the difference this time.

9.4 From the Short Run to the Long Run

In Figure 9.8, we show the aggregate demand curve intersecting the short-run aggregate supply curve at an output level y_0. We also depict the long-run aggregate supply curve in this figure. The level of output in the economy, y_0, exceeds the level of potential output, y_0. In other words, this is a boom economy: Output exceeds potential output.

📄 Remember

Potential output is the output level produced by a full-employment economy.

〰 Study Tip

The only way to get better at graphs is to draw them. You should draw and label this graph enough times that it becomes comfortable to you.

What happens during a boom? Because the economy is producing at a level beyond its long-run potential, the level of unemployment will be very low. This will make it difficult for firms to recruit and retain workers. As firms compete for labor and raw materials, the tendency will be for both wages and prices to increase over time. Increasing wages and prices will shift the short-run aggregate supply curve to the left.

Figure 9.9 shows how the short-run aggregate supply curve shifts upward over time. As the economy adjusts, there will be continuing competition for labor and raw materials that will lead to continuing increases in wages and prices. The reason there may be more than one short-run equilibrium as the economy moves to the long run is due to sticky prices.

In the long run, the short-run aggregate supply curve will keep rising until it intersects the aggregate demand curve at a_1. At this point, the economy reaches the long-run equilibrium—precisely the point where the aggregate demand curve intersects the long-run aggregate supply curve.

☞ In this model, the long-run aggregate supply function acts like an attracting magnet. The short-run condition may move away from the long-run equilibrium, but will be attracted by economic forces back to long-run equilibrium.

In summary:

If $y_0 > y_f$, => unemployment ↓ => wages and prices↑ => short run AS ↓ => y ↓ to $y = y_f$

If $y_0 < y_f$, => unemployment ↑ => wages and prices↓ => short run AS ↑ => y ↑ to $y = y_f$

Activity

Calculate the multiplier for the following MPC information:

    a. MPC = 0.2
    b. MPC = 0.5
    c. MPC = 0.9

Answers

    a. 1.25
    b. 2.0
    c. 10.0

Key Terms

Aggregate demand curve (AD): A curve that shows the relationship between the level of prices and the quantity of real GDP demanded.

Aggregate supply curve (AS): A curve that shows the relationship between the level of prices and the quantity of output supplied.

Autonomous consumption spending: The part of consumption spending that does not depend on income.

Consumption function: The relationship between the level of income and consumer spending.

Long-run aggregate supply curve: A vertical aggregate supply curve that represents the idea that in the long run, output is determined solely by the factors of production.

Marginal propensity to consume (MPC): The fraction of additional income that is spent.

Marginal propensity to save (MPS): The fraction of additional income that is saved.

Multiplier: The ratio of the total shift in aggregate demand to the initial shift in aggregate demand.

Short-run aggregate supply curve: A relatively flat aggregate supply curve that represents the idea that prices do not change very much in the short run and that firms adjust production to meet demand.

Short run in macroeconomics: The period of time in which prices do not change or do not change very much.

Stagflation: A decrease in real output with increasing prices.

Supply shocks: External events that shift the aggregate supply curve.

Wealth effect: The increase in spending that occurs because the real value of money increases when the price level falls.

Practice Quiz

(Answers are provided at the end of the Practice Quiz.)

1. According to Keynesian analysis:
    a. wages adjust rapidly and this causes prices to rapidly change as well.
    b. wages adjust slowly and this causes prices to rapidly change in compensation.
    c. wages adjust slowly and this causes prices to slowly change as well.
    d. wages adjust rapidly and this causes prices to slowly change in compensation.

2. An economy is more likely to avoid economic fluctuations if:
    a. prices adjust slowly.
    b. prices adjust quickly.
    c. prices don't send signals to producers and consumers.
    d. prices prevent economic coordination.

3. Which of the following statements is correct?
    a. Flexible wages lead to sticky prices and hamper the economy's ability to bring demand and supply into balance in the short run.
    b. Sticky wages cause sticky prices and hamper the economy's ability to bring demand and supply into balance in the short run.
    c. Sticky wages and sticky prices are an important aspect of economic stability, bringing demand and supply into balance in the long run.
    d. In order to bring supply and demand into balance in the long run, flexible wages and prices must become sticky wages and prices.

4. According to the textbook discussion of the macroeconomic consequences of sticky prices, in the macroeconomic short run, both formal and informal contracts between firms mean that:
    a. changes in supply will be reflected primarily in changes in prices, not output.
    b. changes in demand will be reflected primarily in changes in output, not prices.
    c. changes in supply and demand will be reflected in changes in prices, not output.
    d. changes in factors other than supply and demand will be reflected in changes in output, not prices.

5. Which components of GDP are also components of aggregate demand?
    a. Consumption and investment
    b. Government spending and net exports
    c. All of the above
    d. None of the above

6. The increase in spending that occurs because the real value of money increases when the price level falls is called:
   a. the wealth effect.
   b. the interest rate effect.
   c. the foreign trade effect.
   d. the income effect.

7. A lower domestic price level will result in:
   a. higher imports.
   b. higher exports.
   c. probably both higher imports and higher exports.
   d. lower net exports.

8. Refer to the figure below. A decrease in government spending, all else the same, will shift the AD curve from the initial AD curve to the curve labeled:

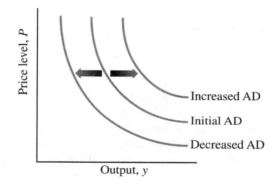

   a. Increased AD.
   b. Decreased AD.
   c. Neither curve. Government spending does not affect the AD curve.
   d. Either curve, depending on the simultaneous changes in taxation.

9. Refer to the figure below. Which of the following best represents the impact of an increase in government spending through the multiplier process?

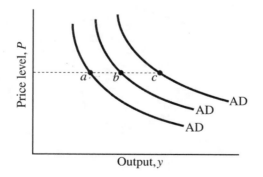

   a. The shift from *a* to *b*, and then to *c*
   b. The shift from *b* to *c*, and back to *a*
   c. The shift from *b* to *a*, and then to *c*
   d. The shift from *c* to *b*, and then to *a*

10. Consider the consumption function $C = C_a + bY$. Which part of this function is called the marginal propensity to consume?
    a. C_a
    b. b
    c. bY
    d. $C_a + bY$

11. The aggregate supply curve depicts the relationship between:
    a.   the number of firms in the economy and the corresponding level of output produced.
    b.   the level of prices and the total quantity of final goods and services that firms are willing and able to supply.
    c.   the number of firms in the economy and the corresponding level of prices.
    d.   the number of firms, the number of workers, and the quantity of final goods that both firms and workers together can supply to the entire economy.

12. In the long run, the level of output is:
    a.   independent of the price level.
    b.   dependent solely on the supply factors.
    c.   the full-employment level of output.
    d.   All of the above

13. In the short run, higher aggregate demand will cause:
    a.   a large increase in the price level, but no change in the level of output.
    b.   a higher price level, but only a slight increase in the level of output.
    c.   a higher level of output, but only a slight increase in the price level.
    d.   a large increase in both the price level and the level of output.

14. Refer to the figure below. The situation of this economy after the supply shock can be called:

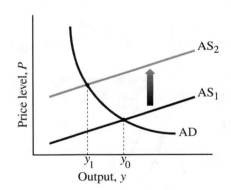

    a.   insufficient demand.
    b.   economic growth.
    c.   stagflation.
    d.   excess supply.

15. Refer to the figure below. In this economy there will be a tendency for:

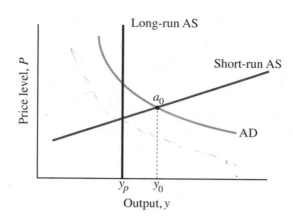

a. prices to fall and wages to rise over time.
b. prices to rise and wages to fall over time.
c. both wages and prices to rise over time.
d. both wages and prices to fall over time.

16. This question tests your understanding of Application 1 in this chapter: Price stickiness in retail catalogs. What does the behavior of prices in retail catalogs demonstrate about how quickly prices adjust in the U.S. economy?

    To analyze the behavior of retail prices, economist Anil Kashyap of the University of Chicago examined prices in consumer catalogs. Kashyap tracked several goods over time, including several varieties of shoes, blankets, chamois shirts, binoculars, and a fishing rod and fly. He found that:
    a. The prices of the goods he tracked changed substantially over time. There was considerable price flexibility.
    b. When prices did change, the changes were always relatively small.
    c. Prices of the goods that he tracked were typically fixed for a year or more.
    d. During periods of high inflation, prices tended to change less frequently.

17. Describe the phenomenon of economic fluctuations and articulate Keynes's opinion of the causes that led to the Great Depression.

18. Explain why an aggregate demand curve slopes downward.

19. Explain the logic of the multiplier according to J.M. Keynes.

20. Explain how output and the price level are determined in the long run.

Answers to the Practice Quiz

1. c. In the Keynesian model, wages adjust slowly, causing prices to slowly change as well.

2. b. The price system does not always work instantaneously. If prices are slow to adjust, then the proper signals are not given quickly enough to producers and consumers.

3. b. This statement reflects sticky prices and their macroeconomic consequences. Sticky wages cause sticky prices and hamper the economy's ability to bring demand and supply into balance in the short run.

4. b. In the macroeconomic short run, both formal and informal contracts between firms mean that changes in demand will be reflected primarily in changes in output, not prices.

5. c. In our study of GDP accounting, we divided GDP into four components: Consumption spending (C), investment spending (I), government purchases (G), and net exports (NX). These four components are also four parts of aggregate demand because the aggregate demand curve really just describes the demand for total GDP at different price levels.

6. a. The increase in spending that occurs because the real value of money increases when the price level falls is called the wealth effect.

7. b. A lower price level makes domestic goods cheaper relative to foreign goods. As domestic goods become cheaper, exports will rise and imports will fall, thereby improving the trade balance.

8. b. An increase in taxes, a decrease in government spending, or a decrease in the money supply will result in a decrease in aggregate demand.

9. a. Initially, the shift from a to b equals the increase in government spending. But after a brief period of time, total aggregate demand will increase by more than the initial increase in government spending, over to c.

10. b. The marginal propensity to consume is the amount by which consumption rises for each additional dollar of income. It is also the slope of the consumption function.

11. b. The aggregate supply curve depicts the relationship between the level of prices and the total quantity of final goods and services that firms are willing and able to supply.

12. d. In the long run, the level of output, y^*, is independent of the price level. Output depends solely on the supply factors—capital, labor—and the state of technology. In the long run, the economy operates at full employment and changes in the price level do not affect this.

13. c. In the short run, firms are assumed to supply all the output demanded, with small changes in prices. The short run aggregate supply curve has a small upward slope. Higher aggregate demand will cause a higher level of output, and only a slight increase in the price level.

14. c. Supply shocks are external events that shift the aggregate supply curve. Adverse supply shocks can cause a recession (a fall in output) with increasing prices. This phenomenon is known as stagflation.

15. c. Aggregate demand intersects the short-run aggregate supply curve at an output level that exceeds the potential level of output. In other words, this is a boom economy. As firms compete for labor and raw materials, there will be a tendency for both wages and prices to increase over time.

16. c. Kashyap found considerable price stickiness. Prices of the goods that he tracked were typically fixed for a year or more (even though the catalogs came out every six months).

17. Economic fluctuations, also called business cycles, are movements of GDP away from potential output. Insufficient demand for goods and services was a key problem of the Great Depression, identified by British economist John Maynard Keynes in the 1930s. Led by Keynes, many economists since his time have focused attention on economic coordination problems. The price system does not always work instantaneously. If prices are slow to adjust, then the proper signals are not given quickly enough to producers and consumers.

18. An aggregate demand curve slopes downward, meaning that a lower price level will result in a higher level of aggregate spending. There are three reasons for the increase in spending, as follows: The increase in spending that occurs because the real value of money increases when the price level falls is called the wealth effect. The interest rate effect: With a given money supply in the economy, a lower price level will lead to lower interest rates and higher consumption and investment spending. The impact of foreign trade: A lower price level makes domestic goods cheaper relative to foreign goods.

19. The logic of the multiplier goes back to Keynes. He believed that as government spending increases and the aggregate demand curve shifts to the right, output will subsequently increase too. Increased output also means increased income for households and higher consumption. It is this additional consumption spending that causes the further shift in the aggregate demand curve.

20. The intersection of aggregate demand and aggregate supply determines the price level and the equilibrium level of output. In the long run, an increase in aggregate demand will raise prices, but leave the level of output unchanged. In the long run, output is determined solely by the supply of capital and the supply of labor, not the price level.

10
Fiscal Policy

Chapter Summary

In 2005, the federal government budget deficit was $331 billion. In other words, the U.S. government spent $331 billion more than its revenue from taxes. In this chapter, we study how governments can use **fiscal policy**—changes in taxes and spending that affect the level of GDP—to stabilize the economy. We explore the logic of fiscal policy and explain why changes in government spending and taxation can, in principle, stabilize the economy. The chapter also provides an overview of spending and taxation by the federal government. These are essentially the tools that the government uses to implement its fiscal policies. Here are the main points of the chapter:

- Increases in government spending or decreases in taxes will increase aggregate demand.
- Decreases in government spending or increases in taxes will decrease aggregate demand.
- Because of the multiplier, the total shift in the aggregate demand curve will be larger than the initial shift. Policy makers need to take the multiplier into account as they formulate policy.
- Both inside lags (the time it takes to formulate policy) and outside lags (the time it takes the policy to work) limit the effectiveness of active fiscal policy.
- The largest component of federal spending is entitlements and mandatory programs.
- The largest components of federal revenues are income taxes and social insurance contributions collected from individuals.
- Government deficits act as an automatic stabilizer that helps to stabilize the economy in the short run.
- In the short run, fiscal policy actions taken to combat a recession will increase the deficit; in the long run, deficits are a concern because they may lead to crowding out of investment spending.
- Active fiscal policy has been periodically used in the United States to stimulate the economy; at other times, concerns about deficits have limited the use of fiscal policy.

Applying the Concepts

After reading this chapter, you should be able to answer these three key questions:
1. Why are the United States and many other countries facing dramatically increasing costs for their government programs?
2. How does the U.S. government make short- and long-term budget projections?
3. How much did the 2001 tax cuts stimulate consumer spending?

☞ Study Tip

This chapter is primarily informational. As such, you should take time to really study the key terms at the end of the chapter. Outlining the chapter will also help you summarize the major points. Lastly, review the "Applying the Concepts" questions and keep them in mind as you read the textbook. This will give real-life applications of the concepts you are studying.

10.1 The Role of Fiscal Policy

In this section, we will explore how the government can shift the aggregate demand curve by using fiscal policy. Fiscal policy consists of the government's ability to tax and spend.

💣 Caution!

Anything affecting C, I, G, or NX other than the price level will cause shifts of the aggregate demand curve. Price level changes will cause movement along the aggregate demand curve. Changes in government spending (G) directly affect AD. Changes in taxes (T) affect disposable personal income which, in turn, affects consumption spending (C).

Government spending and taxes will shift the aggregate demand curve. Government spending is a component of aggregate demand. If government spending increases, then aggregate demand increases, shifting the AD curve to the right. Government spending decreases aggregate demand, shifting the curve to the left.

Changes in taxes affect aggregate demand indirectly. If the government lowers taxes on consumers and firms, they will have more income at their disposal and will increase their consumption spending and investment spending.   Because consumption and investment spending are components of aggregate demand, aggregate demand will increase as well. Increases in taxes will have the opposite effect.

In Figure 10.1, panel A shows that an increase in government spending shifts the aggregate demand curve from AD_0 to AD_1, restoring the economy to full employment. This is an example of expansionary policy. Decreasing taxes would have the same effect.   Panel B shows that an increase in taxes decreases aggregated demand, shifting the aggregate demand curve to the left, from AD_0 to AD_1, and restoring the economy to full employment. This is an example of contractionary policy. Decreasing government spending would have the same effect.

☞ Study Tip

The best way to understand graphical analysis is to draw the graphs. First draw the graphs in an equilibrium condition. Then show what happens to aggregate demand after a variable such as government spending or taxes changes.

> **Study Tip**
>
> The concept of the multiplier is the same concept you learned in Chapter 9. Review pages 199–200 if you need a refresher on the computing of the multiplier.

You learned about the multiplier in Chapter 9. This multiplier effect occurs because an initial change in output will affect the income of households, and thus change consumer spending. For example, an increase in government spending of $10 billion will initially raise household incomes by $10 billion and lead to increases in consumer spending. In turn, the increase of income increases consumer spending and will raise output and income further, leading to further increases in consumer spending.

Fiscal policy can be used to stabilize an economy. **Stabilization policies** are policy actions taken to move the economy closer to full employment or potential output. Expansionary and contractionary policies are examples of stabilization policies. Stabilization policies are difficult to implement for two big reasons:

1. Lags, or delays, in stabilization policy. Lags arise because decision makers are often slow to recognize and respond to changes in the economy, and fiscal policies and other stabilization policies take time to operate.
2. Economists simply do not know enough about all aspects of the economy to be completely accurate in all their forecasts.

Economists recognize two broad classes of lags. **Inside lags** refer to the time it takes to formulate a policy. They happen for two reasons. First, it takes time to identify and recognize a problem. Second, once a problem has been diagnosed, it still takes time before the government can take action.

☞ In the U.S., any change in fiscal policy requires substantial agreement among 435 members of the House of Representatives, 100 members of the Senate, and 1 president. No wonder the inside lag for fiscal policy is so long.

Outside lags refer to the time it takes for the policy to actually work. Even when policy makers agree on a policy, it takes time to implement the policy. For example, if taxes are to be increased, then it may not happen until the next fiscal year. Figure 10.2 shows the problem caused by lags. Panel A shows an example of successful stabilization policy, where the economy is moved closer to full employment output. Panel B shows the consequences of ill-timed policies. An ill-timed policy moves the economy further away from full employment output.

Forecasts are critical to stabilization policy. Uncertainties can cause greater problems than the problem itself. Economists are careful before recommending active stabilization policies.

10.2 The Federal Budget

The federal budget—the document that describes what the federal government spends and how it pays for that spending—provides the framework for fiscal policy. Consider the following facts about the budget:

*   In 2005, total federal spending was approximately 20.2 percent of GDP, or $2.47 trillion.
*   Federal taxes were 17.5 percent of GDP.
*   With a U.S. population of about 300 million, total federal spending amounted to approximately $8,230 per person.
*   Fiscal year 2005 began on October 1, 2004, and ended on September 30, 2005.

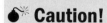 Visit www.whitehouse.gov/omb/budget to find the current federal budget information for the United States. This site provides you complete information about the federal budget.

The two major components of federal spending are purchases of goods and services and transfer payments. Table 10.1 summarizes federal spending for the 2005 fiscal year. There are three categories of spending within the federal budget.

1. **Discretionary spending** is spending on all the programs that Congress authorizes on an annual basis that are not automatically funded by prior laws.
2. **Entitlement and mandatory spending** is all spending that Congress has authorized by prior law. Social Security, Medicare, and Medicaid are in this category of spending.
3. Net interest is interest that the government pays the public on the government debt held by the public.

● Caution!

Transfer payments—such as Medicare and Medicaid—are not a component of GDP because they do not represent any currently produced goods or services.

Let's review an Application that answers one of the key questions we posed at the start of the chapter:

1. Why are the United States and many other countries facing dramatically increasing costs for their government programs?

APPLICATION 1: INCREASING LIFE EXPECTANCY AND AGING POPULATIONS SPUR COSTS OF ENTITLEMENT PROGRAMS

As life expectancies increase, the population ages and new medical technologies become available to help people live longer. Economists and budget analysts predict that spending on federal retirement and health programs will grow extremely rapidly. Today, Social Security, Medicare, and Medicaid constitute approximately 9 percent of GDP. Experts estimate that in 2075—when children born today are in their retirement years—spending on these programs will be approximately 21 percent of GDP. Strategies for dealing with this issue include raising taxes, savings and investment, and entitlement spending reform.

Table 10.2 shows the revenues the federal government received in fiscal year 2005 in both dollar terms and as a percent of GDP. Federal revenues are broken up into the following categories:

1. Individual income taxes
2. Social insurance taxes
3. Corporate taxes
4. Excise, estate, and other taxes

Supply-side economics is a school of thought that emphasizes the role taxes play in the supply of output in the economy. The **Laffer curve** shows the relationship between the tax rates and tax revenues. High tax rates could lead to lower tax revenues if economic activity is severely discouraged. According to the Laffer curve, lower tax rates may actually increase tax revenues.

Virtually all economists today believe Laffer's tax revenue idea won't work when it comes to broad-based income taxes or payroll taxes. For these types of taxes, cutting rates from their current levels would simply reduce the revenues that the government collects.

Budget deficits occur when government spending exceeds tax revenues during a fiscal year. Financing the shortfall requires borrowing from the public. **Budget surpluses** occur when government spending is less than tax revenues in a given year.

Taxes and transfer payments that stabilize GDP without requiring explicit actions by policy makers are called **automatic stabilizers**. How do these stabilizers work? Tax revenues will fall sharply during a recession as national income falls. At the same time, government transfer payments for programs such as unemployment insurance and food stamps will also tend to increase during a recession. The government deficit itself, in effect, offsets part of the adverse effect of the recession and thus helps stabilize the economy. The opposite happens in the case of an economic boom.

Let's review an Application that answers one of the key questions we posed at the start of the chapter:

5. How does the U.S. government make short- and long-term budget projections?

APPLICATION 2: HOW GOVERNMENTS USE BUDGET BASELINES TO FORECAST DEFICITS

When Congress and the president consider the proper course of fiscal policy, they must consider the future state of the budget—will there be a deficit or surplus and how big will the deficit or surplus be? But to make these forecasts, it is necessary to make explicit assumptions about what spending and tax policies will be in place. These assumptions are known as *budget baselines*.

Are deficits bad? The short answer to this question is "It depends." Of course we can't live on the answer "It depends." On what does this question depend? Deficits may be bad or good depending on the economic circumstances facing the economy at the time. For example, during a recession, running a deficit would actually move the economy out of the recession by stimulating aggregate demand.

On the other hand, deficits may cause problems in a fully employed economy. An example we discussed in Chapter 7 is crowding out. When the economy is at full employment, deficit spending is likely to crowd out an equal amount of investment and consumption spending. The opportunity cost of the deficit may be decreased investment and consumption spending.

☞ Visit www.cbo.gov—U.S. Congressional Budget Office Web—for the details of the budget that makes up deficits.

 Principle of Opportunity Cost

The opportunity cost of something is what you sacrifice to get it.

Another form of crowding out may happen in the financial markets. As the government runs large deficits, it will have to borrow increasing amounts of money from the public by selling U.S. government bonds. In the financial markets, the government will be in increased competition with businesses that are trying to raise funds from the public to finance their investment plans, too. This increased competition from the government will make it more difficult and costly for businesses to raise funds and, as a result, investment spending will decrease.

☞ Policy makers often debate the deficit and the debt. For contrasting perspectives of the federal budget, look at the following Web sites:
www.cbpp.org
www.ncpa.org/newpd/index.php

10.3 Fiscal Policy in U.S. History

Contrary to popular belief, the U.S. government did not use fiscal policy during the Great Depression. Policymakers understood the concept of fiscal policy, but they did not use it because they were afraid of deficits and how those deficits could affect the economy. Yet the outbreak of World War II generated increased government spending. Economists debate whether World War II pulled the United States out of the Great Depression.

☞ The view of the economy during the Great Depression was based on a classical model. Many policy makers believed that the economy would return to equilibrium, and so government intervention would cause the economy to destabilize even more.

It was not until the presidency of John F. Kennedy during the early 1960s that modern fiscal policy came to be accepted. Walter Heller, the chairman of the president's Council of Economic Advisers under John F. Kennedy, was a forceful advocate of active fiscal policy. Heller advocated for tax cuts to stimulate aggregate demand.

Two other factors led the Kennedy administration to support the tax cut:
1. Tax rates were extremely high at the time. The top individual tax rate was 91 percent, compared to about 40 percent today. The corporate tax rate was 52 percent, compared to 35 percent today.
2. Heller convinced Kennedy that even if a tax cut led to a federal budget deficit, it was not a problem. In 1961, the federal deficit was less than 1 percent of GDP, and future projections indicated that the deficit would disappear as the economy grew because of higher tax revenues.

While difficult to measure for sure, the growth of GDP from 1963 through 1966 at a 4 percent rate suggests the tax cuts did have a positive effect on the economy. As the Vietnam War began and military spending increased, unemployment fell to very low levels. From 1966 to 1969, the overall unemployment rate fell below 4 percent. As the economy started to overheat from government spending, a surcharge of 10 percent was levied against demand on goods and services. The impact of the surcharge was minimal since consumers saw it as temporary. The surcharge did not decrease consumer spending as much as economists had initially estimated. Why did this happen? According to economists, consumers often base their spending on an estimate of their long-run average income, or **permanent income**, not on their current income. The temporary, one-year tax surcharge during the Vietnam War had a similar effect. Because consumers knew the surcharge was not permanent, they didn't alter their spending habits very much.

During the 1970s, there were many changes in taxes and spending, but no major changes in overall fiscal policy. A recession in 1973 led to a tax rebate and other incentives in 1975, but, by and large, changes to fiscal policy were mild.

Reagan's tax cuts in the 1980s were significant. The tax cuts were justified on the basis of improving economic incentives and increasing the supply of output rather than increasing aggregate demand. In other words, the tax cuts were supply-side motivated. Taxes can have important effects on the supply of labor, saving, and economic growth. By the mid-1980s, large government budget deficits began to emerge, and policy makers became concerned.

During the late 1990s, President Bill Clinton proposed a "stimulus package" that would increase aggregate demand, but it was defeated in Congress. Clinton later successfully passed a major tax increase that brought the budget into balance. By the year 1998, the federal budget actually began to show surpluses rather than deficits.

Here is a summary of George W. Bush's tax policies from 2001–2003:

- During his first year in office in 2001, President George W. Bush passed a 10-year tax cut plan that decreased tax rates, in part to eliminate the government surpluses and return revenues to households, but also to stimulate the economy that was slowing down as the high-tech investment boom was ending.
- After the September 11, 2001, terrorist attacks, President Bush and Congress became less concerned with balancing the federal budget and authorized new spending programs to provide relief to victims and to stimulate the economy, which had entered into a recession prior to September 11.
- In May 2003, President Bush signed another tax bill to stimulate the sluggish economy and, in particular, to increase investment spending. This bill had many distinct features, including moving up some of the previously scheduled cuts in tax rates that were part of the 2001 tax bill, increasing the child tax credit, and lowering taxes on dividends and capital gains.

Figure 10.3 plots the course of spending, taxes, and the deficit since 1996 and shows the recent reemergence of deficits.

Let's review an Application that answers one of the key questions we posed at the start of the chapter:

3.   How much did the 2001 tax cuts stimulate consumer spending?

APPLICATION 3: SURVEYS SHOW MUCH OF THE 2001 TAX CUTS WERE SAVED

In 2001, approximately 90 million U.S. households received tax rebate checks from the government. These checks were up to $300 for a single taxpayer or $600 for joint, or married, filers. The tax rebate was just the first installment of a multiyear tax reduction for households stemming from a new tax bill passed that year. Professors Matthew Shapiro and Joel Slemrod surveyed households using the University of Michigan Survey Research Center Monthly Survey. They asked a nationally representative set of households whether they were more likely to spend the rebate, save it, or pay down existing debts. Shapiro and Slemrod surveyed households both when the rebate checks were being mailed and following their arrival. They found that less than 25 percent of households were likely to spend the rebate.

☞ Visit the Heritage Foundation Web site, www.heritage.org/research/taxes/issues 2004.cfm, or the Brookings Institution Web site, www.brookings.edu/comm./policybriefs/pb101.htm, for additional information regarding the Bush tax cuts and their impacts on spending and saving.

Activity

Name two examples of discretionary spending and two examples of entitlement and mandatory spending.

Answers

Discretionary spending would include national defense, state department, and education spending among others. Entitlement and mandatory spending would include Social Security, Medicare, and Medicaid.

Key Terms

Automatic stabilizers: Taxes and transfer payments that stabilize GDP without requiring policy makers to take explicit action.

Budget deficit: The amount by which government spending exceeds revenues in a given year.

Budget surplus: The amount by which government revenues exceed government expenditures in a given year.

Contractionary policies: Government policy actions that lead to decreases in aggregate demand.

Discretionary spending: The spending programs that Congress authorizes on an annual basis.

Entitlement and mandatory spending: Spending that Congress has authorized by prior law, primarily providing support for individuals.

Expansionary policies: Government policy actions that lead to increases in aggregate demand.

Fiscal policy: Changes in government taxes and spending that affect the level of GDP.

Inside lags: The time it takes to formulate a policy.

Laffer curve: A relationship between the tax rates and tax revenues that illustrates that high tax rates could lead to lower tax revenues if economic activity is severely discouraged.

Medicaid: A federal and state government health program for the poor.

Medicare: A federal government health program for the elderly.

Outside lags: The time it takes for the policy to actually work.

Permanent income: An estimate of a household's long-run average level of income.

Social Security: A federal government program to provide retirement support and a host of other benefits.

Stabilization policies: Policy actions taken to move the economy closer to full employment or potential output.

Supply-side economics: A school of thought that emphasizes the role that taxes play in the supply of output in the economy.

Practice Quiz

(Answers are provided at the end of the Practice Quiz.)

1. Which of the following would be a fiscal policy the government might want to use in a recession?
   a. Increasing the money supply and lowering interest rates
   b. Decreasing income tax rates
   c. Decreasing government purchases of goods and services
   d. All of the above

2. Government policies that decrease aggregate demand are called:
   a. recessionary policies.
   b. contractionary policies.
   c. fiscal policies.
   d. expansionary policies.

3. Refer to the figure below. Which type of fiscal policy would cause this move of the AD curve?

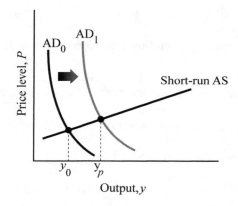

   a. Higher taxes
   b. Higher government spending
   c. A decrease in the money supply
   d. An increase in production costs as a result of higher oil prices

4. Stabilization policy is _____ because there are _____ between recognition and response to changes in the economy
   a. simple...excellent tools to establish the difference
   b. difficult...time lags
   c. easy...multipliers
   d. impossible...too many variables to account for

5. Refer to the figure below. Which side shows an ideal stabilization policy?

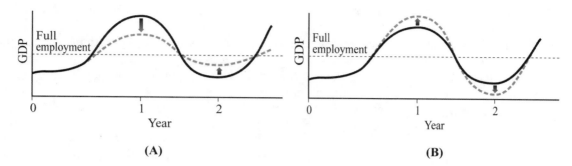

(A)   (B)

a. A
b. B
c. Both A and B
d. Neither A nor B

6. There are _____ lags, which refer to the time it takes to formulate a policy, and _____ lags, which refer to the time it takes for the policy to actually work.
a. inside; outside
b. postulating; effective
c. formulating; speculative
d. theoretical; realistic

7. The actual document that describes what the federal government spends and how it pays for it is called:
a. The Economic Report of the President.
b. Economic Indicators.
c. The Federal Budget.
d. The Monetary Policy Report.

8. The fiscal year runs:
a. from July 1st to June 30th.
b. from January 1st to December 31st.
c. from April 16th to April 15th.
d. from October 1st to September 30th.

9. All the programs that Congress authorizes on an annual basis, which are not automatically funded by prior laws passed by Congress, are called:
a. entitlements.
b. mandatory spending.
c. discretionary spending.
d. means-tested spending.

10. _____ provides health care to all individuals once they reach the age of 65, while _____ provides health care to the poor, in conjunction with the states.
a. Medicare; Medicaid
b. Social Security; Medicare
c. Medicare; Social Security
d. Medicaid; Medicare

11. This question tests your understanding of Application 1 in this chapter on life expectancy and entitlement programs. Which of the following statements is true?
   a. As people live longer in many countries, government is going to find it more difficult to find entitlement programs for the elderly.
   b. Increased taxes would increase the revenue government has for these programs and encourage greater economic growth.
   c. The U.S. has the most severe problem in the world with a rapidly aging population and rising government spending on entitlement programs for the elderly.
   d. Increasing the retirement age would have no effect on the financial burden of entitlement programs for the elderly as the savings would be insignificant.

12. Among the sources of revenue for the federal government are individual income taxes. As of 2005, how much of the receipts (in billions) and what percent of GDP is estimated to represent individual income taxes?
   a. 927 and 7.6%
   b. 794 and 6.5%
   c. 153 and 1.2%
   d. 269 and 1.2%

13. If the federal government's expenditures are greater than its revenue, there is a _____ _____.
   a. budget deficit
   b. budget surplus
   c. budget baseline
   d. bond purchase

14. In addition to estate taxes and customs duties, which of the following taxes is a relatively minor contributor?
   a. The withholding of a portion of workers' paychecks
   b. Social insurance taxes
   c. Corporate taxes
   d. Estate and gift taxes

15. *Crowding out* refers to:
   a. the problem arising from having to consult with a large number of people in order to get fiscal policy approved in time to help the economy.
   b. the decline in private expenditures that results from an increase in government purchases.
   c. the ever-decreasing amount of induced expenditures that eventually stops the multiplier of government purchases.
   d. the increase in government expenditures following an increase in GDP from rising consumption or investment expenditures.

16. Taxes and transfer payments that stabilize GDP without requiring explicit actions by policymakers are called:
   a. discretionary fiscal policy.
   b. expansionary fiscal policy.
   c. automatic stabilizers.
   d. social insurance stabilizers.

17. When the economy is at full employment, a cut in household taxes will:
    a. tend to decrease consumer spending.
    b. increase consumption but reduce another component of GDP.
    c. increase investment but reduce consumption.
    d. increase consumption, and usually other components of GDP as well, through the multiplier effect.

18. During the Great Depression,
    a. there was a large fiscal expansion, as the government ran substantial budget deficits.
    b. there was a large accumulation of revenues, as the government ran substantial budget surpluses.
    c. there was no net fiscal expansion, as taxes were sufficient to cover government spending.
    d. there was fiscal expansion at first, which then turned into fiscal contraction.

19. A tax on consumption will not decrease consumption as much as expected if the tax is:
    a. temporary.
    b. permanent.
    c. too high.
    d. too low.

20. Which of the following presidents was able to bring the federal budget into balance?
    a. Kennedy
    b. Reagan
    c. Clinton
    d. G. W. Bush

21. Explain the impact of budget deficits for the economy in the long run.

22. List and briefly describe the types of fiscal stabilization policies available to the government, and briefly explain the difficulties associated with stabilization policies.

Answers to the Practice Quiz

1. b. Policy advocates argue that the government needs expansionary policies during a recession; that would include raising government spending and/or cutting taxes.

2. b. Government policies that decrease aggregate demand are called contractionary policies.

3. b. Higher government spending, which is a component of aggregate demand, causes the aggregate demand curve to shift to the right.

4. b. Stabilization policy is difficult because there are time lags between recognition and response to changes in the economy, and because we simply do not know enough about all aspects of the economy.

5. a. Here, the size of the fluctuations is dampened by stabilization policy.

6. a. There are inside lags, which refer to the time it takes to formulate a policy, and outside lags, which refer to the time it takes for the policy to actually work.

7. c. The federal budget is the actual document that describes what the federal government spends and how it pays for it. It provides the framework for fiscal policy.

8. d. The government runs its budget on a fiscal year basis, from October 1 to September 30.

9. c. Discretionary spending constitutes all the programs that Congress authorizes on an annual basis, which are not automatically funded by prior laws passed by Congress.

10. a. Medicare provides health care to all individuals once they reach the age of 65. Medicaid provides health care to the poor, in conjunction with the states.

11. a. The developed countries in general have experienced rising life spans, increasing the percent of the population that is elderly and increasing the number of years these individuals collect entitlement benefits. This makes it much more difficult to fund these programs.

12. a. This is the federal revenue derived from individual income taxes, which is also the largest source of revenue for the federal government.

13. a. The federal government's budget shows the relation between its expenditures and its tax revenue. If the federal government's expenditures are greater than its revenue, there is a budget deficit. If the federal government's expenditures are less than its tax revenue, there is a budget surplus.

14. c. The corporate tax is a tax levied on the earnings of corporations. This tax raised less than 7.5% of total federal revenues during fiscal year 2003.

15. b. A decline in private expenditures as a result of an increase in government purchases is called crowding out.

16. c. Taxes and transfer payments that stabilize GDP without requiring explicit actions by policymakers are called automatic stabilizers.

17. b. When the economy is at full employment, a cut in household taxes will tend to increase consumer spending. However, since output is fixed at full employment, some other component of output must be reduced, or crowded out.

18. c. Although government spending increased during the 1930s, taxes increased sufficiently during that same period, with the result that there was no net fiscal expansion.

19. a. Consumers often base their spending on an estimate of their long-run average income or permanent income, not on their current income.

20. c. Clinton successfully passed a major tax increase that brought the budget into balance.

21. In the long run, large budget deficits can have an adverse effect on the economy. When the economy is at full employment, a cut in household taxes will tend to increase consumer spending. However, since output is fixed at full employment, some other component of output must be reduced, or crowded out. This is an example of the principle of opportunity cost.

22. Both expansionary policies and contractionary policies are examples of stabilization policies, actions to move the economy closer to full employment or potential output. Government policies that increase aggregate demand are called expansionary policies. Government policies that decrease aggregate demand are called contractionary policies. Stabilization policy is difficult because there are time lags between recognition and response to changes in the economy, and because we simply do not know enough about all aspects of the economy.

11

The Income-Expenditure Model

Chapter Summary

The model we develop in this chapter is called the income-expenditure model, sometimes referred to as the *Keynesian cross*. The model was developed by the economist John Maynard Keynes in the 1930s. This chapter will primarily use graphical tools to explain the income-expenditure model. An appendix to this chapter provides an algebraic treatment of the model and shows how some of the key formulas are derived. Here are the main points of the chapter:

- In the income-expenditure model, the level of output in the economy will adjust to equal the level of planned expenditures. This level of output is called equilibrium output.
- Consumption spending consists of two parts. One part is independent of income, but can be influenced by changes in wealth or consumer sentiment. The other part depends on the level of income.
- Increases in planned expenditures by households, the government, or the foreign sector lead to increases in equilibrium output.
- Because of the multiplier, the final increase in equilibrium output is larger than the initial increase.
- Policy makers can use multipliers to calculate the appropriate size of economic policies.
- Higher tax rates, by reducing the multiplier, can reduce fluctuations in GDP.
- Increases in exports lead to increases in equilibrium output; increases in imports lead to decreases in equilibrium output.
- The income-expenditure model can be used to derive the aggregate demand curve.

Applying the Concepts

After reading this chapter, you should be able to answer these four key questions:
1. How do increases in the value of homes affect consumer spending?
2. Why does real GDP typically increase after natural disasters?
3. How influential a figure was John Maynard Keynes?
4. Why do foreign countries like U.S. growth?

11.1 A Simple Income-Expenditure Model

To determine equilibrium output, we need to understand the behavior of firms. Figure 11.1 illustrates the behavior of firms with a 45° line from the origin. In the income-expenditure model, the 45° line represents where planned expenditure equals actual output. Because firms are willing to supply whatever is demanded without raising prices very much, demand is the key factor in determining the level of output, or GDP.

As we consider demand, we will focus on consumption spending (C) and investment spending (I). Total demand or **planned expenditures** in this model will be $C + I$. In the income-expenditure model, the level of output in the economy will adjust to equal the level of planned expenditures. The level of output is called the **equilibrium output**. The following equation shows this relationship:

☑ Key Equation

Equilibrium output $= y^* = C + I =$ planned expenditures

Figure 11.2 can help us understand how the level of equilibrium output, or GDP, in the economy is determined. On the expenditure-output graph, we draw the line representing planned expenditures, $C + I$, which is a horizontal line, because both C and I are fixed amounts. The intersection of the 45° line with the planned expenditures line at point a determines equilibrium output, y^*. Later we will add other components of aggregate demand and demonstrate its effects on the income-expenditure model.

What if production is greater or lesser than equilibrium output? Figure 11.3 illustrates how adjustment would occur:
- If there is excess production, the 45° line is greater than planned expenditures. Output that is not purchased piles up as business inventories. Businesses see inventories rising and reduce production in the next period to meet demand.
- If there is insufficient production, the 45° line is lower than planned expenditures. When people purchase more output than firms are currently producing, inventories fall. Firm see inventories falling and increase production in the next period.

⤶ Study Tip

Table 11.1shows how adjustment to equilibrium output occurs with numerical data. Notice that production here refers to output produced. The interaction between planned expenditures, $C + I$, and output produced determines the equilibrium output amount.

💣 Caution!

Demand—not prices—drives the production of inputs and products in the short run.

11.2 The Consumption Function

As we build the model toward total planned expenditures, we will start with household consumption. Other components in later sections to be added later as we build toward total planned expenditures. You will remember from Chapter 5, consumption expenditures were $8,844 billion or 70.2 percent of GDP. (See Table 5.1 on page 104.) The following equations are key to understanding consumption behavior.

☑ Key Equations

Consumption Function: $C = C_a + by$, where C_a is autonomous consumption expenditures, b is the marginal propensity to consume (MPC), and y is income.

$$MPC = \frac{\text{additional consumption}}{\text{additional income}}$$

$$MPS = \frac{\text{additional saving}}{\text{additional income}}$$

In Chapter 9, consumption expenditures can be broken into two pieces. Autonomous consumption is consumption expenditures that don't change when income changes. Autonomous consumption is represented in the equation as (C_a). The other term, (by), in the consumption function represents consumer spending dependent on changes in income. This term has two parts to it. The letter b represents the marginal propensity to consume and the letter y represents income. The **marginal propensity to consume**, or MPC, is the fraction of additional income spent on consumption goods. The marginal propensity to save, or MPS, is the remaining fraction of additional income that must be saved.

⌐ Study Tip

Output is also equal to the income that flows to the households. As firms produce output, they pay households income in the form of wages, interest, profits, and rents. Recall the discussion of value added in Chapter 5. Since total income equals total value added, we know total income must also equal total output. We can therefore use y to represent both output and income.

Figure 11.4 shows how the consumption function is graphed in the income-expenditure model. Autonomous consumption (C_a) is graphed as the intercept term. The consumption function has a slope of b equal in value to the marginal propensity to consume (MPC).

Figure 11.5 shows how changes in autonomous consumption and the marginal propensity to consume cause changes in the consumption function. Panel A shows that an increase in autonomous consumption from C_{0a} to C_{1a} shifts the entire consumption function upward. Note that the slope of the consumption function does not change. The consumption function shifts when:
* Consumer wealth changes
* Consumer confidence changes

Panel B shows that an increase in the MPC from b to b' increases the slope of the consumption function. MPC increases pivot the consumption function counterclockwise; MPC decreases pivot the consumption function clockwise.

Let's review an Application that answers one of the key questions we posed at the start of the chapter:

1. How do increases in the value of homes affect consumer spending?

APPLICATION 1: RISING HOME EQUITY, THE WEALTH EFFECT, AND INCREASED CONSUMER SPENDING

From 2000 to 2003, the value of home equity—the difference between the value of homes and the amount of mortgage debt on the property—increased by approximately $2 trillion. Home equity is the single-largest component of net wealth for most families in the United States. A study by the International Monetary Fund (IMF) found that increases in home equity have larger effects on consumption than increases in the stock market. The IMF found that a dollar increase in home equity increased consumption by approximately 7 cents, whereas increases in stock market wealth led to an increase of only 4.5 cents.

11.3 Equilibrium Output and the Consumption Function

Figure 11.6 shows how equilibrium output is determined with a consumption function. Take the following steps in graphing equilibrium output:
1. Draw the consumption function (C).
2. Draw the $C + I$ line parallel to the C line but shifted upward by I units.
3. Draw the 45° line.
4. Where the $C + I$ line crosses the 45° line, determines equilibrium output, y^*.

☑ Key Equation

$$y^* = \frac{C_a + I}{1 - \text{MPC}}$$

In Chapter 8, we defined the relationship between saving and investment. We can also define equilibrium output in terms of savings and investment as follows:

☑ Key Equations

$y = C + S \text{ (Income)} \Rightarrow S = y - C$
$y = C + I \text{ (Output)} \Rightarrow I = y - C$
$S = I$

From these equations, we can derive a savings function that shows the level of savings given a level of income. The **saving function** is derived as follows:

☑ Key Equations

$S = y - C$
$S = y - (C_a + by)$
$S = y - C_a - by$
$S = -C_a + y - by$
$S = -C_a + (1 - b)y$

Figure 11.7 illustrates the impact of the multiplier in the income-expenditure model. When investment increases from I_0 to I_1, equilibrium output increases from y_0 to y_1. The change in output (Δy) is greater than the change in investment (ΔI). The logic behind the multiplier is that spending generates income for additional spending. As this process continues over time, total spending will continue to increase, but in diminishing amounts.

☑ Key Equations

$$\text{Multiplier} = \frac{1}{1 - \text{MPC}}$$

$$\Delta y = \Delta I \left(\frac{1}{1 - MPC} \right)$$

☞ Study Tip

Learn now to apply the multiplier formulas above. They will be similar to fiscal policy applications in section 11.4 in this chapter. Try practice problems in this study guide until you feel comfortable solving these problems.

Let's review an Application that answers one of the key questions we posed at the start of the chapter:

2. Why does real GDP typically increase after natural disasters?

APPLICATION 2: INCREASED INVESTMENT SPENDING RAISES GDP AFTER NATURAL DISASTERS

When Hurricane Katrina devastated the Gulf Coast and New Orleans in 2005, many economists predicted that it would have only small and temporary effects on total U.S. GDP. The basic reason for their prediction was that natural disasters can often stimulate economic activity because people need to buy material to rebuild homes. The purchase of goods and services is new investment spending for the economy, which stimulates GDP both through its direct effect and through the multiplier. Ironically, although the hurricane destroys wealth (in terms of the house), it stimulates new production.

☞ Some economists call spending like this "regrettables" because most people would rather not spend to rebuild a destroyed house.

11.4 Government Spending and Taxation

Using taxes and spending to influence the level of GDP in the short run is known as **Keynesian fiscal policy**. As with investment spending in the previous section, government spending and taxes have multiplier effects. In this section, we will expand planned expenditures to include government spending:

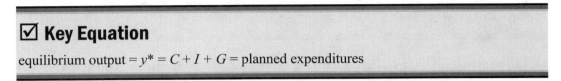

☑ **Key Equation**

equilibrium output = $y^* = C + I + G$ = planned expenditures

Panel A of Figure 11.8 shows how increases in government spending affect GDP. The increase in government spending from G_0 to G_1 shifts the $C + I + G$ line upward and increases the level of GDP from y_0 to y_1.

〰 **Study Tip**

The multiplier for changes in autonomous variables such as autonomous consumption, investment, and government expenditures are all the same as the one shown below.

☑ **Key Equation**

$$\text{Multiplier} = \frac{1}{1 - MPC}$$

Panel B of Figure 11.8 shows how an increase in taxes will decrease the level of GDP. As the level of taxes increases, the demand line will shift downward by b (the increase in taxes). Equilibrium income will fall from y_0 to y_1. The multiplier for taxes is slightly different than the multiplier for government spending.

☑ **Key Equation**

$$\text{Tax Multiplier} = \frac{-MPC}{1 - MPC}$$

The tax multiplier is negative because increases in taxes decrease disposable personal income and lead to a reduction in consumption spending. Any change in taxes does not directly affect spending. Instead it affects disposable income. A tax cut causes disposable income to increase. *Spending* increases by the MPC times the increase in disposable income. That's why the MPC is in the numerator of the tax multiplier equation.

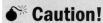

☞ Caution!

Be sure and use negative signs to show tax and spending decreases in your calculations. The multipliers are built to take into account increases and decreases.

Although our income-expenditure model with government is very simple and leaves out many factors, like all models, it illustrates some important lessons:

- An increase in government spending will increase total planned expenditures for goods and services.
- Cutting taxes will increase the after-tax income of consumers and will also lead to an increase in planned expenditures for goods and services.
- Policy makers need to take into account the multipliers for government spending and taxes as they develop policies.

Keynes was a strong advocate for activist fiscal policy. One of Keynes's controversial ideas was that governments could stimulate the economy even if they spent money on wasteful projects. In the *General Theory*, he even remarked (tongue-in-cheek) how lucky the Egyptians were, because the death of the pharaohs would lead to new pyramids being built. Pyramids do not add to the stock of capital to produce regular goods and services. But Keynes's point was that building pyramids does add to planned expenditures and stimulates GDP in the short run.

In the long run, of course, we are better off if government spends the money wisely, such as on needed infrastructure such as roads and bridges. This is an example of the principle of opportunity cost.

 Principle of Opportunity Cost

The opportunity cost of something is what you sacrifice to get it.

Let's review an Application that answers one of the key questions we posed at the start of the chapter:

3. How influential a figure was John Maynard Keynes?

APPLICATION 3: JOHN MAYNARD KEYNES: A WORLD INTELLECTUAL

This Application summarizes the life and accomplishments of John Maynard Keynes. Many have called Keynes the most influential economist of the 20th century. Keynes was a prolific writer and economist following in the footsteps of his father John Neville Keynes. The younger John Maynard Keynes attended Cambridge and King's College. His best known work is *The General Theory of Employment, Interest, and Money*.

Figure 11.9 plots the rate of growth of U.S. real GDP from 1871 to 2005. It is apparent from the graph that the U.S. economy has been much more stable after World War II than before. One reason for this increased stability is automatic stabilizers. To see how automatic stabilizers work in our model, we must take into account that the government levies income taxes by applying a tax rate to the level of income. We will look to after-tax income or personal disposable income. The consumption function changes to account for taxes.

☑ Key Equation

$C = C_a + b(1 - t)y$ where the adjusted MPC $= b(1 - t)$

Changes to the MPC cause the slope of the consumption function to change. Figure 11.10 shows how an increase in the tax rate would affect the income expenditure model. Raising the tax rate lowers the adjusted MPC and reduces the slope of this line. The $C + I + G$ line with taxes intersects the 45° line at a lower level of income.

Automatic stabilizers help stabilize economic fluctuations. Permanent income and expectations that the government will take action to stabilize the economy also contribute to economic stability.

11.5   Exports and Imports

An increase in exports means that there's an increase in the demand for goods produced in the United States. An increase in imports means that there is an increase in foreign-produced goods purchased by U.S. residents. Importing goods rather than purchasing them from our domestic producers reduces the demand for U.S. goods.

To modify our model to include the effects of world spending on exports and U.S. spending on imports, we need to take two steps:
1. Add exports X, as another source of demand for U.S. goods and services.
2. Subtract imports, M, from total spending by U.S. residents. We will assume that imports, like consumption, increase with the level of income.

☑ Key Equations

$M = my$ where m is the **marginal propensity to import.**
$b - m = $ marginal propensity to consume adjusted for imports.

Figure 11.11 shows how equilibrium output is determined including the international sector. Figure 11.12 shows the impacts on equilibrium output with changes in exports and changes in the marginal propensity to import. Panel A shows that an increase in exports will increase the level of GDP. Panel B shows that an increase in the marginal propensity to import will decrease the level of GDP.

Let's review an Application that answers one of the key questions we posed at the start of the chapter:

4. Why do foreign countries like U.S. growth?

APPLICATION 4: THE LOCOMOTIVE EFFECT: HOW FOREIGN DEMAND AFFECTS A COUNTRY'S OUTPUT

From the early 1990s until quite recently, the United States was what economists term the "locomotive" for global growth. As the U.S. economy grew, our demand for foreign products increased. Imports increase as an economy grows, and U.S. imports also increased along with output during this period. Because the U.S. economy is such an important part of the world economy, its demands for foreign goods—U.S. imports—fueled exports in foreign countries and promoted their growth.

> ### ᜇᜄ᜔ Study Tip
>
> A basic fact of international trade is that one country's imports must be the exports of other countries in the world. If U.S. imports increase, then exports from some of the other countries must also increase.

11.6 The Income-Expenditure Model and the Aggregate Demand Curve

In Figure 11.13, we see how the income-expenditure model provides the foundation for the aggregate demand curve, which will enable us to analyze both changes in output and prices. As the price level falls from P_0 to P_1, planned expenditures increase. Output increases from y_0 to y_1. The aggregate demand curve shows the combination of prices and equilibrium output.

> ### ᜇᜄ᜔ Caution!
>
> Anything affecting C, I, G, or NX other than the price level itself will cause shifts of the aggregate demand curve. Price level changes will cause movement along the aggregate demand curve.

Figure 11.14 shows what happens when a variable other than the price level changes. For example, the increase in government expenditure will raise the equilibrium output, from y_0 to y_1. Because the price level has not changed, we have a higher level of output at the same level of price. This means that the aggregate demand curve would shift to the right, from AD_0 to AD_1.

> ### ᜇᜄ᜔ Study Tip
>
> If you want to know how the equations are derived mathematically, refer to the appendix of this chapter for detailed analysis.

Activity

Suppose you have a consumption function of $C = 200 + 0.8(y)$ and investment $I = 300$.
a. Calculate the equilibrium output y^*.
b. Determine the savings function.
c. At y^*, what is the savings amount?

Answers

a. Use the following key equation; $y^* = \dfrac{C_a + I}{1 - \text{MPC}}$

$$y^* = \frac{200 + 300}{1 - 0.8} = 2500$$

b. $S = y - C$
$S = y - (200 + 0.8y)$
$S = y - 200 - 0.8y$
$S = \text{-}200 + 0.2y$

c. $S = \text{-}200 + 0.2(2500)$
$S = 300$

Another way to solve for this answer is to use the $S = I$ identity and know that investment was 300. In these simple models, S will always be equal to I regardless of the level of equilibrium income.

Key Terms

Autonomous consumption: The part of consumption that does not depend on income.

Consumption function: The relationship between consumption spending and the level of income.

Equilibrium output: The level of GDP at which planned expenditure equals the amount that is produced.

Marginal propensity to consume (MPC): The fraction of additional income that is spent.

Marginal propensity to import: The fraction of additional income that is spent on imports.

Planned expenditures: Another term for total demand for goods and services.

Saving function: The relationship between the level of saving and the level of income.

Practice Quiz

(Answers are provided at the end of the Practice Quiz.)

1. The income-expenditure model was originally developed by the economist _____ and later extended and refined by many economists.
   a. Adam Smith
   b. John Maynard Keynes
   c. Milton Friedman
   d. Joseph Schumpeter

2. Refer to the figure below. In the income-expenditure model, what happens at y^*?

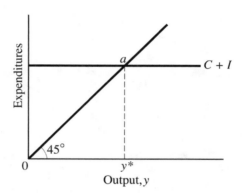

   a. Output equals the change in inventories.
   b. Output equals planned expenditures.
   c. The amount of output demanded equals the amount of output in inventories.
   d. All of the above

3. Refer to the figure below. When is production expected to fall?

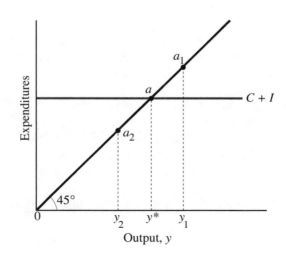

a.   At y^*
b.   At y_1
c.   At y_2
d.   There isn't sufficient information to answer the question.

4.   Consider the consumption function $C = C_a + bY$. Which part of this function is called the marginal propensity to consume?
a. C_a
b. b
c. bY
d.   The entire consumption function, $C_a + bY$, is equivalent to the marginal propensity to consume.

5.   Refer to the figure below. Which graph correctly depicts an increase in wealth?

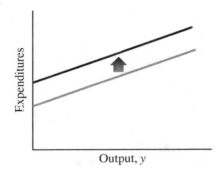 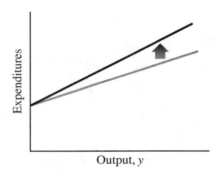

a.   The graph on the left
b.   The graph on the right
c.   Both graphs
d.   Neither graph

6.   This question tests your understanding of Application 1 in this chapter: Rising home equity, the wealth effect, and increased consumer spending. How do increases in the value of homes affect consumer spending?

From 2000 to 2003, the value of home equity—the difference between the value of homes and the amount of mortgage debt on the property—increased by approximately $2 trillion. Home equity is the single-largest component of net wealth for most families in the United States.

Which of the following assertions about home equity is correct?
a.   Compared to wealth holdings in the stock market, which are widely spread across the income spectrum, home-equity wealth tends to be concentrated in the highest income brackets.
b.   Increases in home equity have larger effects on consumption than increases in the stock market.
c.   It appears that households believe that increases in stock market values are more likely to be permanent than increases in home equity.
d.   At the higher end of the income distribution, households are more likely to spend—not save—after an increase in wealth.

7. Refer to the figure below. Which point best represents $(C_a + I)$?

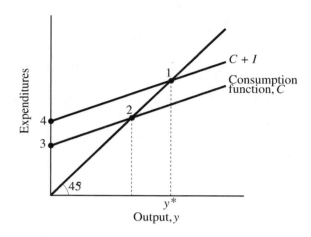

a. Point 1
b. Point 2
c. Point 3
d. Point 4

8. The relationship between the level of income and the level of savings is called:
    a. the savings function.
    b. the marginal propensity to save.
    c. the savings multiplier.
    d. the demand for savings.

9. Which of the following affects the level of GDP in the short run through its influence on the demand for goods and services?
    a. The level of government spending
    b. The level of taxation
    c. Both the level of spending and the level of taxation
    d. Neither the level of spending nor the level of taxation

10. This question tests your understanding of Application 3 in this chapter: John Maynard Keynes: A world intellectual. How influential a figure was John Maynard Keynes?

    Which of the following were among Keynes's ideas that challenged the conventional wisdom of his time?
    a. Keynes argued that economies could automatically recover from economic downturns.
    b. Keynes believed that economies could recover from downturns by themselves, without the help of the government or anyone else.
    c. Keynes believed that monetary policies could be very effective during deep recessions.
    d. Keynes argued that governments needed to adopt active policies, such as increased public works, in order to stimulate the economy.

11. Which of the following is the multiplier of government spending?
    a. $1/MPC$
    b. $1/(1 - MPC)$
    c. $- MPC/(1 - MPC)$
    d. change in y / change in G

12. The U.S. economy has been much more stable after World War II than before. The reason is that:
    a. government taxes and transfer payments, which increase fluctuations in real GDP, grew slowly after the war.
    b. government taxes and transfer payments, which help to reduce fluctuations in real GDP, grew sharply after the war.
    c. government taxes have roughly equaled transfer payments, thereby reducing fluctuations in GDP after the war.
    d. government taxes and transfer payments, which increase fluctuations in real GDP, have remained stable after the war.

13. Refer to the figure below. The shift in the function could have been caused by:

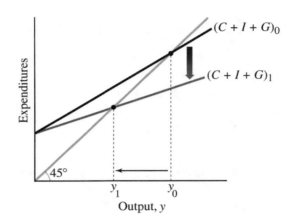

    a. an increase in government spending.
    b. a decrease in government spending.
    c. an increase in tax rates.
    d. a decrease in tax rates.

14. To modify our model to include the effects of exports and imports, we need to:
    a. add exports and imports to total spending.
    b. subtract exports and imports from total spending by U.S. residents.
    c. add exports and subtract imports from total spending.
    d. subtract exports and add imports to total spending.

15. Refer to the figure below. The slope of this function equals:

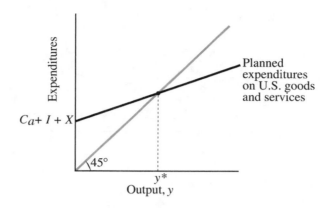

a. $1/(1 - b)$
b. $1/(1 - b + m)$
c. $b - m$
d. $1 - b + m$

16. Refer to the figure below. Which graph best depicts the impact of an increase in exports?

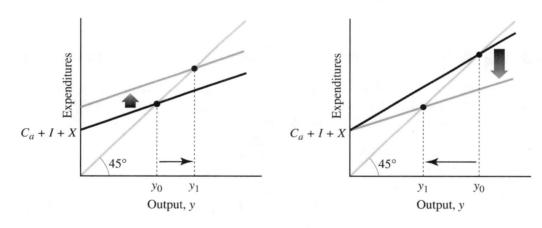

a. The graph on the left
b. The graph on the right
c. Both graphs
d. Neither graph

17. Refer to the figure below. Which move illustrates an increase in the price level in this graph?

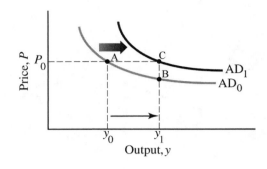

   a.   A move from A to B
   b.   A move from A to C
   c.   A move from B to A
   d.   A move from C to A

18. The consumption function is $1000 + .75Y$. Find the level of consumption resulting from national income if GDP is currently $8000 billion.
   a. $1000 billion
   b. $6000 billion
   c. $7000 billion
   d. $9000 billion

19. Describe in words the meaning of the multiplier of autonomous planned investment spending.

20. Refer to the table. Use the numbers on the table to determine the value of autonomous consumption, the marginal propensity to consume (MPC), the marginal propensity to save (MPS), construct the consumption function, and construct the saving function.

Aggregate Income Y	Consumption C	Saving S
0	50.0	-50
50	87.5	-37.5
100	125.0	-25
150	162.5	-12.5
200	200.0	0
250	237.5	12.5
300	275.0	25

21. When the expectations and spending decisions of buyers and sellers do not coincide with each other, production may be too low for full employment. Explain what this Keynesian argument means.

22. Explain the impact of the foreign sector on the income-expenditure model.

Answers to the Practice Quiz

1. b. The income-expenditure model was originally developed by the economist John Maynard Keynes in the 1930s and later extended and refined by many economists.

2. b. At equilibrium output y^*, output equals planned expenditures, $C + I$, and inventories are not changing.

3. b. If output were higher than equilibrium (y_1), it would exceed demand and production would fall.

4. b. The marginal propensity to consume is the amount by which consumption rises for each additional dollar of income. It is also the slope of the consumption function.

5. a. An increase in wealth causes autonomous consumption to increase from C_{0a} to C_{1a} and shifts up the entire consumption function.

6. b. A study by the International Monetary Fund found that increases in home equity have larger effects on consumption than increases in the stock market. In particular, it found that a dollar increase in home equity increased consumption by approximately 7 cents, whereas increases in stock market wealth led to an increase of only 4.5 cents.

7. d. Point 4 is the value of $(Ca + I)$, or autonomous expenditures.

8. a. The level of savings in the economy is not fixed, and how it changes depends on the real GDP. The savings function is the relationship between the level of income and the level of savings. The fraction that the consumer saves is determined by his or her marginal propensity to save (MPS).

9. c. Both the level of government spending and the level of taxation, through their influence on the demand for goods and services, affect the level of GDP in the short run.

10. d. Keynes provided the rationale for activist fiscal policy today.

11. b. This is the number by which a change in government spending will change equilibrium income.

12. b. Government taxes and transfer payments, which help to reduce fluctuations in real GDP, grew sharply after the war.

13. c. An increase in tax rates decreases the slope of the $C + I + G$ line. This lowers output and reduces the multiplier.

14. c. To modify our model to include the effects of exports and imports, we need to take two steps: Add exports, X, to other sources of spending as another source of demand for U.S. products. Subtract imports, M, from total spending by U.S. residents. Consumers will import more goods as income rises.

15. c. The fraction m is known as the marginal propensity to import. We subtract this fraction from b, the overall marginal propensity to consume, to obtain the MPC for spending on domestic goods, $b - m$.

16. a. An increase in exports (X) affects the intercept of the expenditure function.

17. a. In this graph, a decrease in the price level causes a move along the aggregate demand curve, from point A to point B.

18. b. The level of consumption resulting from the level of national income will be 75% of national income. $8000 times .75 is $6000.

19. The multiplier of autonomous planned investment shows the change in equilibrium income resulting from a change in autonomous planned investment spending. Each dollar of additional investment yields more than one dollar of additional income. In a closed economy without taxation, this multiplier equals $1/(1 - MPC)$. If the MPC equals 0.8, for example, then the multiplier equals 5. In other words, for each additional dollar of investment spending, equilibrium income will rise by five dollars.

20. The value of autonomous consumption equals 50, or the value of consumption when income equals zero. The marginal propensity to consume (MPC) is the slope of the consumption function. Using any two pairs of income and consumption values, the MPC = 0.75. Using any two pairs of income and saving values, the MPS = 0.25, or $1 - MPC$. The consumption function equals $C = 50 + 0.75Y$, and the saving function equals $S = -50 + 0.25Y$.

21. Since households and firms are two different groups of people, the spending and saving decisions of households are divorced from the investment and production decisions of business firms. For example, suppose that business expectations became pessimistic. Business firms would reduce planned investment, regardless of how low interest rates dipped. If firms were unwilling to use household saving to invest, then saving would be too high. If saving is too high, consumption is too low, and some of the goods produced by the firm remain unsold. This, in turn, would prompt business firms to reduce output and employment in future periods. This was the Keynesian argument, which, combined with the existence of sticky wages, helped to explain the persistence of unemployment. If a reduction in output and employment fails to put downward pressure on prices and wages, then the economy could remain stuck at a level of output below the potential output for an extended period.

22. Exports is an autonomous component of expenditure. Exports depend on the income of foreigners, not domestic income. Regardless of the level of domestic income, exports remain the same. Imports depend on the level of domestic income. As domestic income rises, imports rise by an amount called the marginal propensity to import (MPI). For example, for each additional dollar of income, domestic consumers may spend 20 cents on foreign goods, making the marginal propensity to import 0.2. The marginal propensity to import ends up in the denominator of the multiplier for the economy. As the marginal propensity to import increases, the multiplier becomes smaller, rotating the aggregate expenditure function clockwise, and decreasing the level of output and income. While exports contribute to higher GDP, imports cause the contrary. The effect of net exports on equilibrium output and income is positive as long as exports exceed imports.

12

Investment and Financial Markets

Chapter Summary

An *investment,* broadly defined, is an action that creates a cost today but provides benefits in the future. In this chapter, we broaden the definition of investment to include actions taken by anyone—individuals, firms, and governments—to improve one's well-being in the future. The chapter discusses theories of investment and how decisions are made to invest or not. Present value is the primary tool you will use to analyze investments. The concept of interest rates and how they relate to investment purchases will be discussed. The chapter closes with a discussion of financial intermediaries and how they facilitate investment. Here are the main points of the chapter:

- Investments incur costs today but provide benefits in the future.
- Investment spending is a volatile component of GDP because expectations about the future are uncertain and ever changing.
- We use the concept of present value to compare the costs and benefits of investments that occur at different points in time. The present value of a payment K, t years in the future, at in interest rate of i is:

$$\text{Present Value} = \frac{K}{(1+i)^t}$$

- The real interest rate equals the nominal interest rate minus inflation.
- Investment spending depends inversely on real interest rates.
- Financial intermediaries reduce the risk and costs of making investments by pooling the funds of savers and monitoring the projects of borrowers.

Applying the Concepts

After reading this chapter, you should be able to answer these four key questions:
1. How do fluctuations in energy prices affect investment decisions by firms?
2. How can understanding the concept of present value help a lucky lottery winner?
3. Why are there different types of interest rates in the economy?
4. How does the government affect the home mortgage market today?

> ### ♦※ Caution!
>
> Up until now, we have defined the term investment as purchases of real capital. In this chapter, we will expand the investment definition more broadly. For this chapter, investment is an action that costs an individual, firm, or government now but provides benefits in the future.

12.1 An Investment: A Plunge into the Unknown

Investment happens in a world of uncertainty. Some investors will react optimistically to this uncertainty. Other investors will react pessimistically. In general, when the future is uncertain, firms become cautious and may postpone making investment decisions such as purchasing additional computers, expanding an office or plant, or creating a new line of products.

Figure 12.1 plots total investment spending as a share of U.S. GDP from 1970 to 2005. You need to notice two things about Figure 12.1:

1. From 1970 to 2005, the share of investment as a component of GDP ranged from a low of about 11 percent in 1975 to a high of over 18 percent in 2000—a dramatic 7-percentage-point difference.
2. Swings in investment spending often occurred over short periods of time. For example, during recessions (noted by the shaded areas in the figure), investment spending fell sharply. During booms, investment spending rose sharply. In other words, investment spending is highly **procyclical**. It increases during booms and falls during recessions.

So what are the reasons or theories that explain the behavior of investors? Consider the following theories:

*   The **accelerator theory** of investment spending: Firms base their expectations of the future on what is happening currently in the economy. When real GDP growth is expected to be high, firms anticipate that investing in plants and equipment will pay off later, so they increase their total investment spending.
*   Animal spirits of investors: John Maynard Keynes said the sharp swings in optimism and pessimism related to investment spending were often irrational, reflecting, perhaps, our most basic, primal instincts.
*   The **multiplier-accelerator** model showed that a downturn in real GDP leads to an even sharper fall in investment, which further reduces GDP via the multiplier.

Psychology or expectations about future real GDP growth are not the only factors that affect investment. Because investments are really trade-offs—something in the present traded for something in the future—the "terms" affecting the trade-off are also important. These terms are interest rates, which we discuss next. Recall the following key principle:

Principle of Opportunity Cost
The opportunity cost of something is what you sacrifice to get it.

12.2 Evaluating the Future

☞ I was asked the following question, "If you could have anything you wanted, what would it be?" I said a sure knowledge of the future, even one day. I would know exactly how to behave if I knew what would happen in the future. There would be no guesswork. But we don't have that luxury. Thus, in evaluating the benefits of an investment, we need to have a process to evaluate future benefits over time. The main tool used to evaluate such future benefits is present value analysis.

Let's review an Application that answers one of the key questions we posed at the start of the chapter:

1. How do fluctuations in energy prices affect investment decisions by firms?

APPLICATION 1: ENERGY PRICE UNCERTAINTY REDUCES INVESTMENT SPENDING

Economists Hui Guo and Kevin Kliesen found evidence that volatility in oil prices adversely affects GDP growth. One important channel by which volatility of oil prices can hurt the economy is by creating uncertainty for firms making investment decisions. This may not only affect the decision to invest, but in what kind of investment to undertake.

☞ Consider the 2002 election between George W. Bush and Al Gore, Jr. The election was held up to count and recount the votes in Florida. The stock market moved very little during that period of time of the recount. Investors knew what to expect with either Bush or Gore as president. But investors held off investing until the election was decided.

☞ The accounting scandal of former energy giant Enron created uncertainty. When the federal government charged upper management of Enron with falsifying reports on the financial health of the company, investors would no longer trust the company's reports. The federal trials and convictions of upper management at companies like Enron were needed to restore people's confidence in investing.

Think about the example in the textbook about loaning money. Suppose that a good friend comes to you and says, "I need some cash, badly. If you give me $100 today, I can give you back $105 next year. Do we have a deal?" How would you decide whether to accept this deal? The tool you would use to analyze this situation is a present value calculation. **Present value** is the maximum amount a person is willing to pay today to receive a payment in the future. Recall the following key principle:

Principle of Opportunity Cost
The opportunity cost of something is what you sacrifice to get it.

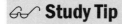 **Study Tip**

The opportunity cost of holding money is the interest rate. In other words, the interest rate is the price you pay for using someone else's money. You have to be compensated by a certain amount before you would be willing to lend your money.

So what determines the present value? It depends on how much you want to have at the end of the year. If you take the deal, you will have $5 more at the end of the year than now ($105 - $100). If we use the present value concept, the question to consider is, "Can I get more lending it somewhere else?" If not, then you have found the maximum amount someone would pay you for your money.

The next question to consider is, "Is $5 enough of a gain in a year or not?" The interest rate represents the opportunity cost of using funds. You have to be compensated enough to be willing to lend your money to another person. In the example, if you could have $105 by putting the money in the bank, then you would be indifferent on lending or putting it in the bank. Either way, you would end up with $105 at the end of the year.

The following key equation shows how to calculate present values:

☑ Key Equation

$$\text{Present Value} = \frac{K}{(1+i)^t},$$

where K is an amount paid t years in the future, i is the interest rate, and t is the time interval.

In the example that involved your friend, her payment (K) is $105, the interval of time (t) in which she's going to pay it is one year. Using the present value formula, the present value of $105 in one year is $100:

$$\text{Present Value} = \frac{\$105}{(1+.05)^1} = \$100$$

ᕲ Study Tip

Page 267 shows examples of present value calculations. Review and work through the examples on the page and see if you can come up with the same answers. If you need more practice, use the end-of-chapter exercises and MyEconLab.

What happens if the interest rate changes from 5 percent to 10 percent? Returning to our original example with your friend, if your friend still promises you $105 after one year, but the interest rate is double, how much would you be willing to loan her today? Using the formula, you would loan your friend only $95.45 today:

$$\text{Present Value} = \frac{\$105}{(1+.10)^1} = \$95.45$$

Let's summarize our discussion of present value:

1. The present value—the value today—of a given payment in the future is the maximum amount a person is willing to pay today for that payment.

2. As the interest rate increases, the opportunity cost of your funds also increases, so the present value of a given payment in the future falls. In other words, you need *less* money today to get to your future "money goal."

3. As the interest rate decreases, the opportunity cost of your funds also decreases, so the present value of a given payment in the future rises. In other words, you need *more* money today to get to your money goal.

Let's review an Application that answers one of the key questions we posed at the start of the chapter:

2. How can understanding the concept of present value help a lucky lottery winner?

APPLICATION 2: OPTIONS FOR A LOTTERY WINNER

The lucky winner of a lottery was given an option. She could either receive $1 million a year for 20 years, for a total of $20 million, or simply receive $10 million today. Why would anyone take the $10 million today? Depending on the interest rate, the $10 million today might be more valuable than the $20 million paid over 20 years. Indeed, if interest rates were 10 percent, you could take the $10 million today, put it in the bank, and earn $1 million in interest (10 percent of $10 million) forever—not just for 20 years! With an 8 percent interest rate, the present value of an annual payment of $1 million every year for 20 years is $9.8 million. So if interest rates exceed 8 percent, it is better to take the $10 million.

Another variable to consider before you lend your money is the effect of price changes. You will lose purchasing power if you don't take into account price changes. This reminds us of one of our key principles, the real-nominal principle.

 Real-Nominal Principle

What matters to people is the real value of money or income—its purchasing power—not the face value of money or income.

Nominal interest rates are interest rates quoted in the market. The **real interest rate** is the nominal interest rate minus the inflation rate.

 **Key Equation**

Real rate = Nominal rate − Inflation rate

While these types of calculations are straightforward, the actual outcomes can be tricky. We don't know with certainty what the inflation rate will be. Investors use what they expect the inflation rate to be to calculate the real interest rate. For example, I may expect inflation to be 4 percent next year. I have to have a real interest rate of 3 percent to fund my project. I have to find a financial investment what will pay at least 7 percent to afford to do my project. Remember we are dealing with expectations, so they may not be perfect. We just have to make our best educated guesses in these calculations.

Let's review an Application that answers one of the key questions we posed at the start of the chapter:

3. Why are there different types of interest rates in the economy?

APPLICATION 3: INTEREST RATES VARY BY RISK AND LENGTH OF LOAN

There are many different interest rates in the economy. Loans vary by their riskiness and by their maturity (the length of the loan). Riskier loans and loans for longer maturities typically have higher interest rates. Figure 12.2 depicts the movement in three interest rates from 2002 to 2005 for three types of investments: corporate AAA bonds (loans to corporations that are good credit risks), 10-year U.S. Treasury bonds (loans to the government for 10 years), and six-month Treasuries (loans to the U.S. government for six months).

⬤※ Caution!

In the first few pages of this chapter, we learned that interest rates are a price people pay us to borrow our money. In other words, the interest rate is also a rate of return. From the view of the borrower, the interest rate is a cost of borrowing. For example, when you use your credit card, the interest rate you pay on your card is a cost to you. But that same interest rate is a rate of return to your bank for use of their funds.

12.3 Understanding Investment Decisions

A simple rule of investing is to invest in a project if the cost you incur today is less than or equal to the present value of the future payments from the project. For example, if the present value of a project is $1,000, then you would not want to spend more than $1,000 for the project or you would be losing money. On the other hand, if you could get the project for less than $1,000, you would be making more money on the project.

Table 12.2 shows different projects with costs and returns. The interest rate will determine what projects you should undertake and what projects you should reject. Suppose you have an interest rate of 4 percent. You would undertake projects C, D, and E and reject projects A and B. In other words, if you must have a 4 percent rate of return on your projects, then you would reject any projects that don't pay at least 4 percent. What if the interest rate went to 6 percent? You would undertake projects D and E, but reject projects A, B, and C. Notice what happens: As the interest rate increases, less investment projects are purchased. As the interest rates decreases, the more investment projects are purchased. This relationship is shown in Figure 12.3.

Taxes and tax benefits may influence investor decisions in addition to real interest rates. Dale Jorgensen at Harvard University developed the neoclassical theory of investment. The **neoclassical theory of investment** states that both real interest rates and taxes are important determinants of investment.

Many investors make decisions based on the performance of the stock market. If the prices of stocks are rising, investment capital purchases also increase. To understand this relationship, we need to see how firms finance new projects. There are basically three ways to finance projects:
1. Use retained earnings
2. Borrow through banks of issuing bonds
3. Issue shares of stock

As the price of a company's stock increases, there are fewer shares needed to generate the funds to finance a project. This supports the Q-theory of investment, developed by James Tobin. The **Q-theory of**

investment links investment spending to stock prices. Figure 12.4 shows the Q-theory relationship. The Standard & Poor's index of 500 stock prices and investment spending move generally in the same direction. Notice the behavior of both graphs before and after the year 2000.

Stock prices were increasing, thus making it possible for firms to finance their investment in real capital. People were optimistic that this would continue for a long time. However, some people saw things differently. Alan Greenspan, former Federal Reserve chairman, described investors during this period as having "irrational exuberance." Investors started to sell off their stock, thinking that the prices would start to decline. As the stock market declined, investment projects were not undertaken. This is consistent with the Q-theory of investment.

☑ Key Equation

Stock price = present value of expected future dividends payments

---

12.4 How Financial Intermediaries Facilitate Investment

Households tend to be more risk-averse than firms. Households want to access money when they need it without risking losses of value. Meanwhile, firms tend to be more risk-taking. They see the rewards of taking risks and may use their funds to purchase capital giving them a higher rate of return. In summary, households tend to be risk-averse and firms tend to be risk-taking. What does this mean for investment?

Risk-averse households seek very high rates of return before they are willing to give up their funds. For example, households must be compensated for the loss of liquidity. Liquidity means an asset is easily convertible into money on short notice. Risk, loss of liquidity, and costs of negotiation are reasons for seeking high interest rates. Households must also be compensated for the risk they may not get their funds back. At the same time, firms seek low interest rates so they can finance their investment projects. If left to themselves, very few funds would be channeled from households to firms. Figure 12.5 shows how this stalemate occurs. So how do funds get from households to firms? Through organizations called financial intermediaries.

Financial intermediaries are organizations that receive funds from savers and channel those funds to investors. Figure 12.6 shows how these organizations channel funds from households to firms. How do financial intermediaries channel these funds from households to investors? Basically, they resolve the issues of risk-averse households. First, financial intermediaries provide liquidity for households. Deposits in banks, credit unions, and brokerages provide liquidity for households. Second, they reduce the risk faced by diversification. They don't put all their eggs in one basket. They diversify their types of lending so that they minimize the risk. If one sector goes poorly, they won't lose all their assets. Financial intermediaries lend to different independent projects to prevent loss of assets. Lastly, they reduce costs of negotiation and spread those costs among a larger number of investors.

Financial intermediaries are successful in channeling assets from households to investors. But sometimes they can fail. When bad times hit the economy, people panic and want their money. If one or two people ask for their funds, banks can provide their funds in full. But if a lot of depositors want their funds at once, the bank can't give back all their deposits. This causes further panic, which reduces the confidence in the system, making it more unstable. This is called a **bank run**. This happened during the Great Depression.

One way to reduce the fear of bank runs is to provide deposit insurance. This insurance guarantees that depositors will have their funds even during a time of panic. Deposit insurance guarantees the government will reimburse depositors for amounts up to $100,000 in each account at each bank should their banks fail.

☞ Deposit insurance takes many forms. The FDIC insures deposits for banks and savings and loan institutions. The NCUA insures deposits at credit unions.

Let's review an Application that answers one of the key questions we posed at the start of the chapter:

4.   How does the government affect the home mortgage market today?

APPLICATION 4: FANNIE MAE AND FREDDIE MAC FACILITATE HOMEOWNERSHIP: BUT DO THEY INCREASE RISK?

Fannie Mae and Freddie Mac are agencies that facilitate home mortgages. Here is how they operate: First, they purchase home mortgages from savings and loan associations (S&Ls) and banks that have made loans to homeowners. This frees up money and allows the S&Ls and banks to make additional home loans to other borrowers. Second, Fannie Mae and Freddie Mac package together the mortgages they purchase and then sell guaranteed, mortgage-backed securities to investors who want to hold a diversified portfolio of home mortgages. Finally, to obtain funds to buy the mortgages from banks and S&Ls, they borrow money from other investors in the market.

Does this activity decrease risk in the home mortgage market? Fannie and Freddie behave like other financial intermediaries and can suffer from the same type of issues they face.

Activity

Suppose that you have a real rate of interest of 4 percent. The expected inflation rate is 5 percent. You have to decide whether or not to invest in a project. The future payments of the project are $1000 in the first year and $2000 in the second year.
a.   Calculate the present value of the project.
b.   Would you take the project if the cost today was $2000?

Answers

a.   The first thing you need to calculate is the nominal interest rate. This is computed by the following equation:

Nominal interest rate = real interest rate + expected inflation rate
        9%   =   4%   +   5%

The present value of the project is computed with the following equation:

$$\text{Present Value} = \frac{\$1000}{(1+.09)^1} + \frac{\$2,000}{(1+.09)^2} = \$2,600.79$$

b.   Since the project's present value is $2,600.79 and the cost today for the project is $2,000, then you should take the project.

Key Terms

Accelerator theory: The theory of investment that says that current investment spending depends positively on the expected future growth of real GDP.

Bank run: Panicky investors simultaneously trying to withdraw their funds from a bank they believe may fail.

Corporate bond: A bond sold by a corporation to the public in order to borrow money.

Deposit insurance: Federal government insurance on deposits in banks and savings and loans.

Expected real interest rate: The nominal interest rate minus the expected inflation rate.

Financial intermediaries: Organizations that receive funds from savers and channel them to investors.

Liquid: Easily convertible into money on short notice.

Multiplier-accelerator model: A model in which a downturn in real GDP leads to a sharp fall in investment, which triggers further reductions in GDP through the multiplier.

Neoclassical theory of investment: A theory of investment that says both real interest rates and taxes are important determinants of investment.

Nominal interest rates: Interest rates quoted in the market.

Present value: The maximum amount a person is willing to pay today to receive a payment in the future.

Procyclical: Moving in the same direction as real GDP.

Q-theory of investment: The theory of investment that links investment spending to stock prices.

Real interest rate: The nominal interest rate minus the inflation rate.

Retained earnings: Corporate earnings that are not paid out as dividends to its owners.

Practice Quiz

(Answers are provided at the end of the Practice Quiz.)

1. An investment, broadly defined, is:
    a. the purchase of stocks, bonds, and other financial securities that yield interest.
    b. the purchase of a machine or a tool to be used in the production process.
    c. a risk-taking activity that may yield substantial returns.
    d. an action that creates a cost today but provides benefits in the future.

2. According to the *accelerator theory*, firms anticipate that their investments in plant and equipment will be profitable:
    a. when the government reduces the capital gains tax.
    b. when the depreciation of plant and equipment is low.
    c. when the growth of inventories is expected to increase in the future.
    d. when real GDP growth is expected to be high.

3. When investment spending is plotted as a share of U.S. GDP, between 1970 and 2005, we discover that:
    a. swings in investment have occurred over long periods of time.
    b. during recessions, investment spending has fallen sharply.
    c. investment spending is highly countercyclical, i.e., moves in the opposite direction to the economy.
    d. All of the above

4. This question tests your understanding of Application 1 in this chapter: Energy price uncertainty reduces investment spending. How do fluctuations in energy prices affect investment decisions by firms? The primary reason why volatility in oil prices affects GDP is that:
    a. volatile oil prices appear to affect consumption decisions more than investment decisions.
    b. firms stop all investments in energy-saving technologies when oil prices are volatile.
    c. if energy prices remain high, it may be profitable to invest in new energy-saving technology, but if prices fall, these investments would be unwise.
    d. if future oil prices are uncertain, both exports and imports will tend to fall.

5. The relationship between the present value of a given payment in the future and the interest rate is an example of a key principle of economics. Which one?
    a. The principle of opportunity cost
    b. The principle of diminishing returns
    c. The principle of voluntary exchange
    d. The real-nominal principle
    e. The marginal principle

6. What is the impact of an increase in the interest rate on present value?
    a. Present value will rise.
    b. Present value will fall.
    c. Present value will remain the same.
    d. Present value may fall or rise, depending on the value of t.

7. The interest rate quoted in the market is called the _____ interest rate, and the _____ interest rate is what you actually earn after inflation has taken its toll.
    a. nominal; real
    b. real; nominal
    c. discounted; prime
    d. prime; discounted

8. When deciding whether to make an investment:
    a. only the real interest rate should be compared with the real expected benefits.
    b. the real rate of interest should be compared with the nominal expected benefits.
    c. only the nominal interest rate should be compared with the nominal expected benefits.
    d. it is reasonable to use either nominal or real interest rates and expected benefits as long as one is consistent.

9. This question tests your understanding of Application 3 in this chapter: Interest rates vary by risk and length of loan. Which of the following assertions about the relationship between interest rates, risk, and maturity is correct?
   a. Riskier loans and loans for longer maturities typically have lower interest rates.
   b. Interest rates for corporate bonds are lower than the rates for 10-year Treasury bonds.
   c. Corporations are less likely to pay back their loans than the U.S. government.
   d. The U.S. government typically pays higher rates when it borrows for shorter periods of time (six months) than for longer periods of time (10 years).

10. Refer to the table below. Using the information on the table, the estimate of the expected real rate of interest for the United States equals:

EXPECTED REAL RATES OF INTEREST FOR FIVE COUNTRIES		
Country	3-Month Interest Rate	Inflation Rate Forecast for 2006
Australia	5.7%	2.8%
Canada	4.0%	2.1%
Denmark	2.8%	1.9%
Switzerland	1.3%	1.2%
United States	5.0%	3.0%

Source: The Economist, April 22, 2006.

   a. 8.0%.
   b. the same as the 3-month interest rate, or 3%.
   c. 2.0%.
   d. an average of the 3-month interest rates listed for the other countries, or close to 3.8%.

11. Fill in the blanks in this sentence: The investment rule is: Invest in a project if the cost you incur today is _____ than or equal to the _____ of the _____ payments from the project.
   a. less; present value; future
   b. less; future value; present
   c. more; present value; present
   d. more; future value; future

12. What is the relationship between investment and real interest rates, all other things being equal?
   a. A positive relationship
   b. A negative relationship
   c. No such relationship exists.
   d. A linear relationship

13. Economists have found that, all other things being equal, when the level of the stock market is high:
   a. investment spending also tends to be high.
   b. investment spending also tends to be low.
   c. investment spending tends to disappear.
   d. investment spending increases then decreases.

14. The present value of expected future dividend payments is equal to:
    a.   the interest rate the firm offers on its corporate bonds.
    b.   the return on its investment projects.
    c.   the price of stock.
    d.   the market rate of interest.

15. Which of the following statements is correct?
    a.   Households save for the same reasons that firms invest.
    b.   Households try to minimize risk and have their savings readily accessible, or liquid.
    c.   Firms are usually averse to risk and usually need funds for a short period of time.
    d.   All of the above

16. Diversification in investment is:
    a.   desirable because it reduces risk to savers and allow investors to obtain funds on better terms.
    b.   desirable because it prevents investors from earning unreasonable profits.
    c.   undesirable because it reduces risk to investors but adds risk to savers.
    d.   undesirable because it is preferable to invest in a single reliable financial instrument than in too
         many instruments.

17. A bank run is:
    a.   a rush by depositors to invest in a particular financial instrument offered by a financial
         intermediary.
    b.   a rush by borrowers to get loans before interest rates rise.
    c.   an attempt by depositors to try to withdraw their money simultaneously.
    d.   All of the above

18. How does a firm determine which investment projects to undertake and which ones to leave for later?

19. The nominal interest rate equals the real interest rate plus the expected rate of inflation. What
    implications does this equality have for lenders and borrowers? Give an example.

20. Briefly explain the role of financial intermediaries.

Answers to the Practice Quiz

1.   d. An investment, broadly defined, is an action that creates a cost today but provides benefits in the
     future.

2.   d. The accelerator theory focuses on real GDP growth. When real GDP growth is expected to be high,
     firms anticipate that their investments in plant and equipment will be profitable and therefore increase
     their total investment spending.

3.   b. Swings in investment have occurred over short periods of time. During recessions, investment
     spending fell sharply. During booms, investment spending rose sharply. This means that investment
     spending is highly procyclical.

4.   c. Volatility of oil prices can hurt the economy by creating uncertainty for firms making investment
     decisions. With this uncertainty, firms may delay such investments because they can't tell whether it
     will be profitable or not. This reduced investment lowers GDP.

5. a. This principle associates the use of money for one use with what the same amount could have earned in alternative uses. As the interest rate increases, the opportunity cost of your funds also increases, so the present value of a given payment in the future falls.

6. b. The present value of a given payment in the future decreases as the interest rate increases. Similarly, when interest rates fall, the present value of a given payment in the future increases.

7. a. The interest rate quoted in the market, which is called the nominal interest rate, and the real interest rate, which is what you actually earn after inflation has taken its toll.

8. d. Imagine comparing a 10% nominal interest rate to a nominal expected 11% rate of return; we are 1% ahead. If the inflation rate is 3%, then the real interest rate is 7% and the real expected rate of return is 8%; we are still 1% ahead.

9. c. Rates for corporate bonds are higher than the rates for 10-year Treasury bonds. That's because corporations are less likely to pay back their loans than the U.S. government.

10. c. Estimates of the expected real rate of interest in each country are found by subtracting the inflation rate forecast from the 3-month interest rate.

11. a. Investment rule: Invest in a project if the cost you incur today is less than or equal to the present value of the future payments from the project.

12. b. There is a negative relationship between real interest rates and investment. High real interest rates will deter investment spending.

13. a. Economists have found that, all other things being equal, when the level of the stock market is high, investment spending also tends to be high.

14. c. The present value of expected future dividend payments is equal to the price of a firm's stock.

15. b. It is difficult to bring savers and investors together. Households save for different reasons than firms invest. Households try to minimize risk and have their savings readily accessible, or liquid, while firms are risk takers and need funds that will be tied up for a long time.

16. a. Financial intermediaries help bring savers and investors together. By using their expertise and the powers of diversification, financial intermediaries reduce risk to savers and allow investors to obtain funds on better terms.

17. c. When depositors panic, they try to withdraw their money simultaneously. This is called a bank run.

18. A business firm has a menu of desirable investment projects, each associated with an expected rate of return. To make an investment decision, the firm compares the expected rate of return on the investment to the real rate of interest, or the opportunity cost of purchasing capital. As long as the expected rate of return on an investment is greater than the real interest rate, the investment project should be undertaken. This is why changes in interest rates affect investment directly. A decrease in the interest rate, for example, makes additional investment projects more attractive.

19. If expectations of the rate of inflation are incorrect, borrowers and lenders may be better off or worse off as a result. For example, if you take out a loan at a stated (or nominal) interest rate of 10%, and the bank expected to earn a real interest rate of 5%, the bank must be anticipating an inflation rate of 5%. But what if the inflation rate turns out to be 8% instead of 5%? The bank will earn only 2% real return on the loan. If the bank wanted to earn 5% real return, it should have charged 13%. Therefore, lenders are worse off as a result of inflation rates that are greater than anticipated, and borrowers are better off.

20. Financial intermediaries help bring savers and investors together. By using their expertise and the powers of diversification, financial intermediaries reduce risk to savers and allow investors to obtain funds on better terms. Households save for different reasons than firms invest. Households try to minimize risk and have their savings readily accessible, or liquid. Firms are risk takers and need funds that will be tied up for a long time. If entrepreneurs had to obtain funds directly from households, households would demand extraordinarily high interest rates to compensate for the costs of negotiation, risk, and lack of liquidity. By pooling the funds of savers and making loans to individual businesses, financial intermediaries reduce the costs of negotiation. They also acquire expertise in both evaluating and monitoring investments. Finally, some financial intermediaries also provide the liquidity households demand.

13

Money and the Banking System

Chapter Summary

In this chapter, we'll look carefully at how money is defined and the role that it plays in the economy. The overall quantity of money in circulation affects the performance of an economy. We will also see how money is created in the banking system. Lastly, we will look at the bankers' bank—the Federal Reserve (the "Fed")—and how it is organized. Here are the main points of the chapter:

- Money consists of anything that is regularly used to make exchanges. In modern economies, money consists primarily of currency and deposits in checking accounts.
- Banks are financial intermediaries that earn profits by accepting deposits and making loans. Deposits, which are liabilities of banks, are included in the money supply.
- Banks are required by law to hold a fraction of their deposits as reserves, either in cash or in deposits with the Federal Reserve. Total reserves consist of required reserves plus excess reserves.
- If there is an increase in the supply of reserves in the banking system, the supply of money will expand by a multiple of the initial increase in reserves. This multiple is known as the money multiplier.
- Decisions about the supply of money are made at the Federal Open Market Committee (FOMC), which includes the seven members on the Board of Governors and the president of the New York Federal Reserve Bank, as well as four of the 11 other regional bank presidents, who serve on a rotating basis.
- In a financial crisis like those that occurred in 1987 and 2001, the Fed can help stabilize the economy. Former Fed chairmen Paul Volcker and Alan Greenspan have been powerful and important figures in the national economy.

Applying the Concepts

After reading this chapter, you should be able to answer these four key questions:
1. What fraction of the stock of U.S. currency is held overseas?
2. Who were the two men who served as chairman of the Federal Reserve from 1979 to 2006, and what were their principal accomplishments?
3. How did the Fed successfully respond to the major stock market crash in 1987?
4. How did the Fed manage to keep the financial system in operation immediately following the attacks on September 11, 2001?

13.1 What Is Money?

Economists define **money** as any items that are regularly used in economic transactions or exchanges and accepted by buyers and sellers. Let's consider some examples of money used in that way. Clearly, currency is money because people can use it to purchase coffee, newspapers, candy, movie tickets, and other goods. Checks also function as money because people use them to pay suppliers, such as utility suppliers. In some ancient cultures, people used precious stones in exchange for goods such as food and clothing. In more recent times, gold bars have served as money. During World War II, prisoners of war did not have currency, but they did have rations of cigarettes, so they used them like money, trading them for what they wanted. Regardless of what the item is that is used for money, money has three basic properties, which we discuss next.

Money is given by buyers to sellers in economic exchanges; therefore, it serves as a **medium of exchange**. Without a medium of exchange, only barter would exist. The number of transactions would slow down dramatically. **Barter**, the exchange of one good or service for another, presents obvious problems. Barter requires a **double coincidence of wants**. A buyer and seller must have exactly what the other wants for an exchange to occur. Exchanges would be inhibited if double coincidence of wants were always required for trade. By serving as a medium of exchange, money solves this bartering problem. You can sell something for money, then hold on to the money until you find what you want to buy with the money. With money, there is no need for a double coincidence of wants. This is why money exists in all societies: It makes economic transactions much easier. Recall the voluntary exchange principle.

 Voluntary Exchange Principle
A voluntary exchange between two people makes both people better off.

In summary, money allows individuals to make exchanges easily. Without money, exchanges would be inhibited. Most transactions that make both people better off would not be possible.

Another purpose of money is to serve as a unit of account. A **unit of account** is a standard unit in which prices can be stated and the value of goods and services can be compared. In our economy, money is used as the unit of account because prices are all quoted in terms of money. It is useful to have the medium of exchange also be the unit of account so that prices for all goods and services are quoted in terms of the medium of exchange that is used in transactions—in our case, money.

The last purpose of money is its role as a liquid store of value. A **store of value** is the property of money that it preserves value until it is used in an exchange. Many assets, such as stocks, bonds, or real estate, serve as a store of value. But money is a liquid store of value. It is easily exchanged in transactions, but holds value over time. Money is actually a somewhat imperfect store of value because of inflation. As prices increase, while the nominal value of the money doesn't change, the real value of money or purchasing power falls.

Money has evolved over time. In earlier centuries, money could take many forms: gold bars, silver, beads, knives, and tobacco. These are examples of **commodity money** systems in which an actual commodity (gold or silver) serves as money. At some point, governments began issuing paper money. However, the paper money was backed by an underlying commodity, for example, so many ounces of gold. Under a traditional **gold standard**, an individual could present paper money to the government and receive its stated value in gold. In other words, paper money could be exchanged for gold. Prior to 1933 in the United States, individuals could exchange their dollars for gold. **Fiat money** has no intrinsic value—it is simply created by a government decree. A government will issue paper money and make this money the official legal tender of the society. In the United States today, if you take a $100 bill to the government, you will not receive any gold or silver—just another $100 bill in return.

How is the amount of money in a country measured? In the United States, the Federal Reserve or the Fed measures the amount of money in the economy. These measures are called monetary aggregates. The most basic measure of money in the United States is called **M1**. It is the sum of currency in the hands of the public, demand deposits, other checkable deposits, and travelers' checks. Figure 13.1 shows their relative percentages. Note that currency is the largest form of M1 balances. M1 does not include all the assets that are used to make economic exchanges. M2 includes all M1 plus deposits in savings accounts, deposits in money market mutual funds, and time deposits of less than $100,000. Figure 13.2 shows percentages of each category. Notice that savings deposits make up the largest part of M2 balances, even greater than M1.

◆✳ Caution!

Credit cards are not money. Although used as a medium of exchange, credit cards are debt instruments. Debit cards serve as electronic checks but do not create an independent source of money. People who use debit cards are accessing funds in already existing checking account balances.

Let's review an Application that answers one of the key questions we posed at the start of the chapter:

1. What fraction of the stock of U.S. currency is held abroad?

APPLICATION 1: MORE THAN HALF OF U.S. CURRENCY IS HELD OVERSEAS

According to a report from the U.S. Treasury, between 55 and 60 percent of U.S. currency outstanding is held abroad. About 25 percent of the currency held abroad is located in Latin America, 20 percent in Africa and the Middle East, and about 15 percent in Asia. The remaining 40 percent is held in Europe and countries of the former Soviet Union and their trading partners.

☞ In many of the countries cited in the Application, their money does not have the three properties: a medium of exchange, a unit of account, and a liquid store of value. Quite often this is caused by the government printing off too much money. As we discussed in Chapter 6, the printing of money can cause hyperinflation where increased money creates inflation to the point that the money is worthless. Another reason that money loses its value is due to lack of faith in the government to back it. Remember, money has a social dynamic. If members of society don't accept the prescribed money as a medium of exchange, then that money form will not be accepted in exchange for goods and services.

13.2 How Banks Create Money

In this section, we will learn the role that banks play in the creation of money in a modern economy. To understand this role, we first have to look more carefully at the behavior of banks and in particular their balance sheet.

The purpose of looking at a balance sheet is to learn how the bank raises the money and where it goes after it has been raised. Balance sheets have two sides: one for assets and one for liabilities. **Liabilities** are the source of funds for the bank. If you open a checking account and deposit your funds in it, the bank is liable for returning the funds to you when you want them. The bank must also pay you interest on the account, if you keep enough money in it. Your deposits are therefore the bank's liabilities. **Assets**, in contrast, generate income for the bank. Loans made by the bank are examples of its assets, because borrowers must pay interest on the loans the bank collects. When a bank is initially opened, its owners must place their own funds into the bank so it has some startup funds. We call these funds **owners' equity**. If the bank subsequently makes a profit, owners' equity increases; if it loses money, owners' equity decreases.

In Figure 13.3, we show the assets and liabilities of a hypothetical bank. On the liability side, the bank has $2,000 of deposits and owners' equity is $200. Owners' equity is entered on the liability side of the balance sheet because it is a source of the bank's funds. The total source of funds is therefore $2,200—the deposits in the bank plus owners' equity.

On the asset side, the bank holds $200 in **reserves**. These are assets that are not lent out. Reserves can be either cash kept in a bank's vaults or deposits in the nation's central bank, the Federal Reserve. Banks do not earn any interest on these reserves. Hence, they try to keep as little excess reserves on hand as possible and loan out as much as they can. Banks are required by law to hold a specific fraction of their deposits as reserves, called **required reserves**. If a bank chooses to hold additional reserves beyond what is required, these are called **excess reserves**. A bank's reserves are the sum of its required and excess reserves.

💣 Caution!

To avoid confusion, keep in mind that reserves and required reserves are not the same thing. Reserves should be thought of as total reserves to the bank. The bank then has required reserves it must hold by law. The bank can use the remaining reserves or excess reserves for loans or to hold in cash for customers. However, banks can also borrow reserves from other banks. These *borrowed reserves* are counted as part of a bank's total reserves.

Now that we understand the concept of reserves, excess reserves, and required reserves, let's look how money is created through the banking sector. Figure 13.4 shows how banks create money. Let's walk through how this process works. A person deposits $1,000 in cash. The initial deposit is received by the bank. Some of the deposit is held as required reserves and the remainder is excess reserves. The First Bank of Hollywood lends the excess reserves in hopes of gaining interest on the loan. Assuming the reserve ratio is 10 percent, then $100 is held in required reserves and the remaining $900 is loaned out. The Second Bank of Burbank then receives a deposit of the loaned $900. The Second Bank holds in required reserves 10 percent or $90. The remaining $810 is loaned out. This process repeats itself until it becomes unprofitable.

☞ Some students say, "Get real! Banks don't lend amounts less than $20." My response to that question is, "How many of you have a credit card?" A great deal of bank lending takes the form of small lending through credit cards. As of November 1, 2006, credit card debt was $301.7 billion. This represented 42.3 percent of all consumer loans according to www.federalreserve.gov/releases/h8/Current/.

The first three banks in the figure loaned out all of their excess reserves and the borrowers deposited the full sum of their loans. In the real world, though, people hold part of their loans as cash and banks don't necessarily loan out every last dime of their excess reserves. Consequently, a smaller amount of money will be created than what's shown in Figure 13.4.

The original $1,000 cash deposit has created checking account balances throughout Los Angeles. What's the total amount? Adding up the new accounts in all the banks (even the ones we have not named), we have:

$1,000 + $900 + $810 + $729 + 656.10 + … = $10,000

How did we come up with this sum? It's from the following simple formula, which we derive in the appendix to this chapter:

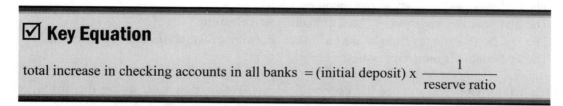

☑ **Key Equation**

$$\text{total increase in checking accounts in all banks} = (\text{initial deposit}) \times \frac{1}{\text{reserve ratio}}$$

Notice that we referred to "change," meaning an increase or decrease. Here's why: In our example, the public, represented by the person who initially made the $1,000 deposit at the First Bank of Hollywood, holds $1,000 less in currency. However, deposits increased by $10,000. Therefore, the money supply, M1, increased by $9,000 ($10,000 − $1,000).

The term 1/reserve ratio in the formula is called the money multiplier. It tells us what the total increase in checking account deposits would be for any initial cash deposit. In the banking system, an initial cash deposit triggers additional rounds of deposits and lending by banks. This leads to a multiple expansion of deposits.

☞ As of 2006 in the United States, banks were required to hold 3 percent in reserves against checkable deposits between $7.8 million and $48.3 million and 10 percent on all checkable deposits exceeding $48.3 million.

This model is simplified in that it is assumed that all deposits go into the banks. In reality, people hold part of their loans as cash. The cash that people hold is not available for the banking system to lend out. The more money people hold in cash, the lower the amount they have on deposit that can be loaned out again.

The money-creation process also works in reverse. Suppose you go to your bank and ask for $1,000 in cash from your checking account. The bank must pay you the $1,000. The bank's liabilities fall by $1,000, but its assets must also fall by $1,000. Withdrawing your $1,000 means two things at the bank: First, if the reserve ratio is 0.1, the bank will reduce its reserves by $100. Second, your $1,000 withdrawal minus the $100 reduction in reserves means that the bank has $900 less to lend out. The bank will therefore reduce its loans by $900. With fewer loans, there will be fewer deposits in other banks. The money multiplier working in reverse decreases the money supply.

However, there is one crucial difference between this example, in which one individual writes a check to another, and our earlier example, in which an individual makes a cash deposit: When Paul receives the check from Freda, the money supply will not be changed in the long run. Here's why: When Freda's check is deposited in Paul's bank, the money supply will begin to expand, but when Freda's bank loses its deposit, the money supply will start to contract. The expansions and contractions offset each other when private citizens and firms write checks to one another.

13.3 A Banker's Bank: The Federal Reserve

Congress created the Federal Reserve System in 1913 after a series of financial panics in the United States. Financial panics can occur when there is bad news about the economy or the stability of financial institutions.

The Federal Reserve has several key functions:
- The Fed is the lender of last resort.
- The Fed supplies currency to the economy.
- The Fed provides a system of check collection and clearing.
- The Fed holds reserves from banks and other depository institutions and regulates banks.
- The Fed conducts monetary policy.

When members of Congress created the Federal Reserve System, they were aware the institution would be very powerful. Consequently, they deliberately created a structure that attempted to disperse the power, moving it away from major U.S. financial centers (such as New York) to other parts of the country. Figure 13.5 shows where each of the 12 Federal Reserve Banks is located. At the time the Fed was created, economic and financial power in this country was concentrated in the East and the Midwest.

There are two other subgroups of the Fed in addition to the Federal Reserve Banks. The **Board of Governors of the Federal Reserve** is the second subgroup. It is the true seat of power in the Federal Reserve System. Headquartered in Washington, D.C., the seven members of the board are appointed for 14-year terms by the president. The chairperson of the Board of Governors serves a four-year term.

✐ Study Tip
Go to www.federalreserve.gov/bios to learn more details about who runs the Federal Reserve.

The third subgroup of the Fed is the **Federal Open Market Committee (FOMC)**, which makes decisions about monetary policy. The FOMC is a 12-person board consisting of the seven members of the Board of Governors, the president of the New York Federal Reserve Bank, who is always a voting member because open market operations are performed at the New York Fed, plus the presidents of four other regional Federal Reserve Banks. The other eight regional bank presidents attend and participate in each FOMC meeting, but are not voting members of the FOMC.

Let's review an Application that answers one of the key questions we posed at the start of the chapter:

2. Who were the two men who served as chairman of the Federal Reserve from 1979 to 2006, and what were their principal accomplishments?

APPLICATION 2: TWO RECENT MAJOR LEADERS OF THE FEDERAL RESERVE BOARD

The two chairmen before the current chairman, Benjamin Bernanke, were Paul Volcker, who served from 1979 to 1987, and Alan Greenspan, who served from 1987 to 2006. In their day, each was the country's major figure in monetary policy. Volcker, who served as the president of the New York Federal Reserve Bank, took a pay cut to come to Washington to fight inflation. Volcker was relentless in his fight against inflation. Although he tamed inflation, the economy was forced through a period of high interest rates and a severe recession. In 1987, President

Ronald Reagan appointed Alan Greenspan. Greenspan was first tested by the 1987 stock market crash (see Application 3) and steered the economy away from a recession. Over the following years, he successfully guided monetary policy. Except for the recessions in the early 1990s and in 2001, the economy grew smoothly and inflation remained under control.

Countries differ in the degree to which their central banks are independent of political authorities. The central banks in both the United States and the United Kingdom operate with considerable independence of elected officials. In other countries, the central bank is part of the treasury department of the government and potentially subject to more direct political control. Central banks that are not independent will always be under pressure to help finance their country's government deficits by creating money. Independence, on the other hand, typically means less inflation.

13.4 What the Federal Reserve Does During a Financial Crisis

As the lender of last resort, the Fed can quell disturbances in the financial markets.

Let's review two Applications that answer key questions we posed at the start of the chapter:

3. How did the Fed successfully respond to the major stock market crash in 1987?

APPLICATION 3: COPING WITH A STOCK MARKET CRASH: BLACK MONDAY, 1987

On October 19, 1987, known as "Black Monday," the Dow Jones index of the stock market fell a dramatic 22.6 percent in one day. Similar declines were felt in other indexes and stock markets around the world. These declines shocked both businesses and investors. A sharp drop in available credit could, conceivably, plunge the economy into a deep recession. Alan Greenspan had just become chairman of the Federal Reserve that year. He quickly issued a public statement in which he said that the Federal Reserve stood ready to provide liquidity to the economy and the financial system. Banks were told that the Fed would let them borrow liberally. In fact, the Fed provided liquidity to such an extent that interest rates even fell. As a result of Greenspan's action, "Black Monday" did not cause a recession in the United States

☞ There is a large contrast between the 1987 stock market fall and the 1929 stock crash. Although the Federal Reserve was in place in 1929, there was no support in terms of reserves lent to the member banks. As people were losing their assets in the stock markets, the banks were in the same position. Banks had used excess reserves to buy stocks. People ran on the banks to get out what they could before they lost all their financial assets. For this reason, there was a system-wide series of bank failures. The deposits wiped out in these failures accounted for a large part of the contraction of the money supply during the early years of the Great Depression.

4. How did the Fed manage to keep the financial system in operation immediately following the attacks on September 11, 2001?

APPLICATION 4: THE FINANCIAL SYSTEM UNDER STRESS: SEPTEMBER 11, 2001

The Fed was tested again on September 11, 2001, following the terrorist attacks against the United States. Many financial firms keep little cash on hand and expect to borrow on a daily basis to pay their ongoing bills and obligations. When the financial markets closed after September 11, many of these firms were in trouble. To prevent a default avalanche, the Federal Reserve immediately took a number of steps to provide additional funds to the financial system. The first tool that the Federal Reserve used was to allow banks to borrow more.

The difference between the credits and the debits extended by the Federal Reserve is called the "Federal Reserve float." Immediately following September 11, the Federal Reserve allowed this float to increase sharply from $2.9 billion to $22.9 billion. These actions effectively put an additional $20 billion into the banking system. The Federal Reserve also purchased government securities in the marketplace and, as a result, put $30 billion into the hands of private citizens and their banks. It also arranged to provide dollars to foreign central banks such as the Bank of England to meet their own needs and the needs of their own banks to facilitate any dollar transactions they had during this crisis.

Activity

How much will total checking accounts grow if you have an initial deposit of $2,000 in cash and a reserve ratio of 5 percent?

Answer

Using the equation below:

$$\text{total increase in checking accounts in all banks} = (\text{initial deposit}) \times \frac{1}{\text{reserve ratio}}$$

$$\text{total increase in checking accounts in all banks} = \$2,000 \times \frac{1}{.05} = \$40,000$$

Key Terms

Assets: The uses of the funds of a bank, including loans and reserves.

Balance sheet: An account statement for a bank that shows the sources of its funds (liabilities) as well as the uses of its funds (assets).

Barter: The exchange of one good or service for another.

Board of Governors of the Federal Reserve: The seven-person governing body of the Federal Reserve System in Washington, D.C.

Central bank: A banker's bank: an official bank that controls the supply of money in a country.

Commodity money: A monetary system in which the actual money is a commodity, such as gold or silver.

Double coincidence of wants: The problem in a system of barter that one person may not have what the other desires.

Excess reserves: Any additional reserves that a bank holds above required reserves.

Federal Open Market Committee (FOMC): The group that decides on monetary policy: It consists of the seven members of the Board of Governors plus five of 12 regional bank presidents on a rotating basis.

Federal Reserve Bank: One of 12 regional banks that are an official part of the Federal Reserve System.

Fiat money: A monetary system in which money has no intrinsic value, but is backed by the government.

Gold standard: A monetary system in which gold backs up paper money.

Lender of last resort: A central bank is the lender of last resort; the last place, all others having failed, from which banks in emergency situations can obtain loans.

Liabilities: The sources of funds for a bank, including deposits and owners' equity.

M1: The sum of currency in the hands of the public, demand deposits, other checkable deposits, and travelers' checks.

M2: M1 plus other assets, including deposits in savings and loans accounts and money market mutual funds.

Medium of exchange: Any item that buyers give to sellers when they purchase goods and services.

Monetary policy: The range of actions taken by the Federal Reserve to influence the level of GDP or inflation.

Money: Any items that are regularly used in economic transactions or exchanges and accepted by buyers and sellers.

Money multiplier: The ratio of the increase in total checking account deposits to an initial cash deposit.

Owners' equity: The funds provided to a bank by its owners.

Required reserves: The specific fraction of their deposits that banks are required by law to hold as reserves.

Reserve ratio: The ratio of reserves to deposits.

Reserves: The portion of banks' deposits set aside in either vault cash or as deposits at the Federal Reserve.

Store of value: The property of money that it preserves value until it is used in an exchange.

Unit of account: A standard unit in which prices can be stated and the value of goods and services can be compared.

Practice Quiz

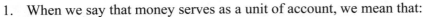

(Answers are provided at the end of the Practice Quiz.)

C 1. When we say that money serves as a unit of account, we mean that:
    a. money eliminates the double coincidence of wants that exists under barter.
    b. exchange is made through the use of money.
    c. prices are quoted in terms of money.
    d. All of the above

2. As of March, 2006, which of the components of the money supply, as measured by M1, was the largest?
    a. Currency held by the public
    b. Demand deposits
    c. Other checkable deposits
    d. Travelers' checks

3. Credit cards are:
    a. part of M1.
    b. part of M2.
    c. both in M1 and in M2.
    d. not part of the money supply.

4. This question tests your understanding of Application 1 in this chapter: according to a report from the U.S. Treasury, between 55 and 60 percent of U.S. currency outstanding is held abroad. In which of the following regions are most of those dollars held?
    a. In Latin America
    b. In Africa and the Middle East
    c. In Asia
    d. In Europe and countries of the former Soviet Union

5. On the balance sheet of a bank:
    a. reserves are on the liability side.
    b. loans are the most important asset.
    c. deposits are the most important asset.
    d. assets plus owners' equity equal liabilities.

6. The name given to the fraction of deposits that banks are legally required to hold in their vaults or as deposits at the Fed is:
    a. reserves.
    b. required reserves.
    c. excess reserves.
    d. total reserves.

7. Suppose that the reserve ratio is 20% and that banks loan out all their excess reserves. If a person deposits $100 cash in a bank, checking account balances will increase by a maximum of:
    a. $20.
    b. $100.
    c. $200.
    d. $500.

8. Assume that banks are always fully loaned and people hold no cash. Given a required reserve ratio of 20%, an infusion of $100 billion in reserves will result in a maximum of:
    a. $100 billion in deposits.
    b. $20 billion in deposits.
    c. $120 billion in deposits.
    d. $500 billion in deposits.

9. Assuming there are no leakages out of the banking system, a money multiplier equal to 10 means that:
    a.   the reserve ratio equals 10.
    b.   an additional $10 of reserves create one dollar of deposits.
    c.   each additional dollar of deposits creates $10 of reserves.
    d.   each additional dollar of reserves creates $10 of deposits.

10. In reality, people hold part of their loans as cash. This makes the multiplier:
    a.   smaller.
    b.   larger.
    c.   the same as if people did not hold cash.
    d.   zero.

11. Which of the following facts is true about the creation of the Federal Reserve System (the Fed)?
    a.   The Fed was created in 1913.
    b.   Creation of the Fed followed a series of financial panics in the United States.
    c.   Congress created the Federal Reserve to be a central bank, serving as a banker's bank.
    d.   All of the above.

12. When we say that one of the functions of the Fed is to be a lender of last resort, we mean that:
    a.   the Fed serves as a clearinghouse for interbank payments.
    b.   the Fed ensures that banks are financially sound.
    c.   the Fed sets reserve requirements.
    d.   the Fed provides funds to troubled banks that cannot find any other sources of funds.

13. How many Federal Reserve districts are there?
    a.   48
    b.   25
    c.   50
    d.   12

14. Fill in the blanks. The Board of Governors of the Federal Reserve has _____ members that are appointed for staggered _____ by the _____ and must be confirmed by the _____.
    a.   seven; 14-year terms; President; Senate
    b.   fourteen; 7-year terms; Senate; President
    c.   twelve; 4-year terms; Congress; President
    d.   fourteen; 4-year terms; House of Representatives; Senate

15. Who is the chairperson of the Federal Open Market Committee (FOMC)?
    a.   The president of the New York Federal Reserve Bank
    b.   The chairperson of the Board of Governors
    c.   Any of the presidents of the Federal Reserve Banks
    d.   Any of the members of the Board of Governors

16. Which body of the Federal Reserve System sets the majority of U.S. monetary policy?
    a. The Board of Governors
    b. The Federal Open Market Committee
    c. The twelve Federal Reserve Banks in each district
    d. The Open Market Desk

17. This question tests your understanding of Application 3 in this chapter: Coping with a stock market crash: Black Monday, 1987. How did the Fed respond to the major stock market crash in 1987?

    On October 19, 1987, known as "Black Monday," the Dow Jones index of the stock market fell a dramatic 22.6 percent in one day. Similar declines were felt in other indexes and stock markets around the world. These declines shocked both businesses and investors. In just 24 hours, many people and firms found themselves much less wealthy.

    How did the Fed react to the stock market crash?
    a. Following the crash, the Fed failed to act as lender of last resort and many banks were forced to close.
    b. The Fed acted promptly to protect the loans and investments of banks and other financial institutions by requiring them to call in borrowers' existing loans and stop making new ones.
    c. The Fed took measures that resulted in a sharp drop in available credit, causing the economy to plunge into a deep recession.
    d. Alan Greenspan quickly issued a public statement in which he said that the Federal Reserve stood ready to provide liquidity to the financial system. Banks were told that the Fed would let them borrow liberally.

18. Define and briefly explain the concept of the money multiplier.

19. Among the missions of the Fed is to serve as a lender of last resort. Briefly explain what this means.

20. Why is central bank independence important for the proper performance of the economy?

Answers to the Practice Quiz

1. c. Unit of account is the property of money that prices are quoted in terms of money. Money provides a convenient measuring rod when prices for all goods are quoted in money terms. Money can be used to compare the relative value of goods, making it easier to carry out economic transactions.

2. a. $735 billion, or 53% of M1, was currency held by the public. With 300 million people in the United States, the $735 billion of currency held by the public amounts to $2,450 per person. However, most people don't hold such a large amount of cash. Much of this currency is held abroad.

3. d. While credit cards are commonly used in our economy to make transactions, they are not part of the money supply.

4. d. 40 percent is held in Europe and countries of the former Soviet Union and their trading partners.

5. b. Loans are usually the largest asset. The business of the bank is to profit from the difference between interest received on loans and interest paid on deposits.

6. b. Required reserves are the fraction of banks' deposits they are legally required to hold in their vaults or as deposits at the Fed.

7. d. The money multiplier is 1/reserve ratio, or $1/0.2 = 5$. Thus, a $100 cash deposit generates $5 * \$100 = \$500$ in new checking accounts.

8. d. Change in deposits = 1/reserve ratio x change in reserves. Then, $1/0.2$ x $100 = 5$ x $100 = \$500$.

9. d. The money multiplier shows the relationship between the final change in deposits and the change in reserves that caused it.

10. a. The multiplier is smaller because this cash is not available for the banking system to lend but there is still a multiplier. As long as people deposit money in banks that then lend at least part of the deposits out, there will be a money multiplier.

11. d. The Federal Reserve System was created in 1913 following a series of financial panics in the United States. Congress created the Federal Reserve to be a central bank, serving as a banker's bank.

12. d. The Fed stands ready to provide funds to a troubled bank that cannot find any other sources of funds.

13. d. The United States was divided into 12 Federal Reserve districts, each of which has a Federal Reserve Bank.

14. a. Headquartered in Washington, D.C., the seven members of the board are appointed for staggered 14-year terms by the President and must be confirmed by the Senate.

15. b. The chairperson of the Board of Governors also serves as the chairperson of the FOMC.

16. b. The FOMC consists of the Board of Governors, the president of the New York Federal Reserve Bank, and, on a rotating basis, four of the presidents of the 11 other district banks.

17. d. In fact, the Fed provided liquidity to such an extent that interest rates even fell. As a result of Greenspan's action, "Black Monday" did not cause a recession in the United States.

18. The money multiplier is the inverse of the required reserve ratio. The money multiplier shows the total increase in checking account deposits for any initial cash deposit. The initial cash deposit triggers additional rounds of deposits and lending by banks, which leads to a multiple expansion of deposits. When people hold part of their loans as cash, the money multiplier is smaller. This cash is not available for the banking system to lend.

19. The Fed is a lender of last resort because it stands ready to provide funds to a troubled bank that cannot find any other sources of funds. Despite the existence of FDIC insurance, banks are still subject to the possibility of bank runs. The Fed is the ideal lender of last resort because it is a nonprofit institution that serves the welfare of the public and because it has an essentially unlimited supply of funds.

20. Central bank independence refers to the ability of central banks to make decisions regarding monetary policy without interference from the government. The government could try to manipulate the money supply in ways that are beneficial for the current administration but harmful for the economy in the long run. For example, suppose that the economy is at full employment, with unemployment at around 5% or so. The Fed could be persuaded to increase the money supply, say 6 to 9 months prior

to an election. By the time the election occurs, the economy could reach a lower rate of unemployment, below the natural rate. Although the reduction in unemployment looks good in the short run, the result in the long run will only be higher inflation. For this reason, the central bank and the executive branch of government should remain distant from each other. Independence increases the credibility of the banking authority, which is interpreted in financial markets as a sign of economic strength.

14

The Federal Reserve and Monetary Policy

Chapter Summary

In this chapter, you'll learn about the role of the Federal Reserve in conducting monetary policy. In the short run, the Federal Reserve can influence interest-rate levels in the economy by changing the money supply. Money markets determine interest rates in the short run. When the Federal Reserve lowers interest rates, investment spending and GDP increase because the cost of funds is cheaper. Here are the main points of the chapter:

- The demand for money depends negatively on the interest rate and positively on the level of prices and real GDP.
- The Fed can determine the supply of money through open market purchases and sales, changing reserve requirements, or changing the discount rate. Open market operations are the primary tool the Fed uses to implement monetary policy.
- The level of interest rates is determined in the money market by the demand for money and the supply of money.
- To increase the level of GDP, the Federal Reserve buys bonds on the open market. To decrease the level of GDP, the Federal Reserve sells bonds on the open market.
- An increase in the money supply will decrease interest rates, increase investment spending, and increase output. A decrease in the money supply will increase interest rates, decrease investment spending, and decrease output.
- In an open economy, a decrease in interest rates will depreciate the local currency and lead to an increase in net exports. Conversely, an increase in interest rates will appreciate the local currency and lead to a decrease in net exports.
- Both lags in economic policies and the need to influence market expectations make successful monetary policy difficult in practice.

Applying the Concepts

After reading this chapter, you should be able to answer these three key questions:
1. What happens to interest rates when the economy recovers from a recession?
2. Is it better for decisions about monetary policy to be made by a single individual or by a committee?

3. What are the advantages and disadvantages of the Federal Reserve becoming more transparent about its actions and decisions and disclosing more information to the public?

14.1 The Money Market

To understand how interest rates are determined in the short run, we need to understand the money market. The **money market** is the market for money where the amount supplied and the amount demanded meet to determine the nominal interest rate. We begin by studying the factors that determine the public's demand for money. Once we understand what affects the demand for money, we can see how the actions of the Federal Reserve determine the supply of money. Then we'll see how the demand and supply of money together determine interest rates.

There are various reasons people demand money balances. Changes in interest rates, prices, and real income (real GDP) determine how much money people hold. People hold money primarily because money makes it easier to conduct everyday transactions. Economists call this reason for holding money the **transaction demand for money**. Recall one of the key principles used throughout the book:

Principle of Opportunity Cost
The opportunity cost of something is what you sacrifice to get it.

The opportunity cost of holding money is the return that you could have earned by holding your wealth in other assets. We measure the opportunity cost of holding money by the interest rate. As interest rates increase in the economy, the opportunity cost of holding money also increases. When the opportunity cost of holding money increases, the public demands less money. The quantity demanded of money will decrease with an increase in interest rates.

> ### ☀ Caution!
>
> Remember, when you have a graph, the variable on one of the axes is the variable that causes movement along a curve. A change in any other variable will cause the curve to shift, increasing to the right or decreasing to the left.

In Figure 14.1, we draw a demand for money curve, M_d, as a function of the interest rate. At higher interest rates, individuals will want to hold less money than they will at lower interest rates because the opportunity cost of holding money is higher. As interest rates rise from r_0 to r_1, the quantity of money demanded falls from M_0 to M_1.

> ### 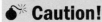 Study Tip
>
> This curve in Figure 14.1 shows the demand for money. If you have difficulties or need a refresher in understanding market demand, refer back to Chapter 4 and review the section on market demand.

The transaction demand for money also depends on two other factors. One is the overall price level in the economy. The demand for money will increase as the level of prices increases. Remember the real-nominal principle:

 **Real-Nominal Principle**

What matters to people is the real value of money or income—its purchasing power—not the face value of money or income.

People need more dollars to buy the same goods when prices increase. The nominal value of the goods increases due to price increases, causing the increase in money demand.

The other factor that influences the demand for money is the level of real GDP or real income. As income increases, individuals and businesses will make more purchases. Similarly, as real GDP increases, individuals and businesses will make more transactions, increasing money demand.

Figure 14.2 shows how changes in prices and GDP affect the demand for money. Panel A shows how the demand for money shifts to the right as the price level increases. At any interest rate, people will want to hold more money as prices increase. Panel B shows how the demand for money shifts to the right as real GDP increases. At any interest rate, people will want to hold more money as real GDP increases. These graphs both show the same result. An increase in prices or an increase in real GDP will increase money demand.

Economists recognize that individuals have a **liquidity demand for money**. People want to hold money so they can make transactions on short notice. The **speculative demand for money** is the demand for money that arises because holding money over short periods is less risky than holding stocks or bonds.

In summary, individuals hold money for three motives: to facilitate transactions, to provide liquidity, and to reduce risk. The amount of money they want to hold will depend on interest rates, the level of real GDP, and the price level.

14.2 How the Federal Reserve Can Change the Money Supply

In this section, we will explore how the Federal Reserve can change the money supply. As we discussed in the last chapter, the banking system as a whole can expand the money supply only if new reserves come into the system. Yet when private citizens and firms write checks to one another, there will be no net change in the supply of money. Because the total amount of reserves in the system is unchanged, the money supply cannot expand. There is one organization, however, that has the power to change the total amount of reserves in the banking system: the Federal Reserve.

☞ Think about exchanging trading cards. The total amounts of cards traded are the same between the people trading unless more cards are added from an outside source. Suppose that 3 friends get together to trade and each has 20 cards to trade. The total amount of cards to be traded would be 60 cards. Notice that the total amount of cards would stay the same regardless of how the trades occurred. You would need to add to the cards from an outside source to increase the total number of cards. The same holds true for checks we write between each other. If I write a $100 check for a friend, she will deposit the check and the money creation process starts. However at the same time that happens, $100 is coming out of my account to honor the check I wrote. The net effect of writing checks to each other doesn't change the total money supply.

The Federal Reserve uses three monetary policy tools to control the money supply:
1. Open market operations
2. Changing reserve requirements
3. Changing the discount rate

The first Fed monetary policy tool we will look at is open market operations. **Open market operations** are the purchase or sale of U.S. government securities by the Fed. There are two types of open market operations:

- In **open market purchases**, the Fed buys government bonds from the private sector.
- In **open market sales**, the Fed sells government bonds to the private sector.

If the Federal Reserve wishes to increase the money supply to stimulate the economy, it buys government bonds from the private sector in open market purchases. As the Fed buys bonds, it gives money to the public that deposits it into the banking system, increasing the money supply. If the Fed wishes to decrease the money supply to slow the economy down, it sells government bonds to the private sector in open market sales. As the Fed sells bonds, it takes money in the exchange from the public and out of the banking system, decreasing the money supply.

Another way the Fed can change the money supply is by changing the reserve requirements for banks. If the Fed wishes to increase the supply of money, it can reduce banks' reserve requirements so they have more money to loan out. This would expand the money supply. To decrease the supply of money, the Federal Reserve can raise reserve requirements. Changing reserve requirements is a powerful tool, but the Federal Reserve doesn't use it very often because it disrupts the banking system.

The last way the Fed can change the money supply is by changing the discount rate. The **discount rate** is the interest rate at which banks can borrow directly from the Fed. They first try to borrow reserves from other banks through the **federal funds market**, a market in which banks borrow and lend reserves to and from one another. If the rate—called the **federal funds rate**—seemed too high to the bank, it could borrow directly from the Federal Reserve at the discount rate. By changing the discount rate, the Federal Reserve can influence the amount of borrowing by banks. If the Fed raises the discount rate, banks will be discouraged from borrowing reserves because it has become more costly. Lowering the discount rate will induce banks to borrow additional reserves. In practice the Fed merely tries to keep the discount rate close to their target for the federal funds rate. The discount rate is rarely used as an independent policy tool.

> ### ᕃᕂ **Study Tip**
>
> To increase the money supply, the Fed does an open market purchase, decreases the reserve requirement, or decreases the discount rate. To decrease the money supply, the Fed does an open market sale, increases the reserve requirement, or increases the discount rate.

☞ Go to the Federal Reserve Web site at www.federalreserve.gov or www.federalreserveeducation.org for more information about how monetary policy tools are used.

14.3 How Interest Rates Are Determined: Combining the Demand and Supply of Money

The demand for money is determined by the public. The supply of money is determined by the Fed. We can see how interest rates are determined in the short run by using a demand-and-supply model of the money market. Figure 14.3 shows a model of the money market. The supply of money is determined by the Federal Reserve, and we assume for simplicity that the supply is independent of interest rates. We represent this independence by a vertical supply curve for money, M_s. In the same graph, we draw the demand for money, M_d. Market equilibrium occurs where the demand for money equals the supply of money, at an interest rate of r^*.

We can use this simple model of the money market to understand the power of the Federal Reserve. Suppose the Federal Reserve increases the money supply through an open market purchase of bonds. In Panel A of Figure 14.4, an increase in the supply of money shifts the money supply curve to the right, leading to lower interest rates. A decrease in the money supply through the Fed's open market sale of bonds, as depicted in Panel B of Figure 14.4, decreases the supply of money, shifting the money supply curve to the left and increasing interest rates.

When the Fed raises interest rates, bond prices fall. As interest rates rise, investors need less money to meet the promised payments in the future, so the price of all these bonds falls. As interest rates fall, investors need more money to meet the promised payments. Therefore, as the Fed changes interest rates, bond prices will move in the opposite direction of interest rates.

☑ **Key Equation**

$$\text{price of bond} = \frac{\text{promised payment}}{1 + \text{interest rate}}$$

Let's review an Application that answers one of the key questions we posed at the start of the chapter:

1.   What happens to interest rates when the economy recovers from a recession?

APPLICATION 1: RISING INTEREST RATES DURING AN ECONOMIC RECOVERY

During 2005, interest rates on three-month Treasury bills rose from 2.3 percent at the beginning of the year to 3.9 percent at the end of the year, as real GDP grew very rapidly. Why should a recovery be associated with higher interest rates? One key to understanding this phenomenon is that the extra income being generated by firms and individuals during the recovery will increase the demand for money. Because the demand for money increases while the supply of money remains fixed, interest rates rise. Another factor is that the Federal Reserve itself may want to raise interest rates as the economy grows rapidly to avoid overheating the economy.

Think about what the Federal Reserve is doing when it conducts the open market purchase. The Federal Reserve is buying bonds from the public. As the Fed buys bonds, it increases the demand for bonds and raises their price. This is another reason bond prices rise as interest rates fall. Similarly, interest rates rise following an open market sale of bonds by the Fed. When the Fed conducts an open market sale, it is selling bonds, increasing the supply of bonds in the market. With an increase in the supply of bonds, the price of bonds will fall.

📖 **Study Tip**

Work through the examples on page 309 of your textbook to understand the relationship between interest rates and bond prices. It is a good application of present value calculations you learned in Chapter 12.

Why is good news for the economy bad news for the bond market? We can understand the behavior of the bond market by thinking about the demand for money. When real GDP increases, the demand for money will increase. As the demand for money increases, the money demand curve will shift to the right. From our model of the money market, we know that increased money demand will increase interest rates. Bond prices move in the opposite direction from interest rates. Therefore, good news for the economy is bad for the bond market.

14.4 Interest Rates and How They Change Investment and Output (GDP)

> **⌒ Study Tip**
>
> The investment demand curve is shown on page 272 of your textbook. You should review this graph as it will be used in this section.

To show how the Fed affects the interest rate, which in turn affects investment (a component of GDP), and finally, GDP itself, we combine our demand and supply for money with the curve that shows how investment spending is related to interest rates. This is shown in Figure 14.5. Panel A in Figure 14.5 shows how interest rates are determined by the demand and supply for money. It is identical to Figure 14.3, which we studied earlier. The graph shows us the equilibrium interest rate for money. Now let's move to Panel B in Figure 14.5. We can see that at the equilibrium interest rate r^*, the level of investment in the economy will be given by I^*.

In Figure 14.6, we show the effects of an increase in the money supply using our money market and investment graphs. As the supply of money increases, interest rates fall from r_0 to r_1. With lower interest rates, investment spending will increase from I_0 to I_1. This increase in investment spending will then increase aggregate demand—the total demand for goods and services in the economy—and shift the aggregate demand curve to the right.

In summary, when the Fed increases the money supply, it leads to lower interest rates and increased investment spending. In turn, a higher level of investment spending will ultimately lead to a higher level of GDP.

> **⌒ Study Tip**
>
> Learn the sequence to understand how each variable affects the next variable. Try and do the same sequencing for the other monetary policy tools.

open market purchases → increase in money supply → fall in interest rates → rise in investment spending → increase in GDP

The Fed can also use its influence to increase interest rates, which will have the exact opposite effect. Investment spending will fall, along with aggregate demand. The aggregate demand curve will shift to the left, and the price level and output in the economy will fall, too. We can again represent this entire sequence of events:

open market sale → decrease in money supply → rise in interest rates → fall in investment spending → decrease in GDP

Suppose the Federal Reserve lowers U.S. interest rates through an open market purchase of bonds. As a result, investors in the United States will be earning lower interest rates and will seek to invest some of their funds abroad. To invest abroad, they will need to sell their U.S. dollars and buy the foreign currency of the country where they intend to invest. This will affect the **exchange rate**—the rate at which one currency trades for another currency in the market. As more investors sell their dollars to buy foreign currency, the exchange rate will fall. A fall in the exchange rate or a decrease in the value of a currency is called **depreciation of a currency**. Lower U.S. interest rates brought on by the Fed will cause the dollar to depreciate. This will ultimately change the demand and supply of goods and services around the globe because it will make U.S. goods cheaper than foreign goods. Let's see why.

As the exchange rate for the U.S. dollar falls, U.S. goods become cheaper and foreign goods become more expensive. The United States then exports more goods and imports fewer goods. Net exports increase, in other words. This increase in net exports increases the demand for U.S. goods and increases GDP. Remember that this all began with an open market purchase of bonds by the Fed that increased the money supply. Here is the sequence of events:

open market purchase	→	increase in money supply	→	fall in interest rates	→	fall in exchange rate	→	increase in net exports	→	increase in GDP

The three new links in the sequence are from interest rates to exchange rates, from exchange rates to net exports, and from net exports to GDP. This sequence also works in reverse. If the Fed conducts an open market sale of bonds, U.S. interest rates rise. As a result, foreign investors earning lower interest rates elsewhere will want to move their money to the United States where they can earn a higher return. As they buy more U.S. dollars, the exchange rate for the dollar will increase, and the dollar will increase in value. An increase in the value of a currency is called **appreciation of a currency**. The appreciation of the dollar will make U.S. goods more expensive for foreigners and imports cheaper for U.S. residents.

When U.S. interest rates rise as a result of an open market sale by the Fed, we expect exports to decrease and imports to increase, decreasing net exports. The decrease in net exports will reduce the demand for U.S. goods and lead to a fall in output. Here is the sequence of events:

open market sale	→	decrease in money supply	→	rise in interest rates	→	rise in exchange rate	→	decrease in net exports	→	decrease in GDP

To summarize, an increase in interest rates will reduce both investment spending (including consumer durables) and net exports. A decrease in interest rates will increase investment spending and net exports. As you can see, monetary policy in an open economy is even more powerful than monetary policy used in a closed economy.

14.5 Monetary Policy Challenges for the Fed

The inside lags for monetary policy are relatively short compared to those for fiscal policy. The FOMC meets eight times a year and can decide on major policy changes at any time and very quickly. It can even give the chairperson of the Board of Governors some discretion to make changes between meetings.

Decisions about monetary policy are made by a committee. How does this affect the effectiveness of monetary policy? There are pros and cons to committee decisions. One advantage for committee decision making is greater information sharing. More people looking at the same problem from different perspectives enrich the decision making process. On the other hand, sometimes committees get bogged down in endless discussion. This may create lags.

The outside lags related to monetary policy, however, are quite long. Most econometric models predict that an interest rate cut will take at least two years for most of its effects to be felt. This delay means that for the Fed to conduct successful monetary policy, it must be able to forecast accurately two years in the future!

Because of the long outside lags for monetary policy and difficulties in forecasting the economy, many economists believe that the Fed should not take a very active role in trying to stabilize the economy. Instead, they recommend that the Fed concentrate on keeping the inflation rate low and stable.

Let's review an Application that answers one of the key questions we posed at the start of the chapter:

2. Is it better for decisions about monetary policy to be made by a single individual or by a committee?

APPLICATION 2: THE EFFECTIVENESS OF COMMITTEES

Alan Blinder, vice-chairman of the Federal Reserve from 1994 to 1996, was convinced that committees were not effective for making decisions about monetary policy. The type of experiment Blinder and his colleague developed was designed to explore how quickly individuals and groups could distinguish changes in underlying trends from random events. The results of the experiment showed that committees perform better than individuals. Committees make decisions as quickly and are more accurate than individuals making decisions by themselves. Moreover, committee decisions were not simply related to the average performance of the individuals who composed the committee—the actual *process* of having meetings and discussions appears to have improved the group's overall performance.

The Fed directly controls only very short-term interest rates in the economy, not long-term interest rates. In fact, when the Fed makes its decisions on monetary policy, it really decides on what the rate should be in the federal funds market—the market in which banks borrow and lend reserves overnight. Once the Fed decides on what rate it wants in the market, it conducts open market operations—buying and selling short-term government bonds—to achieve this rate. Thus, when the Federal Reserve decides the course of monetary policy, it is really just setting a very short-term interest rate for the economy.

The Fed does this by indirectly influencing short-term rates. Here's how: Long-term interest rates are averages of current and expected future short-term interest rates. Long-term interest rates are an average of the current short-term interest rate and expected future short-term rates.

Influencing expectations of the financial markets is an important part of the Fed's job. The Fed does try to communicate its general intentions for future policy actions to the public to help make those policies more effective. However, the public ultimately must form its own expectations of what the Fed is going to do.

Coping with financial market expectations complicates the Fed's task in developing monetary policy. Thus, before the Fed takes any actions on interest rates or even makes any statements about its future intentions, it can see what the market is thinking. The Fed has to decide whether to either take actions consistent with market expectations of its own actions or to "surprise" the market in some way.

Let's review an Application that answers one of the key questions we posed at the start of the chapter:

3. What are the advantages and disadvantages of the Federal Reserve becoming more transparent about its actions and decisions and disclosing more information to the public?

APPLICATION 3: MAKING THE FEDERAL RESERVE MORE TRANSPARENT

In recent years, the Fed has gradually become more open in its deliberations. For many years, the Fed would not even say if it had changed interest rates. These policies began to change slowly in the 1990s. Starting in 2000, after each FOMC meeting the Fed announces its target for the federal funds rate and makes a brief statement explaining its actions. There was enough interest on this very topic for the FOMC to hold a special meeting—the first since 1979—to discuss the issue. The special meeting did not lead to any dramatic change in the Fed's communication policies. But now the members of the FOMC participate in drafting statements. The Fed clearly recognizes that its statements may be just as important as its actions.

☞ A continual concern about the lack of transparency is that trust starts to erode. Central bank independence and effectiveness is a function of trust. If people start to see that the Fed is not open with its communication, they may lose trust in what the Fed is doing. Such a lack of trust can cause Fed policies to become less effective.

The model for monetary policy that we developed in this chapter can be used to understand the behavior of the economy only in the short run, when prices do not change very much. Monetary policy can affect output in the short run when prices are largely fixed, but in the long run, changes in the money supply affect only the price level and inflation. In the long run, the Federal Reserve can only indirectly control nominal interest rates and it can't control *real* interest rates.

Activity

Now that you know how monetary policy works and how it affects various parts of the economy, what would happen when there is an increase in the discount rate? Put together a sequence for

a. A country without trade
b. A country with international trade

Answers

a. The sequence of events in a country without trade when there is an increase in the discount rate is:

increase in discount → rate	decrease in money → supply	rise in interest → rates	fall in investment → spending	decrease in GDP

b. The sequence of events in a country that has international trade when there is an increase in the discount rate is:

increase in discount→ rate	decrease in money → supply	rise in interest → rates	rise in exchange → rate	decrease in net → exports	decrease in GDP

Key Terms

Appreciation of a currency: An increase in the value of a currency.

Depreciation of a currency: A decrease in the value of a currency.

Discount rate: The interest rate at which banks can borrow from the Fed.

Exchange rate: The rate at which currencies trade for one another in the market.

Federal funds market: The market in which banks borrow and lend reserves to and from one another.

Federal funds rate: The interest rate on reserves that banks lend each other.

Illiquid: Not easily transferable to money.

Liquidity demand for money: The demand for money that represents the needs and desires individuals and firms have to make transactions on short notice without incurring excessive costs.

Money market: The market for money in which the amount supplied and the amount demanded meet to determine the nominal interest rate.

Open market operations: The purchase or sale of U.S. government securities by the Fed.

Open market purchase: The Fed's purchase of government bonds from the private sector.

Open market sale: The Fed's sale of government bonds to the private sector.

Speculative demand for money: The demand for money that arises because holding money over short periods is less risky than holding stocks or bonds.

Transaction demand for money: The demand for money based on the desire to facilitate transactions.

Practice Quiz

(Answers are provided at the end of the Practice Quiz.)

1. The money market is the market for money where the amount supplied and the amount demanded meet to determine:
    a. bond prices. ⌄
    b. stock prices.
    c. the nominal interest rate.
    d. the real interest rate.

2. Economists refer to the *transaction demand for money* to describe how money is used to:
    a. buy stocks and bonds.
    b. hold wealth.
    c. buy goods and services.
    d. calculate the purchasing power of income.

3. Fill in the blanks. As interest rates increase, the opportunity costs of holding money _____ and the public will demand _____ money.
   a. increase; more
   b. increase; less
   c. decrease; more
   d. decrease; less

   i↑ ⇒ m s ↓ → ↑n

4. Refer to the figure below. Which of these graphs correctly depicts the impact of an increase in the aggregate price level?

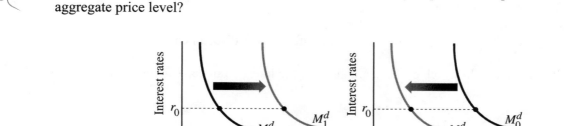

   a. The graph on the left
   b. The graph on the right
   c. Both graphs could do that.
   d. Neither graph would apply.

5. The demand for money that represents the needs or desires of individuals or firms to make purchases on quick notice is called:
   a. spot demand for money.
   b. liquidity demand for money.
   c. expected demand for money.
   d. real money demand.

6. Holding money over short periods may be less risky than holding stocks or bonds. This is an example of:
   a. precautionary demand for money.
   b. transactions demand for money.
   c. liquidity demand for money.
   d. speculative demand for money.

7. If the Federal Reserve wishes to increase the money supply to stimulate the economy, it will conduct:
   a. an open market sale.
   b. an open market purchase.
   c. an increase in the required reserve ratio.
   d. an increase in the discount rate.

8. Which of the following is among the tools the Fed has available to change the money supply?
    a. Changing reserve requirements
    b. Changing the prime lending rate
    c. Buying and selling currencies in foreign exchange markets
    d. All of the above

9. The discount rate is:
    a. the rate at which banks can borrow from the Fed.
    b. the rate at which banks can borrow from each other.
    c. the interest rate that commercial banks offer to their best customers.
    d. the rate at which the present value of a given sum of money is discounted.

10. Refer to the figure below. In which of these graphs does the interest rate have a tendency to rise?

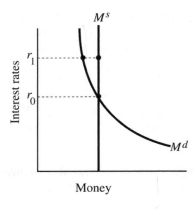
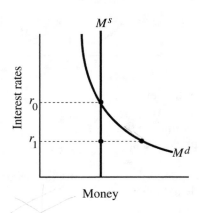

    a. In the graph on the left
    b. In the graph on the right
    c. In both graphs
    d. In neither graph

11. If a bond promises to pay $120 a year from now, and the interest rate is 6%, what is the price of the bond?
    a. $2,000
    b. $113.20
    c. $72
    d. $20

12. This question tests your understanding of Application 1 in this chapter: Rising interest rates during an economic recovery. What happens to interest rates when the economy recovers from a recession?

    Why should a recovery be associated with higher interest rates?
    a. Interest rates increase during a recovery because the demand for money increases as the economy generates more jobs and income.
    b. During recoveries, interest rates usually rise as a result of increases in the money supply.
    c. Usually, a combination of higher demand for money and higher supply of money results in higher interest rates during an economic recovery.
    d. A combination of lower demand for money and higher supply of money during recessions leads to higher interest rates.

13. Fill in the blanks. When the Fed buys bonds, in order to _____ interest rates, it is _____ the demand for bonds, thus the price of bonds tends to _____.
    a. raise; increasing; rise
    b. lower; increasing; fall
    c. lower; increasing; rise
    d. lower; decreasing; fall

14. Refer to the figure below. Which of the following statements best describes this scenario?

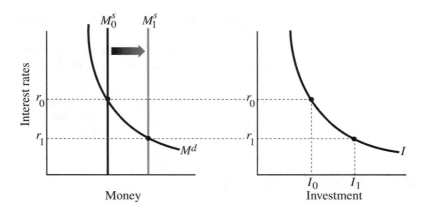

    a. When interest rates rise, investors need less money to obtain the same promised payments in the future, so the price of bonds falls.
    b. An increase in real GDP causes the demand for money to rise, putting upward pressure on interest rates.
    c. Lower interest rates brought on by the Fed will cause the dollar to appreciate.
    d. An open market purchase leads to an increase in the money supply, which causes interest rates to fall and investment spending to rise.

15. Through its impact on interest rates, an increase in the money supply will result in:
    a. appreciation of the dollar.
    b. depreciation of the dollar.
    c. either an increase or a decrease in the value of the dollar, depending on the magnitude of change in interest rates.
    d. neither appreciation nor depreciation of the dollar. Changes in the money supply do not affect the value of the dollar.

16. Fill in the blanks. Because of the _____ in forecasting the economy, many economists believe that the Fed _____ take a very active role in trying to stabilize the economy.
    a. advances; should
    b. advances; should not
    c. difficulties; should
    d. difficulties; should not

17. The most important tool to control the amount of reserves in the banking system, and therefore the money supply, is open market operations. Briefly describe an open market purchase by the Fed.

18. In addition to open market operations, the Fed has other tools of monetary policy available to change the money supply, but it does not use those other tools often. Why not?

19. Explain the impact of expansionary monetary policy on the foreign sector, and particularly on the value of the dollar?

20. Bond prices change in the opposite direction from changes in interest rates. Use a numerical example to explain why.

21. Why is it that good news for the economy is bad news for the bond market and perhaps for the stock market as well?

22. Trace the impact of an open market sale by the Fed, to show eventually what happens to GDP.

23. Monetary policy is even more powerful in an open economy than in a closed economy. Take the case of a decision by the Fed to adopt expansionary monetary policy to explain why.

24. After the economic slowdown that started around the third quarter of 2000, the Fed lowered interest rates eleven times in the following year, 2001. What concerns would you have, if any, about the effort by the Fed to smooth out this economic recession?

Answers to the Practice Quiz

1. c. The money market is the market for money where the amount supplied and the amount demanded meet to determine the nominal interest rate.

2. c. Holding money makes it easier to conduct transactions. Economists call this reason for holding money the transactions demand for money.

3. b. As interest rates increase, the opportunity cost of holding money increases, and the public will demand less money.

4. a. As prices increase, people need to hold more money to buy goods and services so the demand for money shifts to the right.

5. b. The liquidity demand for money is the demand for money that represents the needs or desires of individuals or firms to make purchases on quick notice.

6. d. Demand for "safer" assets that form part of the M2 category of money is called the speculative demand for money. Holding money over short periods may be less risky than holding stocks or bonds.

7. b. If the Federal Reserve wishes to increase the money supply to stimulate the economy, it buys government bonds.

8. a. Banks are asked to hold a smaller or larger fraction of their deposits as reserves.

9. a. The discount rate is the rate at which banks can borrow from the Fed.

10. b. This graph shows a lower interest rate than equilibrium, which causes an excess demand for money. The interest rate would rise.

11. b. The price of a bond equals future promised payment/$(1 + i)t$. This is $120/1.06$.

12. a. The simple model of the money market helps explain why interest rates can rise during an economic recovery. One key to understanding this phenomenon is that the extra income being generated by firms and individuals during the recovery will increase the demand for money. Because the demand for money increases while the supply of money remains fixed, interest rates rise.

13. c. When the Fed buys bonds in order to lower interest rates, it is increasing the demand for bonds, thus the price of bonds tends to rise. Alternatively, an open market sale increases the supply of bonds, causing bond prices to fall and interest rates to rise.

14. d. This is the precise relationship between interest rates, investment, and output.

15. b. A higher money supply leads to lower interest rates and less interest in investing in dollar-denominated assets. Consequently, the demand for dollars will fall and the dollar will depreciate.

16. d. Because of the difficulties in forecasting the economy, many economists believe that the Fed should not take a very active role in trying to stabilize the economy. Instead, they recommend that the Fed concentrate on keeping the inflation rate low and stable.

17. Suppose the Fed purchases $1 million worth of government bonds from the private sector. The Fed writes a check for $1 million and presents it to the party who sold the bonds. The Fed now owns those bonds, and the party who sold the bonds has a check for $1 million. Checks written against the Fed count as reserves for banks. If the reserve ratio is 10%, the bank must keep $100,000 in new reserves, but can make loans for $900,000. And so, the process of money creation begins. Open market purchases increase the money supply. The Fed has unlimited ability to create money because it can write checks against itself to purchase the government bonds without having any explicit "funds." Banks accept it because these checks count as reserves for the bank.

18. The Fed does not increase the reserve requirement often because it can be disruptive to the banking system. Banks would be forced to call in or cancel many of their loans. The Fed does not change the discount rate often because it is difficult to tell exactly how much of an effect the change will have. Also, changes in the discount rate can be largely offset by changes in other interest rates. Relative to the level of other interest rates, a change in the discount rate may be too large in some circumstances, or too small in others. In practice, the Fed keeps the discount rate close to the federal funds rate to avoid large swings in borrowed reserves by banks. The Fed conducts monetary policy by setting targets for the federal funds rate. Once it has set those targets, it uses open market operations to keep the actual federal funds rate on target.

19. All else the same, actions by the Fed to lower U.S. interest rates will make U.S. investments less attractive relative to foreign investments. Foreign investors, then, would decrease their demand for dollar-denominated assets, and consequently the demand for dollars. Less demand for the dollar will lower the value of the dollar, or the exchange rate of the dollar for other currencies, in currency markets throughout the world. This is good news for U.S. producers who now can export their good at relatively lower prices, but bad news for U.S. consumers, as the prices of imports will be relatively higher. As the dollar depreciates, then, exports will rise and imports will fall, improving the nation's trade balance, and thereby increasing GDP.

20. The price of a bond one year from now is the promised payment divided by 1 plus the interest rate. For example, a bond that promises to pay $106 a year from now, with an interest rate of 6% per year, would cost today: $106/(1 + 0.06) = $100. In other words, if you are willing to invest at 6% per year, you would pay $100 today for a promised payment of $106 next year. When the interest rate falls from 6% to 4%, you have to pay $101.92 today to have $106 next year ($106/(1 + 0.04) = $101.92). And, if the interest rate rose from 6% to 8%, for example, you would have to pay only $98.15 to have $106 next year. Notice in this example that when the interest rate decreases, the price of the bond increases; and when the interest rate rises, the price of the bond falls.

21. Because an increase in real GDP causes the demand for money to rise, it puts upward pressure on interest rates. Consequently, bond prices will fall. Also, higher GDP growth leads to higher expectations of inflation which tend to push up nominal interest rates, leading to lower bond prices. Stock prices can also fall despite good economic news. As bond prices fall, bonds become more attractive than stocks, resulting in lower demand for stocks, and lower stock prices.

22. An open market sale of bonds by the Fed drains cash reserves out of the banking system, and lowers the money supply. In the model of the money market, as the money supply shifts to the left, while the demand for money remains the same, the interest rate rises. A higher interest rate will lower investment spending, therefore, shift aggregate expenditure downward and aggregate demand to the left. This decrease in aggregate demand means that the economy will settle in equilibrium at a lower level of output and employment.

23. An increase in the money supply, all else the same, results in a decrease in the market rate of interest. As the interest rate falls, the demand for dollars falls, causing the price of the dollar (or exchange rate) to fall. As the exchange rate falls, exports rise and imports fall. Consequently, net exports will rise. An increase in net exports results in an increase in GDP. Monetary policy is more powerful in an open economy because the increase in net exports is consistent with the intent of the expansionary policy, which is to increase GDP.

24. Successful stabilization policies can reduce the magnitude of economic fluctuations, but ill-timed policies can magnify economic fluctuations. There are inside lags in recognition and implementation of policy, and outside lags, or lags that refer to the time it takes for policy to be effective. Outside lags in monetary policy appear to be longer than inside lags. Economists are not very accurate in forecasting what will happen in the economy. For example, knowing whether a slowdown is temporary or permanent is a classical problem policymakers face when the economy appears to be slowing down. Today, most policymakers understand these limitations and are cautious in using activist policies to smooth out economic fluctuations.

15

Modern Macroeconomics: From the Short Run to the Long Run

Chapter Summary

One of the great debates surrounding macroeconomic policy making centers on the short run versus the long run. Keynes and Friedman embody this debate. Up to this point in the book, we have discussed the short run and the long run separately. Now, however, we'll explain how the economy evolves from the short run to the long run. Here are the main points of the chapter:

- The short run in macroeconomics refers to the period of time in which prices do not change very much. The long run in macroeconomics is when prices have time to fully and completely adjust to economic changes.
- When output exceeds full employment, wages and prices rise faster than their past trends. If output is less than full employment, wages and prices fall relative to past trends.
- The price changes that occur when the economy is away from full employment push the economy back to full employment. Economists disagree on the length of time that this adjustment process takes; estimates range from less than two years to six years.
- Economic policies are most effective when the adjustment process is slow. However, to improve their chances of being reelected, politicians can potentially take advantage of the difference between the short-run effects and the long-run effects of economic policies.
- If the economy is operating below full employment, falling wages and prices will reduce money demand and lower interest rates. The fall in interest rates will stimulate investment and lead the economy back to full employment.
- The reverse occurs when output exceeds full employment. Increases in wages and prices will increase money demand and interest rates. As investment spending falls, the economy returns to full employment.
- In the long run, increases in the supply of money are neutral. That is, increases in the money supply do not affect real interest rates, real investment, or real output. This is known as the long-run neutrality of money.
- Increases in government spending will raise real interest rates and crowd out investment in the long run. Decreases in government spending will lower real interest rates and crowd in investment in the long run.
- The adjustment model in this chapter helps us to understand the debate between Keynes and the classical economists.

Applying the Concepts

After reading this chapter, you should be able to answer these three key questions:
1. What went wrong for the Japanese economy during its decade-long economic downturn?
2. What are the links between presidential elections and macroeconomic performance?
3. What explained the decision by the Japanese government to increase taxes in the 1990s when the economy was still suffering from a recession?

15.1 Linking the Short Run and the Long Run

To begin to understand how the short run and the long run are related, let's return to what we mean by the short run and the long run in macroeconomics.

> 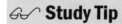 **Study Tip**
>
> This chapter deals with aggregate demand and aggregate supply curves, which you learned about in Chapter 9. If you need to review the graphs, go back to Chapter 9.

In Chapter 9, we explained how in the short run wages and prices are sticky and do not change immediately in response to changes in demand. The **short run in macroeconomics** is the period of time over which prices do not change or do not change very much. The **long run in macroeconomics** is the period of time in which prices have fully adjusted to any economic changes. Long-run, full-employment economics applies after wages and prices have largely adjusted to changes in demand.

In the short run, GDP is determined by the current demand for goods and services in the economy, so fiscal policy—such as tax cuts or increased government spending—and monetary policy—such as adjusting the money supply—can impact demand and GDP. However, in the long run, GDP is determined by the supply of labor, the stock of capital, and the state of technology—in other words, the willingness of people to work and the overall "material" the economy has to work with. Full employment is another characteristic of the long run. Because the economy is operating at full employment in the long run, output can't be increased by changes in demand.

This chapter answers two important questions.
1. How does what happens in the short run determine what happens in the long run?
2. How long is the short run?

Sometimes, we see wages and prices in all industries rising or falling together. For example, prices for steel, automobiles, food, and fuel may all rise together. Why? Wages and prices will all tend to increase together during booms when GDP exceeds its full-employment level or potential output. Wages and prices will fall together during periods of recessions when GDP falls below full employment or potential output.

Table 15.1 summarizes our discussion of unemployment, output, and changes in wages. It is important to emphasize one point: In addition to the changes in wages and prices that occur when the economy is producing at more or less than full employment, there is also typically ongoing inflation in the economy. The difference between equilibrium output level and the potential output level is called the output gap. If the equilibrium output level is greater than potential output, it's called an inflationary GDP gap. If the equilibrium output level is less than potential output, the output gap is called a recessionary GDP gap.

If the economy is producing at a level above full employment, firms will find it increasingly difficult to hire and retain workers, and unemployment will be below its natural rate. Workers will find it easy to get and change jobs. To attract workers and prevent them from leaving, firms will raise their wages. As one firm raises its wage, other firms will have to raise their wages even higher to attract the workers that remain. Wages are the largest cost of production for most firms. Consequently, as labor costs increase, firms have no choice but to increase the prices of their products. However, as prices rise, workers need higher nominal wages to maintain their real wages. This is an illustration of the real-nominal principle.

 Real-Nominal Principle

What matters to people is the real value of money or income—its purchasing power—not the face value of money or income.

This adjustment process leads to wage–price spirals. A **wage–price spiral** is the process by which changes in wages and prices cause further changes in wages and prices. When the economy is producing below full employment or potential output, the process works in reverse. Unemployment will exceed the natural rate. Firms will find it is easy to hire and retain workers, and they can offer workers less. As all firms cut wages, the average level of wages in the economy falls. Since wages are the largest component of firms' costs, when wages fall, prices start to fall, too. In this case, the wage–price spiral works in reverse.

In summary, when output exceeds potential output, wages and prices throughout the economy will rise above previous inflation rates. If output is less than potential output, wages and prices will fall relative to previous inflation rates.

15.2 How Wages and Price Changes Move the Economy Naturally Back to Full Employment

Using aggregate demand and aggregate supply, we can illustrate graphically how changing prices and wages help move the economy from the short to the long run.

First, let's review the graphical representations of aggregate demand and aggregate supply. Recall from Chapter 9 that the **aggregate demand curve** is a curve that shows the relationship between the level of prices and quantity of real GDP demanded.

There are two aggregate supply curves—one for the short run and one for the long run. The **short-run aggregate supply curve** is relatively flat. The shape of the curve reflects the idea that prices do not change very much in the short run and that firms adjust production to meet demand. The **long-run aggregate supply curve**, however, is vertical. The vertical line means that at any given price level, firms in the long run are producing all that they can, given the amount of labor, capital, and technology available to them in the economy. The line represents what firms can supply in the long run at a state of full employment or potential output.

 Caution!

If you don't feel comfortable with the concepts in this section, stop here and review Chapter 9. The remainder of Chapter 15 will use the aggregate demand/aggregate supply model extensively. Drawing this model as shown in Figures 15.1 and 15.2 will help you understand economic behavior.

> ## 👌 Study Tip
> Review the following figures that show what happens in the case of a recession and a boom:
> • Recession – Review Figure 15.1.
> • Boom – Review Figure 15.2.

Now let's look at what happens if the economy is in a slump, producing below full employment or potential output. Panel A of Figure 15.1 shows an aggregate demand curve and the two aggregate supply curves. In the short run, output and prices are determined where the aggregate demand curve intersects the short-run aggregate supply curve—point a. This point corresponds to the level of output y_0 and a price level P_0. Notice that y_0 is a level less than full employment or potential output, y_p. In the long run, the level of prices and output is given by the intersection of the aggregate demand curve and the long-run aggregate supply curve—point c. Output is at full employment y_p, and prices are at P_F. How does the economy move from point a in the short run to point c in the long run? Panel B shows us how. At point a, the current level of output, y_0, falls short of the full-employment level of output, y_p. With output less than full employment, the unemployment rate is above the natural rate. Firms find it relatively easy to hire and retain workers and wages and then prices begin to fall. As the level of prices decreases, the short-run aggregate supply curve shifts downward over time, as shown in Panel B. The short-run aggregate supply curve shifts downward because decreases in wages lower costs for firms. Competition between firms will lead to lower prices for their products.

☞ Have you ever had the hiccups? As you review the graphs, notice that the short-run aggregate supply curve has the hiccups. Why does this happen? Remember from our discussions in Chapter 9 that price stickiness prevents immediate adjustment. As firms adjust to short run conditions of price and wage changes, a new short-run equilibrium will exist. This will continue until output reaches full employment.

But what if the economy is "too hot" instead of sluggish? What will then happen is the process we just described, only in reverse, as we show in Figure 15.2. When output exceeds potential, unemployment will exceed the natural rate. As firms bid for labor, the wage–price spiral will begin, but this time in an upward direction instead of downward, as in Panel B. The short-run aggregate supply curve will shift upward until the economy returns to full employment. That is, wages and prices will rise to return the economy to its long-run equilibrium at full employment.

In summary:
- If output is less than full employment, prices will fall as the economy returns to full employment, as shown in Figure 15.1.
- If output exceeds full employment, prices will rise and output will fall back to full employment, as shown in Figure 15.2.

How long does it take to move from the short run to the long run? Economists disagree on the answer. Some economists estimate that it takes the U.S. economy two years or less, some say six years, others say somewhere in between and others even longer. Because the adjustment process is slow, there is room, in principle, for policy makers to step in and guide the economy back to full employment.

Suppose the economy were operating below full employment at point a in Figure 15.3. One alternative for policy makers would be to do nothing, allowing the economy to adjust itself, with falling wages and prices, until it returns by itself to full employment, point b. This may take several years. During that time, the economy will experience excess unemployment and a level of real output below potential.

Another alternative would be to use expansionary policies, such as open market purchases by the Fed or increases in government spending and tax cuts, to shift the aggregate demand curve to the right. In Figure 15.3, we show how expansionary policies could shift the aggregate demand curve from AD_0 to AD_1 and move the economy to full employment, point c. Notice here that the price level is higher at point c than it would be at point b. The higher price level and bias toward inflation is the price an economy pays for using expansionary policies to speed the recovery from recessions.

☞ Visit the Federal Reserve's Report to the Congress at http://www.federalreserve.gov/boarddocs/hh/ for information about how the Fed uses monetary policy to help the economy adjust.

What if nominal interest rates become so low that they cannot fall any further? Keynes called this situation a **liquidity trap**. When the economy is experiencing a liquidity trap, the adjustment process no longer works. Japan experienced the liquidity trap during the 1990s.

Let's review an Application that answers one of the key questions we posed at the start of the chapter:

1. What went wrong for the Japanese economy during its decade-long economic downturn?

APPLICATION 1: JAPAN'S LOST DECADE

Following World War II, Japan's economy grew rapidly. However, around 1992 it ground to a halt, and by 1993–1994 the country was suffering from a recession. Prices stopped rising, and deflation—falling prices—began in Japan. For Japanese borrowers, falling inflation rates raised the *real* rate of interest they were paying on their preexisting loans, essentially increasing their burden of debt. This made them reluctant to purchase additional goods and services. With fewer loans being made in Japan and fewer goods and services being purchased, aggregate demand was weak.

For a number of years, the United States urged Japan to increase public spending to end its recession. Eventually Japan did try this approach, but policy makers were cautious, because government budget deficits were very large. Nominal interest rates were also very close to zero, making it difficult to use monetary policy to stimulate the economy. Some observers claimed that Japan was suffering from a Keynesian liquidity trap. Restoring the health of the banking system was a major priority. Toward the beginning of the first decade of 2000, the economy began to improve somewhat. Beginning in 2003, the Japanese economy grew by 2.3 percent, up from nearly no growth at all. It was a modest increase in growth, but an increase nonetheless, and it continued for the next several years.

Economists have observed another behavior where fiscal or monetary policy is used for political reasons. Using monetary or fiscal policy in the short run to improve a politician's reelection prospects may produce a **political business cycle**. Here is how a political business cycle might work. About a year or so before an election, a politician might use expansionary monetary policy or fiscal policy to stimulate the economy and lower unemployment. If voters respond favorably to lower unemployment, the incumbent politician may be reelected. After reelection, the politician faces the prospect of higher prices or crowding out. To avoid this, the politician may engage in contractionary policies. The result is a classic political business cycle: Because of actions taken by politicians for reelection, the economy booms before an election but then contracts after the election. Good news comes before the election, and bad news comes later.

Let's review an Application that answers one of the key questions we posed at the start of the chapter:

2.   What are the links between presidential elections and macroeconomic performance?

APPLICATION 2: ELECTIONS, POLITICAL PARTIES, AND VOTER EXPECTATIONS

The original political business cycle theories focused on incumbent presidents trying to manipulate the economy in their favor to gain reelection. Subsequent research began to incorporate other, more realistic factors. The first innovation was to recognize that political parties could have different goals or preferences. The second major innovation was to recognize that the public would anticipate that politicians will try to manipulate the economy. As Professor Alberto Alesina of Harvard University first pointed out, this suggests that economic growth should be less if Republicans win and greater if Democrats win. The postwar U.S. evidence is generally supportive of this theory.

15.3 Understanding the Economics of the Adjustment Process

Recall that when an economy is producing below full employment, the tendency will be for wages and prices to fall. Similarly, when an economy is producing at a level greater than full employment or potential output, the tendency will be for wages and prices to rise. The adjustment process first begins to work as changes in prices affect the demand for money. Recall the real-nominal principle.

 Real-Nominal Principle

What matters to people is the real value of money or income—its purchasing power—not the face value of money or income.

According to this principle, the amount of money that people want to hold depends on the price level in the economy. If prices are cut in half, you need to hold only half as much money to purchase the same goods and services. Decreases in the price level will cause the money demand curve to shift to the left; increases in the price level will shift the money demand curve to the right.

Figure 15.4 shows how the fall in the price level can restore the economy to full employment through money demand, interest rates, and investment without active fiscal or monetary policy. In Panel A, the economy is initially below full employment. The price level falls, stimulating output. In Panel B, the lower price level decreases the demand for money and leads to lower interest rates at point *d*. In Panel C, lower interest rates lead to higher investment spending at point *f*. As the economy moves down the aggregate demand curve from point *a* toward full employment at point *b* in Panel A, investment spending increases along the aggregate demand curve.

Now you should understand why changes in wages and prices restore the economy to full employment. The key is that (1) changes in wages and prices change the demand for money; (2) this changes interest rates, which then affect aggregate demand for goods and services and ultimately GDP.

What can policy makers do if an economy is in a recession but is also in a liquidity trap with nominal rates so close to zero that the natural adjustment process ceases to work? Economists have suggested two solutions to this problem. First, expansionary fiscal policy—cutting taxes or raising government spending—still remains a viable option to increase aggregate demand. Second, the Fed could become extremely aggressive and try to expand the money supply so rapidly that the public begins to anticipate future inflation. If the public expects inflation, the expected real rate of interest (the nominal rate minus the expected inflation rate) can become negative, even if the nominal rate cannot fall below zero. A negative expected real interest rate will tempt firms to invest, and this will increase aggregate demand.

In Figure 15.5, we show the effects of expansionary monetary policy in both the short run and the long run. In the short run, as the supply of money increases, the economy moves from the original equilibrium to point a, with output above potential. But in the long run, the economy returns to point b at full employment but at a higher price level than at the original equilibrium.

Figure 15.6 can help us understand some answers to these questions. Starting at full employment, an increase in the supply of money from M^s_0 to M^s_1 will initially reduce interest rates from r_F to r_0 (from point a to point b) and raise investment spending from I_F to I_0 (point c to point d). We show these changes with the red arrows. The blue arrows show that as the price level increases, the demand for money increases, restoring interest rates and investment to their prior levels—I_F and r_F, respectively. Both money supplied and money demanded will remain at a higher level, though, at point e. When the economy returns to full employment, the levels of real interest rates, investment, and output are precisely the same as they were before the Fed increased the supply of money. The increase in the supply of money had no effect on real interest rates, investment, or output in the long run. Economists call this the **long-run neutrality of money**. In other words, in the long run, changes in the supply of money are neutral with respect to "real" variables in the economy such as labor, capital, and real GDP. For example, if the price of everything in the economy doubles, including your paycheck, you are no better or worse off than you were before.

Another economic phenomenon we observed was crowding out. Starting at full employment, an increase in government spending raises output above full employment. If the economy is at full employment, then expansionary fiscal policy would be inflationary. Using aggregate supply and aggregate supply analysis, we can show crowding out creates upward pressure on wages and prices. As wages and prices increase, the demand for money increases, as shown in Panel A, raising interest rates from r_0 to r_1 (point a to point b) and reducing investment from I_0 to I_1 (point c to point d). The economy returns to full employment, but at a higher level of interest rates and a lower level of investment spending. When policy makers understand crowding out, they must balance the short-run consequences of changes in taxes or spending with the long-run consequences. Sometimes this is quite difficult.

Let's review an Application that answers one of the key questions we posed at the start of the chapter:

3. What explained the decision by the Japanese government to increase taxes in the 1990s when the economy was still suffering from a recession?

APPLICATION 3: AN UNFORTUNATE GAMBLE

As we discussed in the chapter-opening story in Chapter 11, the Japanese government sharply increased taxes on consumption in 1997—just as Japan was in the midst of its prolonged recession. Why did the government do this? The reasons were clear. As the economy slumped, fiscal deficits were increasing, as taxes fell and government spending rose. Policy makers understood that their society was aging rapidly and that this would mean even more demands on the public sector in the near future. They became convinced that the current fiscal deficits plus the inevitable future demands on the government would lead to long-run increases in government spending. Although policy makers were right to consider the long-run consequences of increases in government spending, they made the unfortunate gamble that the short-run effects of the tax increase would not hinder the economy's recovery. They were wrong, because the tax increase prolonged the recession.

15.4 Classical Economics in Historical Perspective

Classical economics refers to a body of economic work developed over time, starting with Adam Smith. Other classical economists—Jean Baptiste Say, David Ricardo, John Stuart Mill, and Thomas Malthus—developed their work during the late eighteenth and nineteenth centuries. Keynes first used the term *classical model* in the 1930s to contrast it with his Keynesian model, which emphasized the difficulties the economy could face in the short run.

Classical economics is often associated with *Say's law,* the doctrine that "supply creates its own demand." To understand Say's law, recall from our discussion of GDP counting in Chapter 5 that production in an economy creates an equivalent amount of income. For example, if GDP is $10 trillion, then production is $10 trillion and $10 trillion in income is generated. The classical economists argued that the $10 trillion of production also created $10 trillion in demand for current goods and services. This meant that there could never be a shortage of demand for total goods and services in the economy, nor any excess.

The debates between Keynesian and classical economists continued for several decades after Keynes developed his theories. In the 1940s, Professors Don Patinkin and Nobel laureate Franco Modigliani clarified the conditions for which the classical model would hold true. In particular, they studied the conditions under which there would be sufficient demand for goods and services when the economy was at full employment. Both economists emphasized that one of the necessary conditions for the classical model to work was that wages and prices be fully flexible—that is, that they adjust rapidly to changes in demand and supply.

In the chapter-opening story, we contrasted John Maynard Keynes with Milton Friedman. Where does he fit into this story? Contrary to Keynes, Friedman believed that the wage–price adjustment mechanism that restored the economy to full employment was reasonably effective. Moreover, he felt that activist government policies often made things worse, not better. For that reason, he preferred that the government not engage in activist stabilization policies.

Activity

Suppose the economy is below full employment in the short run and isn't adjusting to full employment. You are the chief adviser to the ruler of your country. What would you suggest to your ruler? Show what would happen using aggregate supply/aggregate demand graphs. What would happen to prices and output?

Answer

Since the economy is not adjusting, then you might suggest expansionary fiscal or monetary policy. This would cause aggregate demand to increase, shifting to the right. This would be similar to Figure 15.3 in your text. Prices would increase slightly and output would increase to full employment.

Key Terms

Aggregate demand curve: A curve that shows the relationship between the level of prices and the quantity of real GDP demanded.

Crowding out: The reduction in investment, or other component of GDP, in the long run caused by an increase in government spending.

Liquidity trap: A situation in which nominal interest rates are so low, they can no longer fall.

Long-run aggregate supply curve: A vertical aggregate supply curve that reflects the idea that in the long run, output is determined solely by the factors of production.

Long run in macroeconomics: The period of time in which prices have fully adjusted to any economic changes.

Long-run neutrality of money: An increase in the supply of money has no effect on real interest rates, investment, or output in the long run.

Political business cycle: The effects on the economy of using monetary or fiscal policy to stimulate the economy before an election to improve reelection prospects.

Short-run aggregate supply curve: A relatively flat aggregate supply curve that represents the idea that prices do not change very much in the short run and that firms adjust production to meet demand.

Short run in macroeconomics: The period of time in which prices do not change or do not change very much.

Wage–price spiral: The process by which changes in wages and prices causing further changes in wages and prices.

Practice Quiz

(Answers are provided at the end of the Practice Quiz.)

1. Which of the following is a characteristic of the short run in the macroeconomics?
   a. Wages and prices are perfectly flexible.
   b. The level of GDP is determined by the supply of goods and services.
   c. Monetary and fiscal policies can have an impact on demand and GDP.
   d. All of the above

2. Which of the following is a characteristic of the economy in the long run?
   a. In the long run, output is determined by the demand for goods and services in the economy.
   b. In the long run, fiscal and monetary policy can have an impact on demand and GDP.
   c. In the long run, capital, labor, and technological progress play a key role in the determination of GDP.
   d. All of the above

3. When the actual rate of unemployment is above the natural rate of unemployment:
   a. prices tend to fall and wages tend to rise.
   b. prices tend to rise and wages tend to fall.
   c. prices and wages tend to fall.
   d. prices and wages tend to rise.

4. The process by which rising wages cause higher prices, and higher prices prompt workers to ask for higher wages is an illustration of this economic principle:
   a. The marginal principle
   b. The real-nominal principle
   c. The principle of diminishing returns
   d. The principle of opportunity cost

5. The process by which rising wages cause higher prices and higher prices feed higher wages in known as:
   a. the bargaining process.
   b. the escalation process.
   c. the wage–price spiral.
   d. the accelerator principle.

6. Fill in the blanks. When unemployment is above the natural rate, output is _____ potential and wages and prices tend to _____.
   a. above; rise
   b. above; fall
   c. below; rise
   d. below; fall

7. Refer to the figure below. Optimally, this economy should operate:

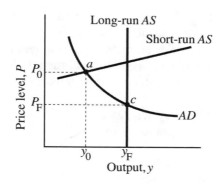

   a.   at y_0, where the economy can reach full employment.
   b.   at y_F, where output coincides with the long-run AS curve.
   c.   at either y_0 or y_F. The economy can do very well in either case.
   d.   at an output level beyond y_F.

8. Refer to the figure below. What is the impact of a decrease in prices and wages on this graph?

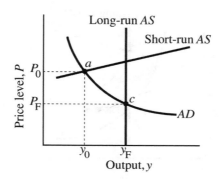

   a.   A shift of the short-run AS curve
   b.   A shift of the long-run AS curve
   c.   A leftward shift of the AD curve
   d.   A rightward shift of the AD curve

9. When the economy is operating below full employment, which of the following can return the economy to full employment with a lower price level?
   a.   An increase in government spending
   b.   A decrease in taxation
   c.   Changes in wages and price that move the economy naturally back to full employment
   d.   All of the above

10. The liquidity trap refers to:
   a.   the need for wages to rise as prices continue to rise.
   b.   the tendency of governments to spend out of control, leaving the country illiquid.
   c.   the failure of nominal interest rates to fall once they reach a certain level.
   d.   the problem that banks face when there is a panic run.

11. This question tests your understanding of Application 1 in this chapter: Japan's lost decade. Why did the natural adjustment process fail to work for the Japanese economy during its decade-long economic downturn? Which of the following accompanied the Japanese deflation of the 1990s?
    a. A steady increase in wholesale prices and real-estate prices
    b. For Japanese borrowers, falling inflation rates raised the real rate of interest they were paying on their preexisting loans, essentially increasing their burden of debt.
    c. Deflation led to very high nominal interest rates, making it difficult to use monetary policy to stimulate the economy.
    d. During the deflation, the banking system gained significant strength, but it wasn't sufficient to bring the economy out of a prolonged recession.

12. A decrease in the price level leads to a(n) _____ the demand for money and a(n) _____ the aggregate demand curve.
    a. increase in; increase in
    b. move along; increase in
    c. decrease in; increase in
    d. decrease in; move along

13. Refer to the figure below. Starting at point a, what is the impact of an increase in the money supply?

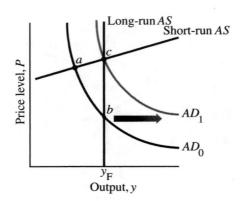

    a. The increase in the money supply is what causes the aggregate demand curve to shift, sending the economy to point c.
    b. The increase in the money supply would bring the economy to point b.
    c. There would be no impact on this economy. The economy remains at point a.
    d. The economy would move from a to c in the short run, and then return to point a in the long run.

14. Fill in the blanks. Starting at full employment, an increase in the supply of money will _____ interest rates and _____ investment spending.
    a. increase; raise
    b. increase; lower
    c. reduce; raise
    d. reduce; lower

15. What economists call the long-run neutrality of money refers to the fact that:
    a. an increase in the supply of money has no effect on real interest rates, investment, or output in the long run.
    b. changes in the supply of money are neutral with respect to nominal variables in the economy in the long run.
    c. changes in interest rates, investment, or output have no effect on the money supply in the long run.
    d. in the long run, changes in the money supply neutralize any changes in investment or output.

16. Refer to the figure below. What could have caused the upward shift in the money demand curve?

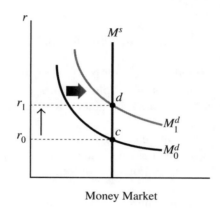

Money Market

    a. An increase in interest rates
    b. An increase in the price level
    c. An increase in the money supply
    d. All of the above

17. The term "classical model" was first used by:
    a. Adam Smith.
    b. John Maynard Keynes.
    c. Alan Greenspan.
    d. Milton Friedman.

18. According to Say's law:
    a. the value of production creates an equivalent amount of income.
    b. there could never be a shortage nor an excess of demand for total goods and services in the economy.
    c. if consumers saved, those savings would eventually turn into investment spending.
    d. All of the above

19. Summarize the differences between the short-run and the long-run in macroeconomics, and the effects of policy on output and employment.

20. Output, wages, and prices rise and fall together. Explain.

21. Suppose that the economy is in short-run equilibrium when output is below the potential level of output. One alternative for the government is to do nothing. What is the other alternative, and what is the difference between the two?

22. In the long run, money is neutral. Explain.

23. Critics of Keynesian economics say that increases in government spending provide only temporary relief and ultimately harm the economy. Explain why.

Answers to the Practice Quiz

1. c. Policies can affect output and employment in the short run but not in the long run.

2. c. In the long run, GDP is determined by the supply of labor, the stock of capital, and technological progress—in other words, the willingness of people to work and the overall "material" the economy has to work with. Full employment is another characteristic of the long run.

3. c. Wages and prices will all tend to increase together during booms when GDP exceeds its full-employment level or potential output. Wages and prices will fall together during periods of recessions when GDP falls below full employment or potential output.

4. b. As prices rise, workers need higher nominal wages to maintain their real wages. This is an illustration of the real-nominal principle.

5. c. The process by which rising wages cause higher prices and higher prices feed higher wages is known as the wage–price spiral.

6. d. When the economy is producing below full employment or potential output, the wage–price spiral works in reverse. Output produced is below potential, and wages and prices tend to fall.

7. b. In the short run, this economy is operating where output is below full employment. Optimally, it should operate at full employment, the long-run equilibrium.

8. a. As long as output is below full employment, prices and wages will fall, shifting the short-run *AS* curve down until full employment is reached.

9. c. Rather than implementing economic policies to increase aggregate demand, policy makers could let the economy naturally return to full employment. This would result in a lower price level in the long run.

10. c. If nominal interest rates become so low that they cannot fall any further, the economy has fallen into what Keynes called a liquidity trap, and the adjustment process no longer works.

11. b. Falling inflation rates result in an increase in the real interest rate on preexisting loans. This causes an increase in the burden of debt and will affect the willingness of people to purchase additional goods and services. With fewer loans being made in Japan and fewer goods and services being purchased, aggregate demand was weak.

12. d. A decrease in the price level leads to a decrease in the demand for money and a move along (not a shift in) the aggregate demand curve.

13. a. As the Fed increases the supply of money, the aggregate demand curve shifts from AD_0 to AD_1. In the long run, the economy returns to long-run equilibrium.

14. c. Starting at full employment, an increase in the supply of money will initially reduce interest rates and raise investment spending.

15. a. Economists call this the long-run neutrality of money. In the long run, changes in the supply of money are neutral with respect to "real" variables in the economy.

16. b. As wages and prices increase, the demand for money increases, raising interest rates and reducing investment.

17. b. The term "classical model" was first used by Keynes to contrast his "Keynesian" or activist model with the conventional economic wisdom of the time that didn't emphasize the difficulties that the economy could face in the short run.

18. d. Say's law is the doctrine that "supply creates its own demand." Since production creates an equivalent amount of income, there could never be a shortage of demand for total goods and services in the economy nor any excess. If consumers saved, those savings would eventually turn into investment spending.

19. In the short run, prices are primarily fixed. Wages and prices do not change—at least not substantially. The level of GDP is determined by the total demand for goods and services. Increases in the money supply, government spending, or tax cuts will lead to an increase in GDP. In the long run, prices are flexible; the level of GDP is determined by the demand and supply for labor, the stock of capital, and technological progress; the economy operates at full employment and the supply of output is fixed. Any increases in government spending must come at the sacrifice of some other use of output.

20. During booms, when GDP exceeds its full employment level, or potential output, wages and prices tend to increase. Firms will offer higher wages because it is more difficult to find, hire, and retain workers. During recessions, when GDP falls below potential output, wages and prices will fall together. When output exceeds potential, wages and prices throughout the economy will rise above previous inflation rates. For example, if the economy had been experiencing 6% annual inflation, prices will rise at a rate faster than 6% per year. If output is less than potential output, wages and prices will fall relative to previous inflation rates.

21. When policy makers do nothing, they allow the economy to adjust itself. A large pool of unemployed workers will put downward pressure on prices. With falling wages and prices, the supply curve will shift downward and to the right until the economy returns to full employment. Rather than waiting for the economy to correct itself, another alternative is to use expansionary fiscal and monetary policies to shift the aggregate demand curve to the right. Both policies result in a return of output to potential output, but the activist policy results in a higher price level than the non-activist policy.

22. In the long run, changes in the money supply are "neutral" with respect to real variables in the economy, that is, they have no effect on real variables, only on prices. However, money is not neutral in the short run. In the short run, changes in the money supply affect interest rates, investment spending, and output. Monetary expansion that initially leads to output above full employment, higher prices and wages, and higher demand for money, eventually results in higher interest rates, lower investment, and a return to full employment. To explain the impact of an increase in the amount of money, suppose that every green dollar was replaced by two blue dollars. Everyone would have twice as many blue dollars as they formerly had of green dollars. Prices and wages quoted in the blue currency would simply be twice as high as for the green dollars. The purchasing power of blue money would be the same as it was for green money; therefore, real wages would be the same.

23. Critics of Keynesian economics say that increases in government spending provide only temporary relief and ultimately harm the economy because it will "crowd out" investment spending in the long run. If government spending crowds out investment spending in the long run, the economy will experience reduced capital deepening and lower levels of real income and wages. On the other hand, decreases in government spending will lead to increases in investment in the long run, which we call crowding-in. Tax cuts can also crowd out investment in the long run. Tax cuts increase consumption; lead to a higher level of GDP; higher prices, wages, and demand for money, thus higher interest rates. Consequently, an increase in consumption will come at the expense of lower investment.

16

The Dynamics of Inflation and Unemployment

Chapter Summary

Economic policy debates often concern inflation and unemployment because they affect us all so directly. In this chapter, we will look at the relationships between inflation and unemployment, examining macroeconomic developments in the United States in the last several decades. We also explore why heads of central banks are known as strong enemies of inflation. Here are the main points of the chapter:

- In the long run, higher money growth leads to higher inflation and higher nominal interest rates.
- A decrease in the growth rate of money will initially lead to higher real-interest rates and higher nominal-interest rates. In the long run, real rates return to their original level; nominal rates are permanently lower because of reduced inflation.
- The rate of inflation increases when actual unemployment falls below the natural rate of unemployment; the rate of inflation decreases when actual unemployment exceeds the natural rate of unemployment. Economists explain this relationship using the expectations Phillips curve.
- How the public forms expectations of inflation and the time frame in which it must form them are important factors in understanding the behavior of inflation and unemployment. Sometimes the public uses rules of thumb to form expectations; other times they may use rational expectations.
- Monetary policy makers need to be cautious about the statements and pronouncements they make because what they say can influence inflation expectations. Conservative central bankers can dampen expectations of inflation.
- The quantity equation and the growth version of the quantity equation show how money, velocity, and nominal income are related.
- Governments sometimes print new money to finance large portions of their budget deficits. Raising funds through printing money is known as seignorage. When governments do this excessively, the result is hyperinflation. Stopping a hyperinflation requires closing the government deficit and ending excessively high rates of money creation.

Applying the Concepts

After reading this chapter, you should be able to answer these three key questions:
1. Do regional differences in unemployment affect the natural rate of unemployment?
2. Can changes in the way central banks are governed affect inflation expectations?
3. Are there bonds that can protect your investments from inflation?

16.1 Money Growth, Inflation, and Interest Rates

An economy can, in principle, produce at full employment with any inflation rate. No "magic" inflation rate is necessary to sustain full employment. To understand this point, consider the long run when the economy operates at full employment. As we have seen, in the long run, money is neutral. If the Federal Reserve increases the money supply at 5 percent a year, annual inflation will be 5 percent. That is, prices in the economy will rise by 5 percent a year.

> ### ⟨⟨ Study Tip
>
> Any change in the money supply will change only prices in the long run. This is the long-run neutrality of money concept you learned in Chapter 15. In the long run, any money supply changes only affect prices.

Let's think about how this economy looks in this "steady state" of constant inflation. The **nominal wages**—wages in current dollars—of workers are all rising at 5 percent a year. However, because prices are also rising at 5 percent a year, **real wages**—nominal wages adjusted for changes in purchasing power—remain constant. Workers suffer from **money illusion**, a confusion of real and nominal magnitudes. Here's the source of the illusion: Because real wages are constant, the only reason their nominal wages are rising by 5 percent a year is the general 5 percent inflation. If there were no inflation, their nominal wages would not increase at all.

People's expectations of inflation affect all aspects of economic life. For example, in the steady-state economy we just described, automobile producers will expect to increase the price of their products by 5 percent every year. They will also expect their costs—of labor and steel, for example—to increase by 5 percent a year. Workers will begin to believe that the 5 percent increases in their wages will be matched by a 5 percent increase in the prices of the goods they buy. Continued inflation becomes the normal state of affairs, and people "build it into" their daily decision-making process. For example, they expect the price of a car to be 5 percent higher next year.

☞ The model in which people form their expectations of the future based on what has happened in the past is called *adaptive expectations*. This model suggests that we basically take past information and adapt our economic behavior for the future.

In Chapter 15, you saw that in the long run, the real rate of interest does not depend on monetary policy because money is neutral. That is, even though the money supply may be higher or lower, the price level will be higher or lower. However, nominal rates of interest do depend on monetary policy because whether the Fed expands or contracts the money supply affects the rate of inflation, which in the long run is determined by the growth of the money supply.

If people expect 5 percent inflation a year, then their demand for money will also increase by 5 percent a year. This is, of course, because people know everything will cost 5 percent more, so they'll need more money in their pockets to pay for the same goods and services. This is an example of the real-nominal principle.

Real-Nominal Principle

What matters to people is the real value of money or income—its purchasing power—not the face value of money or income.

As long as the Fed allows the supply of money to increase by 5 percent—the same amount as inflation—the demand for money and its supply will both grow at the same rate. Because money demand and supply are both growing at the same rate, real interest rates and nominal interest rates will not change.

To continue with our example, suppose the public expects 5 percent annual inflation and both the money supply and money demand grow at 5 percent a year. Now suppose the Fed suddenly decreases the annual growth rate of money to 4 percent, while the public continues to expect 5 percent annual inflation. Because money demand grows at 5 percent but the money supply grows at only 4 percent, the growth in the demand for money will exceed the growth in the supply of money. The result will be an increase in both real interest rates and nominal interest rates.

The economy will eventually adjust to the lower rate of money growth, and inflation will eventually fall from 5 percent to 4 percent per year to match it. In the long run, the *real* rate of interest will eventually fall and return to its previous value. *Nominal* interest rates, which reflect expectations of ongoing inflation, will be 1 percent lower, because inflation has fallen from 5 percent to 4 percent per year.

In summary, in the short run, a policy of tight money leads to slower money growth, higher interest rates, and lower output. But in the long run, reduced money growth results in lower interest rates, lower inflation, and has no effect on the level of output.

16.2 Understanding the Expectations Phillips Curve: The Relationship Between Unemployment and Inflation

From the text reading you learned about A.W. Phillips. Phillips found that lower unemployment was associated with higher inflation. He also noticed that the inflation rate falls when the economy is in a recession and unemployment is high. This inverse relationship became known as the *Phillips curve*. Figure 16.1 shows the Phillips curve relationship.

The relationship between unemployment and inflation, taking into account expectations about inflation, is known as the **expectations Phillips curve**. The expectations Phillips curve included the notion that unemployment varies with *unanticipated inflation*. Actual inflation will then exceed expected inflation. Workers will see their nominal wages increase with the inflation, but because they do not fully expect this sudden inflation, they will think that their real wages have increased. With higher perceived real wages being offered, potential workers will be inclined to accept the jobs firms offer them. As a result, unemployment will fall below the natural rate. That's why we often see an association between increases in the inflation rate and a decrease in the unemployment rate. Table 16.1 summarizes the key points about the expectations Phillips curve.

Two broad classes of theories attempt to explain how the public forms its expectations of inflation. Some economists and psychologists, including Nobel laureate Herbert Simon, believe that the public uses simple *rules-of-thumb* to predict future inflation. A simple rule-of-thumb might be to assume next year's inflation will be the same as this year's inflation. According to this view, it is unreasonable to expect too much sophistication from the public because of the complexity of the economy and forecasting difficulties.

In the 1970s, a group of economists led by Nobel laureate Robert E. Lucas, Jr., from the University of Chicago, developed an alternative view, called the theory of rational expectations. **Rational expectations** theory is the economic theory that analyzes how the public forms expectations in such a manner that, on average, they forecast the future correctly. The rational expectations theory portrayed workers and firms as much more sophisticated and basing their expectations on all the information available to them. According to the theory, the public, on average, anticipates the future correctly. Although the public may make mistakes in specific instances, on average, the public's expectations are rational or correct.

The two approaches—rules-of-thumb versus rational expectations—tend to deliver similar predictions when the economy is very stable and there are no major policy changes. However, when there are major policy changes—for example, when the government introduces new policies to fight inflation or reduce federal deficits—the two approaches predict different outcomes. The rational expectations theory predicts the public will anticipate the consequences of these policies and change its expectations about inflation accordingly; the rule-of-thumb theory says it won't. Which view is correct?

The truth lies somewhere in the middle. On the one hand, sophisticated firms, such as Microsoft or Wal-Mart, do appear to take advantage of available information. On the other hand, there is evidence that a considerable amount of inertia and nonrationality enters into the general public's decision-making process.

Figure 16.1 shows the dynamics of inflation and unemployment from 1986–1993. Inflation rose and the unemployment rate fell below the natural rate. Inflation later fell as unemployment exceeded the natural rate.

What factors can shift the natural rate of unemployment? Economists have identified a number of factors:
- **Demographics.** The composition of the workforce can change, decreasing the natural rate. For example, we know teenagers have higher unemployment rates than adults. If changes in population lead to a lower percentage of teenagers in the labor force, we would expect the natural rate of unemployment to decrease. In the 1990s, there were fewer teenagers than adults in the labor force. This change in demographics appears to have been what caused the natural rate of unemployment to decline in the United States.
- **Institutional changes.** Changes in laws, regulations, and economic institutions can influence the natural rate of unemployment. Suppose the government shortens the length of time unemployed workers can collect benefits. We would then expect the unemployed to return to work more rapidly and the natural rate of unemployment to fall. Some economists have argued that the rise of temporary employment agencies in the United States during the 1990s made the labor market more efficient. Workers were matched more quickly with jobs, and this contributed to the decline of the natural rate. In Europe, a very different set of institutional factors had the opposite result: Generous benefits for the unemployed increased the time they spent unemployed. Restrictions on employers making it difficult to fire workers led to employers hiring fewer of them in the first place. Both these factors raised the natural rate of employment.
- **The state of the economy.** Some economists believe the performance of the economy itself may influence the natural rate of unemployment. Suppose the economy goes into a long recession. During that time, many young people may not be able to find jobs and fail to develop a strong work ethic. Other workers may lose some of their skills during a prolonged period of unemployment. Both factors could lead to longer-term unemployment and an increase in the natural rate of unemployment.
- **Changes in growth of labor productivity.** If the growth rate in labor productivity falls, wages must also rise more slowly because they are tied to productivity increases in the long run. However, if workers don't realize this, they might continue to push for higher nominal wage increases and be less inclined to accept lower nominal wages. This will increase the natural rate of employment. Similarly, if productivity growth is higher than anticipated, wages will rise more quickly, because

firms will be willing to pay more to retain their workers and recruit new ones. As a result of this unexpected productivity growth, workers may not be as aggressive in asking for additional nominal wage increases, because they are pleased with what they are already getting. They will be more inclined to accept these wages, and this will effectively lower the natural rate of unemployment. Some economists believe that this in fact happened in the late 1990s.

Let's review an Application that answers one of the key questions we posed at the start of the chapter:

1. Do regional differences in unemployment affect the natural rate of unemployment?

APPLICATION 1: REGIONAL DIFFERENCES IN UNEMPLOYMENT INCREASE THE NATURAL RATE

At any point in time, some regions of a country may experience difficulties while others prosper. Does this matter when it comes to understanding the behavior of inflation and unemployment? It does, because low unemployment and high unemployment have somewhat different effects on wages. When unemployment is low, firms compete for workers and bid up wages sharply. However, when unemployment is high, it is more difficult for firms to cut wages because workers tend to resist wage cuts. What this means is that even if the total unemployment rate in the country appears to be at the natural rate of unemployment, there could still be upwards inflation pressure if wages increase faster in the low-unemployment regions than they fall in the high-unemployment regions. As a consequence, the greater the differences in unemployment across regions, the higher the natural rate of unemployment will be in the country as a whole.

In 2004, two economists working at the Federal Reserve Bank of St. Louis studied how regional differences in unemployment have varied over time. These economists found that variations were relatively high during the 1980s but fell sharply in the 1990s. This fall in the variations had two implications. First, it meant that the U.S. labor market operated more like a truly national than a regional market in the 1990s. Second, their work strongly suggested that the natural rate of unemployment fell in the 1990s. Based on their analysis, these economists estimated that the effect was quite large and that the natural rate fell by about 2 percentage points—just because differences in unemployment from state to state were smaller.

16.3 How the Credibility of a Nation's Central Bank Affects Inflation

Expectations about the Fed's determination to fight inflation will affect behavior in the private sector. If the Fed is credible or believable in its desire to fight inflation, it can deter the private sector from taking aggressive actions that drive up prices. This is the reason the heads of central banks are conservative, preferring to risk increasing unemployment rather than risk an increase in inflation.

Countries in which central banks are more independent from the rest of the government have, on average, lower inflation rates. As our discussion illustrates, how a central bank influences expectations is important for understanding the behavior of prices and output in an economy. Understanding how the private sector forms its inflation expectations in the first place is also important. Economists have used the theory of rational expectations that we discussed earlier to explain the credibility of central banks.

☞ Sometimes people will respond to information and plan accordingly even to the point of negating the need for the policy to take place. This is called "announcement effect." Some economists argue that sometimes the announcement of a policy is enough for people to take action. This can create lags where the policy becomes ineffective or makes things even worse.

In our example, the theory of rational expectations implies that the union will, on average, anticipate whether the Fed will expand the money supply in the face of wage increases. A credible Fed will tend to deter wage increases by not expanding the money supply. Many economists believed that Fed Chairman Alan Greenspan was more credible than other Fed chairmen in his determination to fight inflation.

Let's review an Application that answers one of the key questions we posed at the start of the chapter:

2. Can changes in the way central banks are governed affect inflation expectations?

APPLICATION 2: INCREASED POLITICAL INDEPENDENCE FOR THE BANK OF ENGLAND LOWERED INFLATION EXPECTATIONS

On May 6, 1997, the Chancellor of Exchequer in Great Britain, Gordon Brown, announced a major change in monetary policy. From that time forward, the Bank of England would be more independent from the government. Although the government would still retain the authority to set the overall goals for policy, the Bank of England would be free to pursue its policy goals without direct political control. Mark Spiegel, an economist with the Federal Reserve Bank of San Francisco, studied how the British bond market reacted to the policy change. He concluded that the announcement did, indeed, cause expectations about inflation to fall by about half a percentage.

 Real-Nominal Principle

What matters to people is the real value of money or income—its purchasing power—not the face value of money or income.

16.4 Inflation and the Velocity of Money

Countries sometimes experience stunning inflation rates. For example, in 15 months from August 1922 to November 1923, the price level in Germany rose by a factor of 10 billion! To explain these extremely high inflation rates and their relationship to money growth, we now introduce a concept that is closely related to money demand: the *velocity of money*.

☑ Key Equation

$$\text{velocity of money} = \frac{\text{nominal GDP}}{\text{money supply}}$$

One useful way to think of velocity is that it is the number of times that money must change hands, or turn over, during a given year for an economy to reach its GDP level. To understand this, consider a simple example. Suppose that nominal GDP is $5 trillion per year and the money supply is $1 trillion. The velocity of money in this economy will be 5. This means that the money supply has to turn over 5 times to purchase the economy's GDP. This leads to an important equation, the **quantity equation**. This equation links money, velocity, prices, and real output. In symbols, we have $M \times V = P \times y$:

☑ **Key Equation**

$M \times V = P \times Y$, where
M is the money supply,
V is the velocity of money,
P is a price index for GDP, and
y is real GDP.

Let's review an Application that answers one of the key questions we posed at the start of the chapter:

3. Are there bonds that can protect your investments from inflation?

APPLICATION 3: INFLATION-INDEXED BONDS IN THE UNITED STATES

In 1997, the U.S. Department of the Treasury created a new financial instrument called the Treasury Inflation-Protected Security, or TIPS. The key feature of TIPS is that the payments to investors adjust automatically to compensate for the actual changes in the Consumer Price Index. Therefore, TIPS provide protection to investors from inflation. Because TIPS compensate for actual inflation, the interest rate on these bonds differs from conventional bonds by the expected inflation rate. By comparing the interest rates on TIPS to other government bonds of similar maturity, economists can estimate the public's expectations of inflation.

M2 is the measure of the money supply that includes currency, demand deposits, savings accounts, time deposits, and deposits in money market mutual funds. Figure 16.4 plots the velocity of M2 in the United States between 1959 and 2005.

The basic quantity equation can be used to derive a closely related formula for understanding inflation in the long run:

☑ **Key Equation**

growth rate of money + growth rate of velocity
= growth rate of prices + growth rate of real output

16.5 Hyperinflation

Economists call very high inflation rates—over 50 percent per month, which is approximately 13,000 percent per year—**hyperinflation**. According to the data in Table 16.2, for a period of one year, Greece had a monthly inflation rate of 365 percent. A monthly inflation rate of 365 percent means the price level rises by a factor of 4.65 each month.

To get a sense of what a 365 percent inflation rate means, suppose that we had inflation of this magnitude in the United States. At the beginning of the month, $1 could buy a large order of French fries. Because prices are rising by a factor of 4.65 each month, by the end of the month it would take $4.65 to buy the same order of French fries, and $1 by the end of the month would be worth only 21.5 cents. After two months, a dollar would be worth only 4.6 cents of its original value. Suppose this inflation continues month after month. After one year, a dollar bill would be worth only 1 millionth of 1 cent!

The value of money deteriorates sharply during hyperinflations and no longer serves as a good store of value. In these extreme circumstances, we would expect that people wouldn't want to hold money very long but would immediately try to spend it. In other words, we would expect the velocity of money to increase sharply during hyperinflations. During hyperinflations, money doesn't facilitate exchange well. Because prices are changing so fast and unpredictably, there is typically massive confusion about the true value of commodities. Different stores may be raising prices at different rates, so the same commodities may sell for radically different prices.

Table 16.3 presents data on three hyperinflations during the 1980s—in Bolivia, Argentina, and Nicaragua—all averaging about 100 percent per month. On the basis of the quantity theory, we suspect that these hyperinflations must have all been caused by money growth. For example, in Greece, the monthly inflation of 365 percent was accompanied by money growth of 220 percent. In Hungary, the monthly inflation of 19,800 percent was accompanied by money growth of 12,200 percent.

If the cause of hyperinflations is excessive money growth, why do governments allow the money supply to grow so fast, risking economic catastrophe? The answer lies in understanding how some governments finance their deficits—the gap between government spending and revenues. Governments can either issue debt or print money. The revenue raised from money creation is called **seignorage**. In principle, governments can do a combination of both—selling bonds and printing money—as long as the deficit is covered:

☞ The German hyperinflation after World War I was severe. In Germany, people would rush out to spend the day's wages as fast as possible, knowing that only a few hours' inflation would deprive today's wages of most of their purchasing power. One source says that people might buy a bottle of wine in the expectation that on the following morning, the empty bottle could be sold for more than it had cost when full. Those with goods to barter resorted to barter to get food; those with nothing to barter suffered.

To end hyperinflation, governments must eliminate their budget deficits by either increasing taxes, cutting spending, or both. This, of course, will cause some economic pain. There is, however, no other remedy. Once the deficit has been cut and the government stops printing money, the hyperinflation will end. Without money growth to feed it, hyperinflation will quickly die of starvation.

Economists who emphasize the role that the supply of money plays in determining nominal income and inflation are called **monetarists**. The most famous monetarist is Milton Friedman, who studied complex versions of the quantity equation and explored the role of money in all aspects of economic life. The work of Friedman and other monetarists was extremely influential in changing opinions of economic thinkers. Moreover, they were also insistent that, in the long run, inflation was a monetary problem. Today, most economists agree with the monetarists that, in the long run, inflation is caused by growth in the money supply.

Activity

Suppose that the growth of real output is 3 percent and the growth rate of velocity is 4 percent. If the growth rate of money increased 10 percent, what would happen to the growth rate of prices?

Answer

Use the key equation:
growth rate of money + growth rate of velocity = growth rate of prices + growth rate of real output
10% + 4% = growth rate of prices + 3%
Solving for the growth rate of prices gives us a value of 11%.

Key Terms

Expectations of inflation: The beliefs held by the public about the likely path of inflation in the future.

Expectations Phillips curve: The relationship between unemployment and inflation, taking into account expectations of inflation.

Growth version of the quantity equation: An equation that links the growth rates of money, velocity, prices, and real output.

Hyperinflation: An inflation rate exceeding 50 percent per month.

Monetarists: Economists who emphasize the role that the supply of money plays in determining nominal income and inflation.

Money illusion: Confusion of real and nominal magnitudes.

Nominal wages: Wages expressed in current dollars.

Quantity equation: The equation that links money, velocity, prices, and real output. In symbols, we have $M \times V = P \times y$.

Rational expectations: The economic theory that analyzes how the public forms expectations in such a manner that, on average, they forecast the future correctly.

Real wages: Nominal or dollar wages adjusted for changes in purchasing power.

Seignorage: Revenue raised from money creation.

Velocity of money: The rate at which money turns over during the year. It is calculated as nominal GDP divided by the money supply.

Practice Quiz

(Answers are provided at the end of the Practice Quiz.)

1. If the Federal Reserve increases the money supply at 5% a year, in the long run there will be:
   a. 5% annual inflation.
   b. something less than 5% annual inflation.
   c. something greater than 5% annual inflation.
   d. no inflation.

2. Suppose that the annual rate of inflation is persistently 5%. After a time, everyone in the economy would begin to expect that the 5% annual inflation that had occurred in the past would continue in the future. Economists call this:
   a. money illusion.
   b. a liquidity trap.
   c. a wage–price spiral.
   d. expectations of inflation.

3. In the long run, the rate of inflation is determined by:
   a. the level of unemployment.
   b. the deviation of output away from potential output.
   c. the growth of real GDP.
   d. the growth of the money supply.

4. In the short run, a policy of tight money leads to:
   a. higher money growth, higher interest rates, and lower output.
   b. slower money growth, higher interest rates, and lower output.
   c. lower interest rates, lower inflation, and no effect on the level of output.
   d. lower interest rates, lower inflation, and lower output.

5. The expectations Phillips curve involves the notion that:
   a. inflation exists in the short run but not in the long run.
   b. real interest rates and nominal interest rates will change with expectations of inflation.
   c. only expected inflation affects output and employment.
   d. unemployment varies with unanticipated inflation.

6. According to the theory of rational expectations:
   a. workers and firms base their expectations on all available information.
   b. the public uses simple rules-of-thumb to predict future inflation.
   c. there is no valid formulation of how individuals form their expectations.
   d. individuals expect tomorrow to be like it was today.

7. What factors cause the natural rate of unemployment to shift over time?
   a. Demographics and the composition of the workforce
   b. Institutional changes
   c. Changes in the growth of labor productivity
   d. All of the above

8. This question tests your understanding of Application 1 in this chapter: Do regional differences in unemployment affect the natural rate of unemployment?

    At any point in time, some regions of a country may experience difficulties while others prosper. For example, high oil prices will simultaneously benefit oil producers in Texas but hurt businesses and consumers in northern states like Vermont that rely heavily on natural gas for heating. Likewise, recessions can affect different parts of the country in different ways.

    Do regional differences in unemployment affect the natural rate of unemployment?
    a. No. Differences in unemployment across regions do not affect the natural rate of unemployment.
    b. Yes. The greater the differences in unemployment across regions, the higher the natural rate of unemployment will be in the country as a whole.
    c. Yes, but only if wages fall in low-unemployment regions and rise in the high-unemployment regions.
    d. No. Economists have found that variations in the unemployment rate across regions is very small, and insufficient to have an effect on the natural rate of unemployment.

9. Refer to the figure below. An increase in the money supply is best described by:

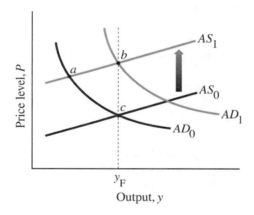

    a. the shift in the *AD* curve.
    b. the shift in the *AS* curve.
    c. the move along the *AD* curve.
    d. None of the above

10. Refer to the figure below. After the upward shift in the AS curve, from AS_0 to AS_1, how can the economy return to full employment at the original price level?

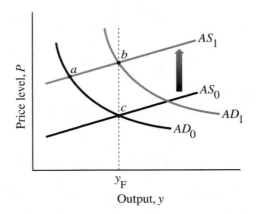

a. If the Fed keeps aggregate demand constant
b. If the Fed increases aggregate demand
c. If the Fed increases the money supply
d. If the Fed decreases aggregate supply

11. Countries that have central banks that are more independent have, on average:
a. higher inflation rates.
b. lower inflation rates.
c. higher rates of output growth.
d. lower rates of output growth.

12. The equation of exchange, or quantity equation, links:
a. the demand for money, the supply of money, and nominal GDP.
b. the money supply, velocity, and nominal GDP.
c. money, prices, interest rates, and real GDP.
d. money to the quantity of output supplied and demanded.

13. To determine the growth rate of prices, we need to know the:
a. growth rate of the money supply.
b. growth rate of velocity.
c. growth rate of real output.
d. All of the above

14. Fill in the blanks. As inflation rises, the price level _____ and each dollar is worth _____.
a. rises; less
b. rises; more
c. falls; more
d. falls; less

15. The history of hyperinflations includes:
a. mostly ancient events. Recently, no country has experienced hyperinflation.
b. recent events. Hyperinflations have occurred in recent times as well as the past.
c. mostly elusive data. No one seems able to identify a single incident.
d. common occurrences in the United States.

16. Which of the following is the most desirable measure to stop hyperinflation?
    a. Eliminate the government deficit.
    b. Print more money.
    c. Stop borrowing from the public.
    d. Eliminate the government.

17. The nominal interest rate equals the real interest rate plus the expected rate of inflation. Explain how an increase in the money supply will affect this equality in the long run.

18. According to the expectations Phillips curve, unemployment varies with unanticipated inflation. Explain.

19. List the factors that affect the natural rate of unemployment.

20. Explain how the credibility of the monetary authority affects the decisions of union workers to ask for higher wages.

21. Budget deficits can be financed by borrowing from the public or printing money. Which of the two causes hyperinflation?

Answers to the Practice Quiz

1. b. In the long run, the inflation rate will be money supply growth minus the growth in real GDP.

2. d. After a time, everyone in the economy would begin to expect that the 5% annual inflation that had occurred in the past would continue in the future. Economists call this "expectations of inflation." Continued inflation becomes the normal state of affairs, and people "build it into" their daily decision-making process.

3. d. Monetary policy affects the rate of inflation, which in the long run is determined by the growth of the money supply.

4. b. In the short run, a policy of tight money leads to slower money growth, higher interest rates, and lower output.

5. d. The relationship between unemployment and inflation when there are expectations about inflation is known as the expectations Phillips curve. The expectations Phillips curve involves the notion that unemployment varies with unanticipated inflation.

6. a. The theory of rational expectations holds that workers and firms base their expectations on all available information.

7. d. Those factors and the state of the economy all affect the natural rate of unemployment.

8. b. It does, because low unemployment and high unemployment have somewhat different effects on wages. When unemployment is low, firms compete for workers and bid up wages sharply. However, when unemployment is high, it is more difficult for firms to cut wages because workers tend to resist wage cuts. What this means is that even if the total unemployment rate in the country appears to be at

the natural rate of unemployment, there could still be upwards inflation pressure if wages increase faster in the low-unemployment regions than they fall in the high-unemployment regions.

9. a. An increase in the money supply lowers interest rates and increases investment spending, causing the aggregate demand curve to shift rightward.

10. a. If the aggregate supply curve shifts from AS_0 to AS_1. If the Fed keeps aggregate demand constant at AD_0, a recession will occur and the economy will eventually return to full employment at the original price level. If the Fed increases aggregate demand, the economy remains at full employment but with a higher price level.

11. b. Central banks that have true independence from the rest of government will be more credible in their commitment to fight inflation. And, in fact, central banks that are more independent have, on average, lower inflation rates.

12. b. The quantity equation is MS times V = nominal GDP. If velocity is predictable, we can use the quantity equation and the supply of money to predict nominal GDP.

13. d. Growth rate of the money supply + growth rate of velocity = growth rate of prices + growth rate of real output.

14. a. For example, with a monthly rate of inflation of 365%, the price level rises by a factor of 4.65 each month. At the end of the month, it will take $4.65 to buy a good that was $1. The dollar is worth only 21.5 cents then. And, at the end of two months, it is worth only 4.6 cents.

15. b. Several countries, like Argentina, Bolivia, and Nicaragua, experienced it during the 1980s.

16. a. To stop hyperinflation, it is necessary to eliminate the government deficit. Once the government stops printing money, the hyperinflation will end.

17. In the long run, changes in the money supply do not affect real variables, including the real interest rate. But nominal rates, which depend on the rate of inflation, will be affected by the growth of the money supply. Because of inflation, countries with higher money growth typically have higher nominal interest rates than the nominal interest rates in countries with lower money growth rates. Money demand is also affected by expectations of inflation. Inflation increases the demand for money to match the expected increase in inflation.

18. The expectations Phillips curve shows the relationship between unemployment and inflation. The impact of recessions and booms on prices and wages is more complex when we take into account ongoing inflation. Suppose the economy is operating at full employment. Wages and prices rise at the rate expected by workers and firms. However, if the economy surges ahead of potential output, the unemployment rate will fall below the natural rate, and inflation will tend to rise. The actual rate of inflation will be higher than the expected (or anticipated) rate of inflation. Similarly, when unemployment is above the natural rate, actual inflation will be lower than expected.

19. Four main factors affect the natural rate of unemployment: 1) Demographics: the composition of the labor force can change the natural rate. For example, if teenagers, who have higher unemployment rates, comprise a higher percentage of the labor force, we would expect the natural rate to increase. 2) Institutional changes: changes in laws, regulations, and economic institutions can influence the natural rate of unemployment. 3) The state of the economy can affect the natural rate when the skills of unemployed workers erode or new workers fail to gain experience and/or a work ethic because of

the lack of jobs. 4) Changes in labor productivity can affect the natural rate of unemployment when workers' demands for payment match the old productivity growth and not the new. If worker productivity is rising faster than before, then with normal wage growth, the labor cost of production will fall and employment can rise above its normal level—the natural rate of unemployment will fall. The opposite would happen when labor productivity rises more slowly.

20. If a union negotiates a very high nominal wage and other unions follow, prices will begin to rise. The aggregate supply curve will shift leftward, causing a recession in the economy. The Fed can do nothing, keeping the money supply constant, and allowing the economy to fall into a recession. Alternatively, the Fed can increase the money supply and raise aggregate demand. This will keep the economy at full employment but lead to higher prices. If union leaders believe that the Fed will not increase aggregate demand, their actions will trigger a recession, so they will hesitate to negotiate higher wages. If the Fed is more likely to increase aggregate demand, the union will increase the nominal wage, resulting in higher prices in the economy. If the Fed is credible in its desire to fight inflation, it can deter the private sector from taking aggressive actions that drive up wages and prices.

21. Hyperinflations occur when governments cannot borrow from the public and resort to printing new money. The public is not interested in buying the bonds of a risky government. To stop hyperinflation, it is necessary to eliminate the government deficit. Once the government stops printing money, the hyperinflation will end.

17

Macroeconomic Policy Debates

Chapter Summary

As a student and citizen, you are inevitably drawn into economic debates. In most cases, the debates are complex, because they involve a mixture of facts, theories, and opinions. Value judgments play a large role in economic debates. In previous chapters, you learned the basic vocabulary of economics and studied different theories of the economy. Now you are ready to examine some of the key policy issues in macroeconomics. Here are the main points of the chapter:

- A deficit is the difference between the government's current expenditures and revenue. The government debt is the sum of all past yearly deficits.
- Deficits can be financed through either borrowing or money creation. Financing deficits through money creation is called monetizing the deficit. It leads to inflation.
- Deficits can be good for the country. Automatic stabilizers and expansionary fiscal policy both work through the creation of deficits.
- The national debt involves two burdens: The national debt can reduce the amount of capital in an economy, leading to lower levels of income; it can also result in higher taxes that future generations will have to pay.
- A number of developed countries have recently changed their monetary policy to emphasize targeting the inflation rate or a range for the inflation rate.
- Although targeting inflation can increase the credibility of a central bank, it does limit the tools left for active stabilization policy.
- A consumption tax would increase the incentives for private saving. However, it is not clear that total savings would necessarily increase, and there would be concerns about the fairness of this form of taxation.

Applying the Concepts

After reading this chapter, you should be able to answer these three key questions:
1. What are the long-term fiscal imbalances for the United States?
2. What does the current chairman of the Federal Reserve think about inflation targeting?
3. What type of tax is the "flat tax"?

᎒Ꮧ **Study Tip**

This chapter deals with macroeconomic issues. This is a chance to apply concepts you learned in previous chapters. If you have forgotten some of the key terms, review them from previous chapters. Also, look for both sides of the issues. Find the pros and cons of the issue.

17.1 Should We Balance the Federal Budget?

To balance a budget, we need to review some terms from Chapter 10. **Government expenditures** include goods and services purchased by the government and transfer payments, such as Social Security and welfare, made to citizens. A **surplus** occurs when the government's tax revenues exceed its expenditures in a given year. The government runs a **deficit** when it spends more than it receives in tax revenues from either taxes or fees in a given year.

ᗌ **Caution!**

Many people confuse the debt and deficits. Remember that the deficit is when the government spends more than it takes in revenue for a fiscal year. The government debt is the total of all yearly deficits over time.

The **government debt** is the *total* of all its yearly deficits. For example, if a government initially had a debt of $100 billion and then ran deficits of $20 billion the next year, $30 billion the year after that, and $50 billion during the third year, its total debt at the end of the third year would be $200 billion.

ᗌ **Caution!**

In this chapter, we focus on the debt held by the public, not the total federal debt, which includes debt held by other governmental agencies. Sometimes popular accounts in the press or on the Web highlight the total federal debt. However, the debt held by the public is the best measure to assess the burden that the federal debt can have on the economy.

☞ Go to the following Web sites for the latest information about the national debt:
- www.publicdebt.treas.gov/opd/odpdodt.htm
- www.brillig.com/debt_clock

The Budget in Recent Decades

Beginning in the 1980s and through most of the 1990s, the federal budget ran large deficits—"deficits as far as the eye can see," as David Stockman, the director of the Office of Management and Budget in President Reagan's administration, put it. Yet in fiscal year 1998, during President Clinton's administration, the federal government ran a budget surplus of $69 billion—its first surplus in 30 years. It continued to run surpluses for the next three fiscal years as well. What caused the change?

The surplus emerged for two key reasons:
1. Economic growth was very rapid and tax revenues—including tax revenues from the sales of stocks and bonds—grew more quickly than anticipated.
2. Federal budget rules were in place that limited total spending.

When President George W. Bush took office in January 2001, the large surplus led him to propose that substantial tax cuts be made. Bush and Congress then passed a 10-year tax cut amounting to $1.35 billion over the course of the decade. Although the tax cuts were large, the Congressional Budget Office (CBO) estimated at that time that the federal government would nonetheless continue to run surpluses through 2010.

Figure 17.1 depicts the debt-to-GDP ratio from 1791 to 2005. Notice, except for the period in the 1980s, the ratio rises sharply during wars and falls during peacetime. With neither a war nor a recession looming on the horizon in early 2001, the CBO predicted the debt-GDP ratio would be relatively low by the end of the decade.

Unfortunately, a series of events intervened to bring deficits back into the picture. The Bush tax cuts, collapse of the stock market, and the recession that began in 2001 sharply reduced tax revenues. Additional tax cuts subsequently passed to stimulate the economy added to the deficit. The terrorist attacks in 2001 also led to higher spending on homeland security and financing the wars that were launched in Afghanistan and Iraq. As a result, in 2006, the CBO forecasted that the debt-to-GDP ratio would not decrease, as previously predicted, but stay in the recent historical range of approximately 40 percent. The federal government ran a budget deficit of over $300 billion in fiscal year 2005, a far cry from surpluses in the late 1990s.

The Budget and Social Security

Federal budget figures include revenue and expenditures from the Social Security system. Over the next decade, the Social Security portion of the budget is expected to run a surplus because of the huge number of baby boomers, those born between 1946 and 1964, currently paying taxes into the system. That surplus won't last forever, though. Some economists argue that Social Security funds should not be included in federal budget figures because the money will be needed to make future Social Security payments to these baby boomers. Over the longer horizon, the surpluses in the Social Security account will disappear and turn to deficits. As our society grows older, spending on both Social Security and Medicare will increase. That increase in spending is causing the CBO to predict emerging federal deficits and sharp increases in the debt-to-GDP ratio to levels comparable to World War II, unless taxes are raised and/or spending is cut significantly.

Five Debates about Deficits

As we have seen, federal budgets are affected by a wide range of factors, including wars, demographic pressures, recessions, and the choices our politicians make on spending and taxes. But what principles should policy makers use to make decisions about cutting and raising taxes and evaluating the national debt? Let's take a look at the debates over the national debt.

Debate One: Do Deficits Lead to Inflation?

In the United States, the Treasury Department issues government bonds to finance the deficit. The Federal Reserve has the option of buying existing government bonds, including those newly issued by the Treasury Department. If the Federal Reserve does purchase the government's bonds, the purchase creates money by taking debt out of the hands of the public in exchange for money. Economists call the purchase by a central bank of newly issued government debt **monetizing the deficit**. If governments finance deficits by creating new money, the result will be inflation.

Debate Two: Is Government Debt a Burden on Future Generations?

The national debt, another commonly used term for total government debt, can impose two different burdens on society, both of which fall on the shoulders of future generations. First, a large debt can reduce the amount of capital in the economy and thereby reduce future income and real wages for its citizens. The result of government deficits is that less savings are available to firms for investment. This illustrates one of our basic principles in economics.

 Principle of Opportunity Cost

The opportunity cost of something is what you sacrifice to get it.

Reduced saving and investment will ultimately reduce the stock of private capital. As a result, there will be less capital deepening. With lower capital per worker, real incomes and real wages will be lower than they otherwise might have been. The government deficit comes at a cost in the future. Second, a large national debt will mean that higher taxes will be imposed on future generations to pay the interest that accumulates on the debt. More income is used to pay the interest on the debt than in more productive purposes. Just like your college loans, the bill eventually comes due—even for the national debt.

Sometimes you hear that these interest payments are not a real burden because "we owe the national debt to ourselves." This is a misleading argument for several reasons. First, we don't owe the interest payments only to ourselves. In 2006, approximately 53 percent of U.S. public debt was held by foreigners. Second, a high proportion of the debt is held by older, wealthy individuals or by institutions, but the taxes levied to service it will be paid by everyone in the United States. Some economists do not believe that government deficits, resulting in government debt, impose a burden on a society. These economists believe in **Ricardian equivalence**, the proposition that it does not matter whether government expenditure is financed by taxes or financed by issuing debt.

Consider the following example. A government initially has a balanced budget. It then cuts taxes and issues new debt to finance the deficit left by the reduction in taxes. Everyone understands that the government will have to raise taxes in the future to service the debt, so everyone increases savings to pay for the taxes that will be increased in the future. If saving rises sufficiently, the public—everyone—will be able to purchase the new debt without reducing the funds they invest in the private sector. Because net investment doesn't decline, there will be no debt burden. As you can see, Ricardian equivalence requires that savings by the private sector increase when the deficit increases. Do savers behave this way? It is actually difficult to provide a definite answer because many other factors must be taken into account in any empirical studies of savings. It appears, however, that during the early 1980s, savings decreased somewhat when government deficits increased. This is precisely opposite to what Ricardian equivalence predicts. As long as Ricardian equivalence does not fully hold true, it's reasonable to assume the government debt imposes a burden on society.

Debate Three: Do Deficits Affect the Size of Government?

Nobel laureate James Buchanan has argued that people are less aware of government deficits than the taxes they're forced to pay. Therefore, financing government expenditures through deficits, rather than through higher taxes, will inevitably lead to higher government spending and bigger government. Buchanan's argument does not hold true for two reasons. First, in recent U.S. history, spending by state and local governments has grown much faster than federal spending. However, state and local governments face many more restrictions when it comes to borrowing money than the federal government faces. For example, many states require legislators to run a balanced budget. Deficit spending isn't allowed.

☞ Many state budgets are divided into two budgets, an operating budget and a capital budget. States often require the operating budget to be balanced, while the capital budget can be financed with bond financing. The federal budget is an omnibus budget, meaning that all spending, operating and capital spending come under one budget. Many states would have deficits if they used an omnibus budget like the federal government.

Second, if Buchanan's argument were true, why did the federal government run surpluses in the late 1990s if politicians trying to get reelected prefer higher government spending and deficits to higher taxes and surpluses? More recent thinking suggests that deficits can be used strategically to actually reduce the growth of government. During the 1980s, for example, the government ran large deficits caused by a combination of a deep recession and major tax cuts. The deficits subsequently made it difficult for politicians to propose new spending programs. Proponents of smaller government, therefore, may wish to cut taxes to reduce surpluses or increase deficits in order to make it more difficult for other politicians to increase government spending. These deficit proponents want to create deficits to prevent "putting sand in Congress's sandbox." Some Congressmen supported President Bush's tax cut in 2001, which reduced the surplus over a 10-year period, precisely for this reason.

Debate Four: Can Deficits Be Good for an Economy?

Deficits automatically emerge during recessions, which also stabilize the economy. Recall how automatic stabilizers work. As incomes fall during a recession, so do tax payments. Moreover, transfer payments such as welfare and food stamps rise. Because government spending increases while tax revenues fall, the deficit must, of course, rise. However, a rising deficit may be what it takes to steer the economy back to full employment.

Professor Robert Barro of Harvard University has argued that it is more efficient to keep tax rates relatively constant than to raise them sharply and then lower them later. Temporarily raising tax rates to very high levels could cause distortions in economic behavior that we would like to avoid. Thus, by running deficits and only gradually raising taxes later to service the debt, we avoid creating excess distortions in the economy.

Let's review an Application that answers one of the key questions we posed at the start of the chapter:

1. What are the long-term fiscal imbalances for the United States?

APPLICATION 1: NEW METHODS TO MEASURE THE LONG-TERM FISCAL IMBALANCES FOR THE UNITED STATES

Over time, there will be an escalating gap between revenues and expenditures, which would have to be met by outright borrowing. How can we measure the size of the gap? Economists Jagadeesh Gokhale of the Cato Institute and Kent Smetters of the University of Pennsylvania have developed a more comprehensive measure of a nation's indebtedness. The method includes estimating the present value of the gap between the government's revenues and expenditures and adding it to the current national debt. This new total measure, which Gokhale and Smetters call the "fiscal imbalance," was calculated in 2003 to be approximately $44 trillion, or four times GDP. This is a huge number. Even during World War II, government debt was only 1.2 times GDP. Gokhale and

Smetters estimate that about 80 percent of the fiscal imbalance will stem from Medicare—rising health-care costs for the elderly. What these numbers suggest is that our current health-care system for retirees will need to undergo fundamental reform to make it more sustainable.

Debate Five: Would a Balanced-Budget Amendment Really Work?

How would a balanced-budget amendment actually work? Many different budgetary Constitutional amendments have been proposed. They all require that, after a phase-in period, Congress propose in each fiscal year a budget in which total revenues (excluding borrowing) cover total expenditures. The amendments also have various escape clauses—for example, to allow borrowing during wartime. Some amendments also allow Congress to suspend the requirement to balance the budget for other reasons, such as during a recession when deficits naturally emerge. Finally, some versions of the amendment would limit the rate of spending increases to the rate at which GDP is growing.

Proponents of the balanced-budget amendment say that it will finally exert discipline on the federal government, preventing large deficits in peacetime, such as those that occurred in the 1980s. With a balanced budget, we could be sure to avoid the effects of deficits: reduced capital formation and shifting tax burdens onto future generations.

Critics of a balanced-budget amendment point to many different problems, such as the following:
- A balanced budget may not allow enough flexibility, or room, for the government to effectively deal with recessions. Under some versions of the amendment, unless three-fifths of Congress votes to suspend requirements, the government would have to cut expenditures or raise taxes during a recession. This would make the recession worse and limit the ability of the government to use fiscal policy to stabilize the economy.
- The Constitution is not the right mechanism to try to enforce complicated budget rules. As various interested parties challenge the actions of Congress, the courts would become heavily involved in federal budget matters.
- Congress could devise special budgets to get around the requirement, for example, by taking some types of spending "off budget," which means simply not counting them as part of the official budget.
- Congress could also find nonbudgetary ways to carry out the policies that it desires. For example, it could issue more regulations or impose mandates or requirements on businesses or other governments to carry out its will. These regulations or mandates could be even more costly to the economy than added deficits.

17.2 Should the Fed Target Inflation?

In Chapter 6, we examined some of the costs of inflation, which include the following:
- Menu costs—the costs firms incur to change their posted prices.
- Shoe-leather costs—the costs individuals and firms pay for the time and resources they spend trying to reduce their holdings of money.
- Distortions in our tax and banking systems because inflation isn't yet factored into them.
- Arbitrary redistributions of money between debtors and creditors from unanticipated inflation.

Debate One: Should the Fed Focus Only on Inflation?

Proponents of inflation targeting argue that the Fed should have only one primary goal: controlling inflation. Other proponents of inflation targeting hold a somewhat less rigid view. Although these proponents believe fighting inflation should be the primary objective of the Fed, or a central bank, they believe an inflation-targeting regimen could be designed to give the central bank some flexibility. For example, the central bank could be required to target a broader range of inflation—say, between 1 and 3 percent—and meet the target several years in the future. This position is consistent with the views of the current chairman of the Federal Reserve, Ben Bernanke.

If monetary policy is geared solely toward controlling inflation, as inflation-targeting proponents would like, and fiscal policies are difficult for Congress and the president to pass, that leaves the government no other tools to fight a recession. Economists also debate the level for an inflation target. Suppose there were general agreement that the ultimate goal should be total price stability—that is, zero inflation. There would still be legitimate questions about what constitutes "stable" prices. Some economists like the idea of the Fed having to meet targets, but they have suggested alternatives to inflation targeting. One alternative would be for the Fed to target the growth rate in nominal GDP instead of inflation. Critics of stabilization policy, of course, believe that not using monetary policy to try to stabilize the economy would actually improve our economic performance.

Let's review an Application that answers one of the key questions we posed at the start of the chapter:

2.   What does the current chairman of the Federal Reserve think about inflation targeting?

APPLICATION 2: BERNANKE ON INFLATION TARGETING

Before he took over as chairman of the Federal Reserve in 2006, Ben Bernanke was an advocate for inflation targeting. While he was a member of the Board of Governors in 2003, Bernanke gave a speech outlining his own views on the merits of inflation targeting. For Bernanke, inflation targeting increased the effectiveness of monetary policy because it provided a long-term anchor for inflation expectations. He called inflation targeting a policy of *constrained discretion.* Under inflation targeting, the Fed could take actions to offset shocks to real output or to the financial system, but it had to keep its long-run inflation targets in clear view. Furthermore, to build confidence in the Federal Reserve, Bernanke advocated that the Fed publish its inflation targets and make available its own forecasts of inflation for the next two years.

Debate Two: If There Were an Inflation Target, Who Would Set It?

In the United Kingdom, which adopted inflation targeting in 1992, the elected government decides on the inflation target for the central bank. These elected officials typically specify a range for the inflation rate that the bank must meet. The central bank is heavily involved in the discussions and has an opportunity to present its views to the public through its publications and published minutes of its meetings. But ultimately, it is the elected government that makes the final decision. In other countries, the central bank has even more influence in setting the inflation target. In New Zealand, for example, the central bank has the responsibility of "achieving and maintaining stability in the general level of prices" without any competing goals, such as stabilizing employment or output. Under current law in the United States, the Fed chairman reports regularly to Congress, but the Fed has considerable power to use monetary policy to stabilize output as well as to fight inflation as it pleases.

17.3 Should We Tax Consumption Rather Than Income?

The U.S. tax system discourages savings. Here's how. In the United States, you must pay taxes on both the wages you earn and the interest you earn on your savings. Suppose that you earn $100 at your job and you have a tax rate of 20 percent. That means you keep $80 after taxes. Now suppose that you save $50 of that money and invest it at 10 percent. At the end of one year, you will have earned an additional $5 on the $50 you saved (10% x $50), but you will get to keep only $4 of it because the government will take $1 in taxes (20% x $5). So, you will have to pay the government $21 in total: $20 on the $100 you earned in wages, plus $1 on the $5 you earned on your savings. If you did not save at all, you would pay only $20 in taxes, not $21.

Not all tax systems work this way. Consumption tax systems do not penalize individuals who save. Sales taxes in the United States and value added taxes abroad are familiar examples of consumption taxes. It is also possible to create a consumption tax from an income tax by not taxing the earnings on savings—just as we do with tax-exempt bonds issued by state and municipal governments. Or, as an alternative, the government could allow savings to be deducted from gross income before the calculation for total taxes owed is made. The key feature of consumption taxation is that you do not face any additional taxes if you decide to save more of your income.

Debate One: Will Consumption Taxes Lead to More Savings?

Taxing consumption instead of savings creates an incentive to save. However, there's no guarantee the incentive will actually result in more money saved in the economy. The tax system imposed on corporations in the United States also creates disincentives to save and invest. Suppose you purchase a share of stock in a corporation. When the corporation earns a profit, it pays taxes on the profit at the corporate tax rate. When the corporation pays you a dividend on the stock out of the profits it earns, you must pay taxes on the dividend income that you receive. Corporate income is taxed twice, in other words—first when it is earned by the corporation and again when it is paid out to shareholders.

Some economists have argued that the corporate taxes lead to less-efficient investment because they result in capital flowing into other sectors of the economy (into real estate, for example) that do not suffer from double taxation. For this reason, in 2003 Congress passed a bill introduced by President Bush that lowered—but did not eliminate— taxes on corporate dividends.

Debate Two: Are Consumption Taxes Fair?

The basic idea behind a consumption tax seems fair. Individuals should be taxed on what they consume—not on what they actually produce. However, moving to a consumption-tax system could clearly favor wealthy and high-income individuals who save the most and earn a lot of income in interest, dividends, rents, and capital gains. Table 17.1 shows estimates based on the capital gains received by different income classes for the year 2003. **Capital gains** are the profits investors earn when they sell stocks, bonds, real estate, or other assets. As you can see, taxpayers with annual incomes exceeding $500,000 earned over half of the economy's capital gains over this period. Obviously, capital assets are highly concentrated among the wealthy. If capital gains and other types of capital income were not taxed, total tax revenue would fall, and the government would have to raise tax rates on everyone to maintain the same level of spending. Excluding capital income from taxation does have its costs. The tax system is one way we have to at least partially reduce inequalities in income.

Critics of consumption taxes worry that moving our tax system in that direction will take away this important tool for social equality. However, other economists believe that high-income individuals already shoulder a very high share of the total tax burden and that we need to focus on designing an efficient system to promote economic growth.

Let's review an Application that answers one of the key questions we posed at the start of the chapter:

3.   What type of tax is the "flat tax"?

APPLICATION 3: THE FLAT TAX IS A TAX ON CONSUMPTION

The "flat tax," designed by Robert E. Hall of Stanford University and Alvin Rabushka of the Hoover Institute, brings the personal income tax and corporate income tax into a single, unified tax system. Under the flat tax, one low, single tax rate applies to both businesses and individuals. Wage payments are deducted by businesses before they pay taxes. In addition, the flat tax would allow businesses to deduct any investment spending they make from their income before the tax is calculated. Because the tax would allow a deduction for investment spending, it can essentially be viewed as a type of consumption tax.

This version of the flat tax has an important feature that ensures that wealthy individuals still pay taxes. Suppose the corporation or business makes an extraordinary return on its investment. Under this version of the flat tax, these extraordinary gains would be taxed in full. Owners of a corporation or business may earn extraordinary gains, but if they do, they will pay taxes on these gains.

☞   According to James Arnold, a BBC business news reporter, more eastern European countries are adopting flat tax systems than western European countries. Many eastern European countries were trying to avoid huge tax evasion by using a flat tax system. Visit the BBC Web site at http://news.bbc.co.uk/2/hi/business/4444717.stm for more details.

Activity

You have learned about inflation targeting. As with the many debates in this chapter, there are two sides to the argument. One question in the debate is, "Should the Fed Focus Only on Inflation?" List one "yes" reason and one "no" reason.

Answer

Some of your answers may include the following:

Debate One: Should the Fed Focus Only on Inflation?

Pro or yes:
- Worrying about other factors—unemployment or the exchange rate—will distract the Fed from its mission and lead to long-run inflationary pressures building in the economy.
- Having a single focus would give the Fed more credibility.

Con or no:
- Monetary policy is useful for fighting recessions. If the Fed is focused on inflation only, stabilization policy would be hindered.
- It is difficult to measure price stability, especially to a specific target.

Key Terms

Capital gains: Profits investors earn when they sell stocks, bonds, real estate, or other assets.

Consumption taxes: Taxes based on the consumption, not the income, of individuals.

Deficit: The amount by which government expenditures exceed government revenue in a given year.

Government debt: The total of all past government deficits.

Government expenditures: Spending on goods and services plus transfer payments.

Monetizing the deficit: Purchases by a central bank of newly issued government bonds.

Ricardian equivalence: The proposition that it does not matter whether government expenditure is financed by taxes or debt.

Surplus: The amount by which government revenues exceed government expenditures in a given year.

Practice Quiz

(Answers are provided at the end of the Practice Quiz.)

1. Which of the following is considered a government expenditure?
    a. The purchase of goods and services by the government
    b. Transfer payments
    c. Social Security and welfare payments
    d. All of the above

2. When the government spends more than it receives in revenues, the sum of the government's yearly deficits is called:
    a. an accumulated deficit.
    b. the government's debt.
    c. a budget balance.
    d. fiscal illusion.

3. Over the next decade and beyond, the Social Security portion of the federal budget is expected to:
    a. run a deficit for a while, but then the deficits will turn to surpluses.
    b. run a surplus for a while, but then the surpluses will turn to deficits.
    c. continuously run deficits.
    d. continuously run surpluses.

4. Which of the following equalities is correct?
    a. Government deficit = government spending – transfer payments
    b. Government deficit = taxes – transfer payments
    c. Government deficit = new borrowing from the public + new money created
    d. Government deficit = accumulated government debt year after year

5. The purchase by a central bank of newly created government debt is called:
   a. open market operations.
   b. monetarist debt relief.
   c. debasing the debt.
   d. monetizing the debt.

6. Which of the following assertions is correct?
   a. A large debt can increase the amount of capital in the economy.
   b. A large debt can increase future income and real wages for its citizens.
   c. The selling of government bonds "crowds out" private investment spending.
   d. All of the above

7. An economist who believes in the Ricardian equivalence is under the impression that:
   a. government deficits impose a burden on society.
   b. it does not matter whether government expenditure is financed by taxes or by issuing debt.
   c. people will stop saving if they anticipate higher taxes in the future.
   d. All of the above

8. According to Nobel laureate James Buchanan, people are:
   a. less aware of government deficits than the taxes they're forced to pay.
   b. highly aware of government deficits, and this will prevent government from spending out of control.
   c. largely indifferent about taxation and government spending.
   d. usually unaware of tax increases.

9. Which of the following statements is correct?
   a. Over short periods, deficits can help the economy to cope with shocks.
   b. Deficits can give government some room to maneuver out of a recession.
   c. Deficits can play a role in tax smoothing.
   d. All of the above

10. This question tests your understanding of Application 1 in this chapter: The long-term fiscal imbalances for the United States. What are the long-term fiscal imbalances for the United States?

    To determine the gap between revenues and expenditures, economists Jagadeesh Gokhale and Kent Smetters developed a method which consists of:
    a. Estimating the present value of the gap between the government's revenues and expenditures and adding it to the current national debt.
    b. finding the "fiscal balance," or the level of revenues necessary to match the level of expenditures in a given year.
    c. adding the yearly value of the debt each year to come up with an estimate of the national deficit.
    d. finding the fiscal deficit, however, because the fiscal gap is so small, an estimate of budget deficit projections could not be found.

11. Which of the following is a cost of inflation?
    a. Menu costs
    b. Shoe-leather costs
    c. Arbitrary redistributions of money between debtors and creditors
    d. All of the above are costs of inflation.

12. Which of the following reflects the growth in real GDP as well as the growth in prices?
    a. The growth rate in nominal GDP
    b. The growth in real GDP
    c. The growth of the money supply
    d. The inflation target

13. In which of the following countries does the government decide on the inflation target for the central bank?
    a. United Kingdom
    b. United States
    c. New Zealand
    d. All of the above

14. It is not clear if a consumption tax will lead to more saving because:
    a. it is unclear whether individuals will allocate their savings to tax-favored investments.
    b. is not clear whether new savings funds are new savings or merely transfers from other accounts.
    c. it is unclear if corporate taxes may lead to less efficient investment.
    d. All of the above

15. In 2003, which of the following income classes earned over half of the economy's capital gains?
    a. $50,000-$75,000
    b. $75,000-$100,000
    c. $200,000-$500,000
    d. $500,000 and over

16. Describe the phenomenon known as monetizing the debt and its relationship to inflation.

17. Can budget deficits be good for the economy? Explain.

18. Should the Fed focus on fighting inflation? What are the benefits and shortcomings of such a proposition?

19. The United States is a country with a low savings rate. Explain why. Also, some economists propose that we move to a consumption tax rather than an income tax. Explain.

Answers to the Practice Quiz

1. d. The purchase of goods and services by the government and the transfer payments (Social Security, welfare, and so on) it makes to its citizens are the government's expenditures.

2. b. The government debt is the total of all of its yearly deficits.

3. b. Over the next decade, the Social Security portion of the budget is expected to run a surplus, but over the longer horizon, as our society grows older, the surpluses will turn to deficits.

4. c. These are the government's two options to finance the deficit.

5. d. The purchase by a central bank of newly created government debt is called monetizing the debt.

6. c. The national debt can pose two burdens for society. First, a large debt can reduce the amount of capital in the economy and thereby reduce future income and real wages for its citizens. Savings flow into capital formation and increase the economy's capital stock. When the government runs a deficit, it sells bonds to the same savers who could have purchased the bonds of private firms. Therefore, the selling of government bonds "crowds out" private investment spending.

7. b. Economists who do not believe that government deficits impose a burden on society believe in the Ricardian equivalence, the proposition that it does not matter whether government expenditure is financed by taxes or by issuing debt because everyone understands that higher debt will result in higher taxes, so people save in anticipation of paying higher taxes in the future.

8. a. Nobel laureate James Buchanan has argued that people are less aware of government deficits than the taxes they're forced to pay, and this inevitably will lead to higher government spending and bigger government.

9. d. Over short periods, deficits can help the economy to cope with shocks, such as oil price increases or a collapse in the stock market. They give the government some room to maneuver out of a recession. Deficits can also play a role in tax smoothing. Professor Robert Barro of Harvard University has argued that it is more efficient to keep tax rates relatively constant than to raise them sharply and then lower them later.

10. a. The method for arriving at a more comprehensive measure of a nation's indebtedness was to estimate the present value of the gap between the government's revenues and expenditures and adding it to the current national debt.

11. d. The costs of inflation include: Menu costs—the costs firms incur to change their posted prices; shoe-leather costs, the costs individuals and firms pay for the time spent trying to reduce their holdings of money; distortions in our tax and banking systems because inflation isn't yet factored into them; and arbitrary redistributions of money between debtors and creditors from unanticipated inflation.

12. a. The growth rate in nominal GDP equals the growth in real GDP plus the growth in prices (inflation).

13. a. In the United Kingdom, it is ultimately the elected government that decides on the inflation target for the central bank. In other countries, such as New Zealand, the central bank has the responsibility of "achieving and maintaining stability in the general level of prices" without any competing goals. In the United States, the Fed has considerable power to use monetary policy to stabilize output as well as to fight inflation as it pleases. But changing the current system to give Congress and the president more power over monetary policy might lead to more inflation, not less.

14. b. It is not clear whether the funds are new savings—meaning reduced consumption—or merely transfers from other accounts.

15. d. Taxpayers with annual incomes exceeding $200,000 earned over half of the economy's capital gains in 2003. Obviously, capital assets are highly concentrated among the wealthy.

16. Monetizing the debt is part of the debate about whether or not deficits lead to inflation. If the Federal Reserve purchases the government bonds issued by the Treasury Department to finance the deficit, that purchase creates money by taking debt out of the hands of the public in exchange for money. Economists call the purchase by a central bank of newly created government debt monetizing the

debt. If a country has no options other than creating money to finance its deficits—in other words, if the public is unwilling to buy its bonds, those deficits will inevitably cause inflation.

17. Yes, in some situations, deficits can be good for the economy. Over short periods, deficits can help the economy to cope with shocks, such as oil price increases or a collapse in the stock market. They give the government some room to maneuver out of a recession. Deficits can also play a role in tax smoothing. Professor Robert Barro of Harvard University has argued that it is more efficient to keep tax rates relatively constant than to raise them sharply and then lower them later. Thus, by running deficits and only gradually raising taxes later to service the debt, we avoid creating excess distortions in the economy.

18. Proponents of inflation targeting argue that the Fed should have only one primary goal: controlling inflation. Commitment to a single goal would give the Fed more credibility and help to keep it free from political pressures. Many other economists strongly object to having the Fed concentrate solely on controlling inflation. There are legitimate questions about what constitutes "stable prices." It is difficult to isolate from prices changes the technological improvements that change the quality of goods rapidly. Some economists like the idea of the Fed having to meet targets, such as to target the growth rate in nominal GDP and thereby both the growth in real GDP as well as the growth in prices (inflation). Critics of stabilization policy believe that attempts to stabilize the economy have done more harm than good over the years by making fluctuations worse. Difficulties include lags, uncertainties about the strength and timing of policies, and difficulties in estimating the natural rate of unemployment.

19. The United States is a country with a low savings rate. Colleges, welfare programs, and even the U.S. tax system discourage savings. Tax systems based on consumption do not penalize individuals who save. Sales taxes and value-added taxes are examples of consumption taxes. The key feature of a consumption tax is that you do not face any additional taxes if you decide to save more of your income. In practice, the U.S. tax system is a hybrid system: halfway between an income tax and a consumption tax. Moving to a consumption tax system could have a major impact on the distribution of income in the economy. If we exempt savings from the income tax, wealthy and high-income individuals who save the most would clearly be favored.

18

International Trade and Public Policy

Chapter Summary

This chapter discusses the benefits of specialization and trade and explores the trade-offs associated with protectionist policies. Here are the main points of the chapter:

- If one country has a comparative advantage vis-à-vis another country in producing a particular good (a lower opportunity cost), specialization and trade will benefit both countries.
- An import ban or an import quota increases prices, protecting domestic industries, but domestic consumers pay the price.
- Because the victims of protectionist policies often retaliate, the protection of a domestic industry can harm an exporting industry.
- A tariff, a tax on imports, generates revenue for the government, whereas an import quota—a limit on imports—generates revenue for foreigners or importers.
- In principle, the laws against dumping are designed to prevent predatory pricing. In practice, predatory pricing laws are often used to shield domestic industries from competition. Allegations of it are hard to prove.
- Under World Trade Organization (WTO) rules, each country may pursue its environmental goals only within its own borders.
- International trade has contributed to the widening gap between the wages of low-skilled and high-skilled labor.

Applying the Concepts

After reading this chapter, you should be able to answer these four key questions:

1. Do tariffs (taxes on imported goods) hurt the poor disproportionately?
2. How much does it really cost to "save" a job that might be lost under free trade?
3. Does the concept of "unfair" competition make sense?
4. What are the most pressing current issues in today's trade negotiations?

18.1 Benefits from Specialization and Trade

Trade (voluntary exchange) between individuals and nations is based on the principle of opportunity cost.

Principle of Opportunity Cost

The opportunity cost of an item is what you must sacrifice to get the item.

Table 18.1 shows the opportunity costs of each good in Shirtland and Chipland. Chipland can produce either 120 shirts in one day or 120 chips in one day. This means that if it gives up production of 120 shirts, it get 120 chips. The opportunity cost of a chip is then one shirt. Similarly, the opportunity cost of a shirt is one chip.

In Shirtland, giving up 108 shirts yields only 36 chips so the opportunity cost of a chip is 3 shirts. This is calculated as the 108 shirts sacrificed divided by the 36 chips gained. Similarly the opportunity cost of a shirt is 1/3 of a chip. This is calculated as the 36 chips sacrificed divided by the 108 shirts gained.

Figure 18.1 shows the production possibilities curves for Shirtland and Chipland. The **production possibilities curve** shows the possible combinations of products that an economy can produce, given that its productive resources are fully employed and efficiently used.

> ### 🗎 Remember
>
> With no trade, an economy's production possibilities frontier also shows the possible consumption possibilities for the economy.

Chipland has the absolute advantage over Shirtland in the production of both chips and shirts. **Absolute advantage** is the ability of one person or nation to produce a product at a lower resource cost than another person or nation. Another way to think of this is that an economy has an absolute advantage in a good when it can produce more of that good in a given amount of time than can another economy.

Trade is based on comparative advantage. **Comparative advantage** is the ability of one person or nation to produce a good at a lower opportunity cost than another person or nation. Since the cost of a shirt is 1/3 of a chip in Shirtland, and one chip in Chipland, Shirtland should produce shirts since it has the comparative advantage, or lower opportunity cost. Chipland should produce chips since it gives up fewer shirts to produce a chip. Chipland has a comparative advantage in chip production because it has a lower opportunity cost for chips.

> ### 🗎 Remember
>
> Even though Chipland can produce more shirts and more chips than Shirtland, it is still in Chipland's best interest to trade with Shirtland. This is because trade is based on comparative advantage—who can produce a good at the lowest opportunity cost.

Based on comparative advantage, Chipland will produce chips and buy shirts. Shirtland will produce shirts and buy chips. The terms of trade can be found from the opportunity costs for the two goods. The **terms of trade** is the rate at which units of one product can be exchanged for units of another product.

How many shirts will Shirtland give up to buy a chip? If Shirtland produced chips on its own, it would give up 3 shirts for each chip. This is Shirtland's opportunity cost, and the most it would be willing to pay for a chip. Chipland gives up one shirt each time it produces a chip and this is the least it would be willing to accept in trade for one chip. As a result, one chip will trade for somewhere between 1 and 3 shirts. Notice that these are simply the opportunity costs of the goods for each nation. Any trade between these two values will make both countries better off.

> ᑭᑊ **Study Tip**
>
> Terms of trade are given by the opportunity costs of goods in the trading countries.

The **consumption possibilities curve** is a curve that shows the combinations of two goods that can be consumed when a nation specialized in a particular good and trades with another nation. We use the consumption possibilities curve to show the gains to Shirtland and Chipland from trading.

In Figure 18.2 Panel A, we have the production possibilities curve for Chipland. Suppose that we start at point *g*, with Chipland producing 120 computer chips per day. If Chipland tried to produce shirts, it would have to give up one chip for each shirt. Suppose the terms of trade are 2 shirts per chip. Now when Chipland gives up a chip, instead of the one shirt it could receive if it produced shirts, it receives 2 shirts from Shirtland in return for selling a chip to Shirtland. At these terms of trade, Chipland is better off as it can now consume 119 chips and 2 shirts instead of the 119 chips and 1 shirt it could produce, and consume, without trade.

Panel B illustrates that Shirtland is better off as well. Starting from point *a*, if Shirtland wanted to produce a computer chip, it would have to give up three shirts without trade. By trading, Shirtland can send 2 shirts to Chipland and receive 1 chip in return. Thus, Shirtland is able to consume 106 shirts and 1 chip with trade instead of the 105 shirts and 1 chip it would have without trade.

> ᑭᑊ **Study Tip**
>
> The consumption possibilities curve shows that trade allows countries to consume combinations of goods they could not produce on their own.

Trade rearranges employment in the two countries as well. As a result of trade, Chipland will choose to buy shirts instead of producing shirts. This means that workers in the shirt industry in Chipland will no longer be needed to make shirts. At the same time, Chipland will specialize in making chips and the chip industry will expand and this will increase the employment of chip makers.

18.2 Protectionist Policies

Figure 18.3 illustrates the effects of an import ban in Chipland. With trade, the shirt market is in equilibrium at point *c* with a price of $12 and a quantity of 80 shirts. All of these shirts are imported as no domestic supplier will sell shirts if the price is below $17. Without imports, the market supply shifts to the left (as the shirts from other countries are no longer offered for sale in Chipland) and the market reaches equilibrium at point *a* with a price of $25 and 60 shirts sold with all 60 shirts coming from domestic suppliers.

An **import quota** is a government-imposed limit on the quantity of a good that can be imported. Import quotas are illegal under international trading laws, however, exporting countries may agree to a voluntary export restraint. A **voluntary export restraint** is a scheme under which an exporting country voluntarily decreases its exports. A voluntary export restraint functions in the same way as an import quota. A **tariff** is a tax on imported goods. At times, governments will issue **import licenses**—rights issued by a government to import goods.

᧡ Study Tip

Any restriction on imports can be analyzed as a decrease in supply in the affected market.

Figure 18.4 illustrates the impact of these trade restrictions. As long as some imports are allowed, the supply curve will shift to the left relative to the free trade supply curve, but will not shift as far left as the zero import case in Figure 19.3 [18.3]. Notice that the restriction on imports leads to an equilibrium at point *d* with a higher price and lower quantity than those under free trade. Point *e* shows the quantity supplied by domestic producers.

The price of shirts will increase to $20 regardless of whether a quota or tariff is used. The difference in the two approaches is who receives the $8 increase in price. With a tariff, this money is collected by the government and so in Figure 19.4 [18.4] the $8 increase in price for the 44 imported units would be collected as tax revenue by the home government. With a quota, importers and producers receive the extra $8 on those units.

Let's review an Application that answers one of the key questions we posed at the start of the chapter:

1. Do tariffs (taxes) on imported goods hurt the poor disproportionately?

APPLICATION 1: THE IMPACT OF TARIFFS ON THE POOR

Studies have found that the poor bear a larger burden from tariffs than do the rich. The first reason is that goods subject to a tariff tend to make up a larger part of the spending of the poor. The second reason is that most tariffs are applied to low priced, imported items, thus raising the price on goods that tend to be purchased more frequently by the poor.

18.3 What Are the Rationales for Protectionist Policies?

There are three primary reasons for restrictive trade policies:
- To shield workers from foreign competition.
- To nurture infant industries until they mature.
- To help domestic firms establish monopolies in world markets.

In many cases, industries affected by trade, such as textiles in the United States, are concentrated in relatively small parts of the United States. Politicians in those areas use trade policy to protect their constituents, even though it may cost other citizens.

Nurturing infant industries is justified in part by the concept of learning by doing. An **infant industry** is one that is at an early stage of development. **Learning by doing** refers to knowledge and skills workers gain during production that increase productivity and lower cost. As the industry matures, costs fall and the protection is less needed.

Airbus is an example of European governments using trade restrictions to assist a domestic firm to gain market share.

Let's review two Applications that answer key questions we posed at the start of the chapter:

2. How much does it really cost to "save" a job that might be lost under free trade?

APPLICATION 2: MEASURING THE COSTS OF PROTECTING JOBS

This Application illustrates the cost of saving U.S. jobs in certain industries. The Application states that each textile job saved from moving abroad costs the United States $199,241. The Application shows the five costliest jobs to save, with jobs in three industries costing the United States over $1 million per year to preserve.

3. Does the concept of "unfair" competition make sense?

APPLICATION 3: PROTECTION FOR CANDLE MAKERS

This Application reprints a satirical petition from the 1800s on behalf of French candle makers for protection from competition from the sun.

18.4 A Brief History of International Tariff and Trade Agreements

This section describes a few major pieces of trade agreement.

The **General Agreement on Tariffs and Trade (GATT)** is an international agreement established in 1947 that has lowered trade barriers between the United States and other nations. The **World Trade Organization** was established in 1995 and oversees GATT and other international trade agreements, resolves trade disputes, and holds forums for further rounds of trade negotiations. The North American Free Trade Agreement (NAFTA) will eliminate all trade barriers between the United States, Canada, and Mexico. The European Union was formed to eliminate trade barriers between member states. The Asian Pacific Economic Cooperation was created to lower trade barriers between 18 member Asian nations. The U.S.-Central American Free Trade Agreement, if approved, will extend NAFTA-like provisions to five Central American countries.

Let's review an Application that answers one of the key questions we posed at the start of the chapter:

4. What are the most pressing current issues in today's trade negotiations?

APPLICATION 4: ONGOING TRADE NEGOTIATIONS

This Application suggests that agricultural trade is the subject of most current trade negotiations. While small countries typically have the comparative advantage in agriculture, many large countries, including the United States, provide heavy subsidies to their agricultural sector that stand in the way of free trade.

18.5 Recent Policy Debates and Trade Agreements

There are three recent policy debates discussed in this chapter:
1. Are foreign producers dumping their products?
2. Do trade laws inhibit environmental protection?
3. Does outsourcing and trade cause income inequality?

Dumping is a situation in which the price a firm charges in a foreign market is lower than either the price it charges in its home markets or the production cost. One reason we might see different prices between countries is price discrimination. **Price discrimination** is the process under which a firm divides consumers into two or more groups and charges a different price for each group buying the same product. A second reason is **predatory pricing**, a pricing scheme under which a firm decreases the price to drive rival firms out of business and increases the price when rival firms leave the market. It is very difficult to determine whether low prices in a market are caused by price discrimination, predatory pricing, or simply more competition in that market.

Environmental concerns arise in trade discussion particularly when the environmental standards in one country cannot be applied to producers in another country. The text demonstrated that the United States can impose certain regulations on foreign producers so long as all domestic producers are held to the same standard. For instance, the United States could limit the allowable levels of exhaust from automobiles as long as all producers that sell in the U.S. market are held to the same standard. A country, however, can't ban the imports of goods produced in other countries by methods of production that the home country outlaws. For example, both the United States, which tried to ban the import of net caught tuna, and the European Union, which tried to ban the import of hormone-treated beef, have been found to be in violation of the WTO over those issues.

Outsourcing refers to firms producing components of their goods and services in other countries. Government can respond by enacting trade barriers to protect low-skilled jobs, or by easing the transition to an economy with fewer low-skilled jobs. To this point, outsourcing has affected low-skilled jobs. It is possible that jobs that require more skills could also be outsourced. There is still much to learn about the effects of outsourcing and international trade on wages and employment.

Activity

Consider Andy, who produces computer programs and hamburgers. In a given week (40 hours), Andy can produce 40 computer programs or 80 hamburgers along a linear production possibilities curve.

a. Find the opportunity cost of computer programs and hamburgers for Andy.
b. Can Andy consume 20 computer programs and 60 hamburgers?
c. Suppose that Laura offers Andy 3 hamburgers for every computer program he writes for her. Will Andy make this trade?
d. Suppose Andy specializes in programs and sells programs to Laura for hamburgers at the terms of trade from part c. Can he consume 20 computer programs and 60 hamburgers?
e. Suppose Laura can only produce 45 hamburgers in a week. Does the fact that Andy has the absolute advantage in hamburger production change his desire to trade with Laura?

Answers

a. One computer program costs Andy 2 hamburgers. One hamburger costs Andy ½ of a computer program.
b. No, this point is outside his production possibilities curve. If Andy consumes 20 computer programs, he can consume at most 40 hamburgers.
c. Yes. It costs Andy 2 hamburgers to write a computer program, so he would gladly accept 3 hamburgers in trade for 1 computer program.
d. Yes. He will produce 40 programs and sell 20 of them. In return for the 20 programs, he will receive 60 hamburgers.
e. No, even though he has the absolute advantage in hamburgers, trade is based on comparative advantage and so this information is not relevant to the decision to trade.

Key Terms

Absolute advantage: The ability of one person or nation to produce a product at a lower resource cost than another person or nation.

Comparative advantage: The ability of one person or nation to produce a good at a lower opportunity cost than another person or nation.

Consumption possibilities curve: A curve showing the combinations of two goods that can be consumed when a nation specialized in a particular good and trades with another nation.

Dumping: A situation in which the price a firm charges in a foreign market is lower than either the price it charges in its home markets or the production cost.

General Agreement on Tariffs and Trade (GATT): An international agreement established in 1947 that has lowered trade barriers between the United States and other nations.

Import licenses: Rights, issued by a government, to import goods.

Import quota: A government-imposed limit on the quantity of a good that can be imported.

Infant industries: Industries that are at an early stage of development.

Learning by doing: Knowledge and skills workers gain during production that increase productivity and lower cost.

Outsourcing: Firms producing components of their goods and services in other countries.

Predatory pricing: A pricing scheme under which a firm decreases the price to drive rival firms out of business and increases the price when rival firms leave the market.

Price discrimination: The process under which a firm divides consumers into two or more groups and charges a different price for each group buying the same product.

Production possibilities curve: A curve that shows the possible combinations of products that an economy can produce, given that its productive resources are fully employed and efficiently used.

Tariff: A tax on imported goods.

Terms of trade: The rate at which units of one product can be exchanged for units of another product.

Voluntary export restraint: A scheme under which an exporting country voluntarily decreases its exports.

World Trade Organization: An organization established in 1995 that oversees GATT and other international trade agreements, resolves trade disputes, and holds forums for further rounds of trade negotiations.

Practice Quiz

(Answers are provided at the end of the Practice Quiz.)

1. Specialization and trade are concepts based on a specific key principle of economics. Which one?
   a. The marginal principle
   b. The principle of diminishing returns
   c. The real-nominal principle
   d. The principle of opportunity cost

2. A *production possibilities curve* shows the possible combinations of:
   a. the goods that can be produced by an economy at full employment over time as the economy grows.
   b. two sets of inputs, or productive resources available to an economy to produce output.
   c. two types of output that can be produced in an economy as full employment is maintained.
   d. quantities of output that are available at various price levels, during a given period, all else the same.

3. Refer to the figure below. Assume that the economy always maintains full employment. What is the opportunity cost of increasing the production of shirts, from 54 to 60?

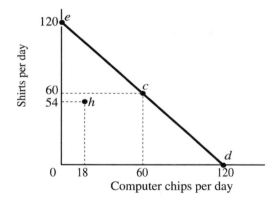

   a. One chip
   b. There is no way to determine the opportunity cost.
   c. Six chips
   d. Three chips

4. We say that a nation has a *comparative advantage* in producing a good if that nation:
   a. fully specializes in the production of that good.
   b. chooses autarky.
   c. has a lower resource cost for the production of that good.
   d. All of the above

5. Refer to the figure below. Which country in this graph has a comparative advantage in the production of shirts?

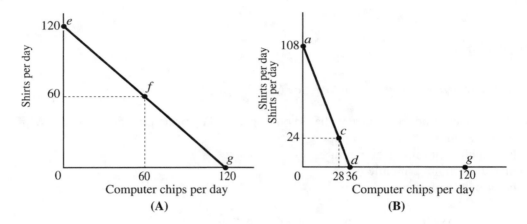

   (A)   (B)

   a. A
   b. B
   c. Neither country
   d. Both countries

6. Only one statement below is entirely correct. Under specialization and trade, the consumption possibilities curve of a nation:
   a. lies below the nation's production possibilities curve because the nation has more options about how much to consume.
   b. lies above the nation's production possibilities curve because the nation has less options about how much to consume.
   c. lies above the nation's production possibilities curve because the nation has more options about how much to consume.
   d. lies below the nation's production possibilities curve because the nation has less options about how much to consume.

7. When a nation voluntarily decreases its exports in an attempt to avoid more restrictive policies, the nation is adopting:
   a. quotas.
   b. tariffs.
   c. import licenses.
   d. voluntary export restraints.

8. Refer to the figure below where one supply curve represents no trade and the other free trade. A country with policies that prevent trade will cause this market to settle in equilibrium at which point?

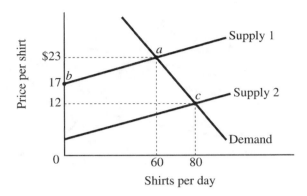

Shirts per day

a. Point *a*
b. Point *b*
c. Point *c*
d. This market may settle in equilibrium at any of the points shown after trade restrictions are imposed.

9. Which of the following is correct about voluntary export restraints (VERs)?
a. Like a quota, a VER increases the price of the restricted good.
b. A VER makes it more difficult for domestic firms to participate in the market.
c. VERs are illegal under global trade rules.
d. All of the above

10. This question tests your understanding of Application 1 in this chapter: The impact of tariffs on the poor. Do tariffs (taxes) on imported goods hurt the poor disproportionately? Which of the following are reasons why tariffs fall disproportionately on the poor in the United States?
a. Within the category of goods for which tariffs are high, the highest tariffs fall on the cheapest products—precisely those that will be purchased by lower-income consumers.
b. Tariffs are usually placed on expensive goods, making those goods even less affordable for the poor.
c. In general, to protect U.S. industries, tariffs are highest on capital-intensive goods; goods that use relatively more capital than labor.
d. Tariffs are placed on goods that represent a higher fraction of the consumption of higher-income households than lower-income households.

11. Refer to the figure below. Which supply curve applies to the case of a tariff relative to supply with free trade or domestic supply alone?

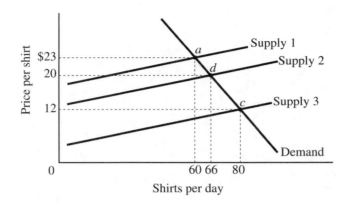

a. Supply 3
b. Supply 1
c. Supply 2
d. None of the above

12. Which of the following are possible reasons why countries restrict trade?
a. To help domestic firms establish monopolies in world markets.
b. To shield workers from foreign competition.
c. To nurture "infant" industries until they mature.
d. All of the above

13. In addition to the nations involved in the WTO, which of the following is an association formed to lower trade barriers and promote international trade?
a. The European Union (EU), which today includes close to 20 countries
b. The leaders of 18 Asian nations have formed the Asian Pacific Economic Cooperation (APEC).
c. The North American Free Trade Agreement (NAFTA) between Canada, Mexico, and the United States.
d. All of the above

14. Based on the evidence concerning antidumping laws and predatory pricing, what is the position of economists about these issues?
a. Economists are skeptical about how frequently predatory pricing actually occurs versus price discrimination.
b. Economists believe that most nations use their antidumping laws to prevent unfair competition, not as protectionist policies in disguise.
c. Economists believe that antidumping laws are hardly ever used because they are an ineffective method of protecting domestic industries.
d. All of the above

15. Nations that use trade restrictions to pursue environmental goals will:
a. find support in the WTO because the WTO wants countries to pursue specific environmental goals.
b. encounter resistance from the WTO.
c. find support in the WTO but only as long as other WTO participants agree with the trade restrictions to be imposed.
d. find that the WTO is neutral, neither supporting nor condemning a country's environmental goals.

16. Trade and specialization mean that individuals and nations:
    a. tighten their borders.
    b. pay no attention to matters of independence and sovereignty, eventually becoming a single nation.
    c. must surrender some of their independence and sovereignty.
    d. forget about borders.

17. Compare autarky equilibrium to equilibrium based on comparative advantage.

18. Protectionist policies are often defended on the grounds that they protect new or infant industries. Comment.

19. What are the WTO rules concerning trade that could harm the environment?

20. How is trade likely to affect the distribution of income?

Answers to the Practice Quiz

1. d. The opportunity cost of something is what you sacrifice to get it. Specialization and trade are based on the idea of sacrificing the production of some goods to concentrate on the production of others, based on comparative advantage.

2. c. The production possibilities frontier shows the possible combinations of two goods that can be produced by an economy, assuming that all resources are fully employed.

3. c. The opportunity cost is the slope of the production possibilities frontier. The information on the axes can be used to establish the value of the slope. The country can produce either 120 shirts when it produces no chips or 120 chips when it produces no shirts. Therefore, this country must give up one chip in order to increase the production of shirts by one. In this case, in order to increase the production of shirts by six, from 54 to 60, the production of chips must decrease by six.

4. a. The comparative advantage for a good means that a country can produce the good for the lower opportunity cost, in other words, give up less of an alternative good in order to make this.

5. b. The opportunity costs are as follows: The opportunity cost of shirts is: 1 chip for country A, and 1/3 chip for country B. Country B has a comparative advantage in the production of shirts because it sacrifices fewer chips to produce one shirt. Country B should therefore produce shirts.

6. c. Each consumption possibilities curve lies above the nation's production possibilities curves, meaning that each nation has more options about how much to consume under specialization and trade.

7. d. A voluntary export restraint (VER) is where a nation voluntarily decreases its exports in an attempt to avoid more restrictive policies.

8. a. Restrictive trade policies would decrease the total supply, causing an increase in the price consumers have to pay for shirts and a decrease in the quantity available for them to buy.

9. a. Like a quota, a VER increases the price of the restricted good, making it more feasible for domestic firms to participate in the market, but is legal under international trade rules.

10. a. In general, to protect U.S. industries, tariffs are highest on labor-intensive goods, goods that use relatively more labor than capital. But these goods tend to be lower priced. That is why tariffs do fall disproportionately on the poor.

11. c. The tariff shifts the supply curve to the left from the free trade scenario of supply curve 3. The market moves upward along the demand curve to point *d*, which is between point *c* (free trade) and *a* (domestic supply only).

12. d. Three possible motivations to restrict trade are: to shield workers from foreign competition, to nurture "infant" industries until they mature, and to help domestic firms establish monopolies in world markets.

13. d. Nations have formed trade associations to lower trade barriers and promote international trade: The North American Free Trade Agreement (NAFTA) between Canada, Mexico, and the United States; the European Union (EU), which today includes close to 20 countries; and the leaders of 18 Asian nations have formed the Asian Pacific Economic Cooperation (APEC).

14. a. Many economists are skeptical about how frequently predatory pricing actually occurs versus price discrimination; they suspect that many nations use their antidumping laws as protectionist policies in disguise. Professor Thomas Prusa of Rutgers University has studied antidumping and found that it is a potent weapon for protecting domestic industries.

15. b. Nations that use trade restrictions to pursue environmental goals will encounter resistance because WTO rules mean that a nation can pursue its environmental goals only within its borders.

16. c. Trade and specialization mean that individuals and nations must surrender some of their independence and sovereignty.

17. Autarky equilibrium is a situation in which the economy chooses how to use its scarce resources to produce a certain amount of goods, in the absence of trade. It is similar to equilibrium based on comparative advantage in that both situations make full and efficient use of resources available. The difference lies in the combinations of output that are produced, and ultimately, in the amounts of goods that can be consumed. When a country chooses to specialize and trade based on comparative advantage, it shifts its production toward the goods for which it is more efficient relative to its trading partner. Once countries specialize and trade, the consumption possibilities frontier rises above the production possibilities frontier. By focusing on what each country does best, world output increases.

18. One possible answer is as follows: It would seem to make sense to protect domestic industries while they achieve the economies of scale and cost per unit of similar foreign competitors. But in reality, infant industries rarely become competitive with their foreign rivals. In the 1950s and 1960s, Latin American countries used tariffs and other policies to protect their young industries, but the industries never became as efficient as the foreign suppliers did. Additionally, once an industry is given tariff protection, it is difficult to take it away.

19. WTO rules concerning trade that could harm the environment state that a country can adopt any environmental standard it chooses, as long as it does not discriminate against foreign producers. For example, the U.S. can limit exhaust emissions of cars, as long as the rules apply equally to all cars—domestic and imports. The U.S. cannot ban imported goods that are produced in factories that generate pollution in other countries. The WTO recognizes that countries differ in the value they place on the environment.

20. Trade could lead to greater inequality of income and wages. If a country increases its exports of products requiring skilled labor, the demand for skilled labor and their wages will rise. And, if the country imports more goods requiring less skilled labor, the wages of unskilled workers will fall.

19

The World of International Finance

Chapter Summary

The value of every currency depends on news and late-breaking developments throughout the world. Rising gas prices, a new terrorist attack, or a change in the leadership of a foreign government can easily affect the price at which currencies trade with one another (the exchange rate). In this chapter, we take a comprehensive and in-depth look at exchange rates as well as other aspects of the international financial system. Understanding our international financial system will help you to interpret the often complex financial news from abroad. Here are the main points of the chapter:

- Exchange rates are determined in foreign exchange markets by supply and demand.
- The real exchange rate is the price of U.S. goods and services relative to foreign goods and services, expressed in a common currency.
- The balance of payments consists of three types of international transactions: current account transactions, financial account transactions, and capital account transactions.
- The sum of the current account balance, the financial account balance, and the capital account is zero.
- Governments can attempt to change exchange rates by buying or selling currencies in the foreign exchange market. Purchasing a currency will cause the currency to appreciate, while selling a currency will cause it to depreciate.
- A system of fixed exchange rates can provide a better environment for business but requires that countries keep their inflation rates and interest rates within narrow limits.

Applying the Concepts

After reading this chapter, you should be able to answer these four key questions:
1. Can the price of hamburgers around the world give us a clue as to the proper value for exchange rates?
2. What factors may allow the United States to continue running large trade deficits with the rest of the world?
3. Why did a group of European countries adopt a common currency?
4. What are the causes of financial collapses that occur throughout the globe?

19.1 How Exchange Rates Are Determined

ᇰᕋ Study Tip

Studying international currency markets is a study of reciprocals. What happens in one country has an inverse effect in the other country. For example, consider the U.S. and Japan. If the Japanese yen is increasing in value relative to the U.S. dollar (appreciating), then the U.S. dollar must also be decreasing in value relative to the yen (depreciating). It is very important when you set up currency markets that you identify which pairs of currencies you are going to analyze.

The Japanese yen is not money in the U.S. There is no single currency that is an acceptable medium of exchange in all countries. Therefore to conduct international transactions between countries, an individual or business must exchange one currency for another. The **exchange rate** is the price at which we can exchange one currency for another. Fluctuations in the exchange rate can have a huge impact on the quantities of goods and services countries import or export and the overall trade balance.

Consider the exchange rate between U.S. dollars and foreign currencies. An increase in the value of a currency relative to the currency of another nation is called an **appreciation of a currency**. The U.S. dollar has become more expensive in terms of yen. The price of the dollar has risen, in other words. Because the dollar has increased in value, we say that the dollar has appreciated against the yen. A **depreciation of a currency** is a decrease in the value of a currency relative to the currency of another nation. If the exchange rate falls from 100 to 90 yen per dollar, you'll get fewer yen for each dollar you exchange.

ᇰᕋ Study Tip

Be sure you understand that if one currency appreciates, the other must depreciate. For example, if the dollar appreciates against the yen, the yen must depreciate against the dollar.

How are exchange rates determined? The exchange rate between U.S. dollars and euros is determined in the foreign-exchange market, the market in which dollars trade for euros. To understand this market, we can use demand and supply. Figure 19.1 shows the demand and supply curves for dollars in exchange for euros. Notice that the exchange rate is denominated in euros per dollar as we are looking at the international market for dollars.

☞ If you are looking for a good exchange rate calculator, visit http://www.x-rates.com.

The supply curve represents the quantity supplied of dollars in exchange for euros. If U.S. individuals or firms want to buy European goods or assets, they must exchange dollars for euros. As they buy euros, they sell dollars. In other words, as U.S. individuals or firms demand euros, they supply dollars. As the value of the dollar increases, more dollars will be supplied to the currency market in exchange for euros. Therefore, the supply curve slopes upward.

The demand curve represents the quantity demanded of dollars in exchange for euros. If European individuals or firms want to buy U.S. goods or assets, they must trade euros for dollars. To buy U.S. goods, Europeans will need dollars. As the Europeans buy dollars, they sell euros. In other words, Europeans demand dollars and supply euros. As the exchange rate for the U.S. dollar falls, dollars become cheaper in terms of euros. Therefore, the demand curve for dollars in exchange for euros slopes downward. Total demand for dollars will increase as the price of the dollar falls, or depreciates, against the euro. This makes U.S. goods and assets less expensive for European residents, because each euro buys more U.S. dollars.

In Figure 19.1, equilibrium occurs at an exchange rate of 0.8 euro per dollar. At this price, the willingness to trade dollars for euros just matches the willingness to trade euros for dollars. The foreign exchange market is in balance, and the price of euros in terms of a dollar is $(1/0.8) = \$1.25$.

Changes in demand or changes in supply will change equilibrium exchange rates. Figure 19.2 shows how an increase in demand, a shift of the demand curve to the right, will increase, or appreciate, the exchange rate. U.S. dollars will become more expensive relative to euros as the price of U.S. dollars in terms of euros increases. Two factors will increase the demand curve for dollars, shifting the demand curve to the right: First, higher U.S. interest rates. With higher returns in U.S. markets, investors throughout the world will want to buy dollars to invest in U.S. assets. Second, lower U.S. prices.

💣 Caution!

Remember for savers, the interest rate is a rate of return. For borrowers of funds, the interest rate is a cost of capital. The examples in this chapter, interest rates, are rates of return. If interest rates represented the cost of borrowing, then U.S. interest rate increases would decrease the demand for U.S. assets, causing a decrease in demand for dollars, shifting the demand curve to the left.

Figure 19.3 shows the effects of an increase in the supply of dollars, a shift in the supply curve to the right. An increase in the supply of dollars will lead to a fall, or depreciation, of the value of the dollar against the euro. What will cause the supply of dollars to increase? Higher European interest rates and/or lower European prices.

ᨃ Study Tip

Changes of the supply curve reflect changes in the foreign economy, while changes in the domestic economy cause changes in the demand curve.

Let's summarize the key facts about the foreign exchange market, using euros as our example:
- The demand curve for dollars represents the demand for dollars in exchange for euros. The curve slopes downward. As the dollar depreciates, there will be an increase in the quantity of dollars demanded in exchange for euros.
- The supply curve for dollars is the supply of dollars in exchange for euros. The curve slopes upward. As the dollar appreciates, there will be an increase in the quantity of dollars supplied in exchange for euros.
- Increases in U.S. interest rates and decreases in U.S. prices will increase the demand for dollars, leading to an appreciation of the dollar.
- Increases in European interest rates and decreases in European prices will increase the supply of dollars in exchange for euros, leading to a depreciation of the dollar.

19.2 Real Exchange Rates and Purchasing Power Parity

In general, however, prices do change over time, so we need to adjust the exchange rate determined in the foreign exchange market to take into account changes in prices. This adjustment is an application of the real-nominal principle.

Real-Nominal Principle

What matters to people is the real value of money or income—its purchasing power—not the face value of money or income.

Economists have developed a concept called the *real exchange rate* that adjusts the market exchange rates for changes in prices. The **real exchange rate** is the price of U.S. goods and services relative to foreign goods and services, expressed in a common currency. We measure it by expressing U.S. prices for goods and services in foreign currency and comparing them to foreign prices. Here is the formula for the real exchange rate:

☑ Key Equation

$$\text{real exchange rate} = \frac{\text{exchange rate} \times \text{U.S. price index}}{\text{foreign price index}}$$

We can use this equation to help understand the factors that change the real exchange rate. First, an increase in U.S. prices will raise the real exchange rate. When foreign prices and the exchange rate are held constant, an increase in U.S. prices will raise the relative price of U.S. goods. Second, an appreciation of the dollar when prices are held constant will also increase the price of U.S. goods relative to foreign goods. And if foreign prices fall, U.S. goods will become more expensive as well.

☞ Another way to look at the real exchange rate is for comparison purposes when buying goods and services. Suppose you were going to buy a BMW and could choose to buy it here in the U.S. or in Germany. If the cost of buying the car in the U.S. was $40,000 and cost of buying the car in Germany was 50,000€, where would you buy the car? Before you could make that decision, you would want to know the real exchange rate. Assume that the nominal exchange rate is 1.5€/$. Purchasing the car in the U.S. would be the same as spending 60,000€ ($40,000 x 1.5€/$). You would want to buy the car in Germany since it is less expensive in comparison.

Economists have found that a country's net exports (exports minus its imports) will fall when its real exchange rate increases. For example, if the U.S. real exchange rate increases, the prices of U.S. goods will increase relative to foreign goods. This will reduce the quantity of U.S. exports, because U.S. goods will have become more expensive; it will also increase the quantity of imports to the United States, because foreign goods will have become cheaper. As a result of the decrease in U.S. exports and the increase in U.S. imports, net exports will decline.

Figure 19.4 plots an index of the real exchange rate for the United States against net exports as a share of GDP from 1980 to 2005, a period in which there were large changes in the real exchange rate and net exports. The index, called a *multilateral real exchange rate,* is based on an average of real exchange rates with all U.S. trading partners. Notice that when the multilateral real exchange rate increased, U.S. net exports fell. As you can see in the figure, starting in both 1983 and 1996, the real exchange rate increased sharply. Subsequently, net exports as a share of GDP fell.

The tendency for easily tradable goods to sell at the same price when expressed in a common currency is known as the **law of one price**. Metals, agricultural commodities, and computer chips are tradable goods that follow the law of one price. If all goods were easily tradable and the law of one price held exactly, exchange rates would reflect no more than the differences in the way the price levels are expressed in the two countries. For example, if a basket of goods in Europe costs 3,000 euros and the identical basket costs $3,750 in the United States, an exchange rate of 0.8 euros to one dollar would make the costs the same in either currency.

According to the theory of **purchasing power parity**, a unit of any given currency should be able to buy the same quantity of goods in all countries. In our European–United States example, the theory of purchasing power parity predicts a market exchange rate of 0.8 euro per dollar. At that exchange rate, European and U.S. goods would sell for the same price if their products were expressed in a common currency. Research has shown that purchasing power parity does not hold precisely.

Let's review an Application that answers one of the key questions we posed at the start of the chapter:

1. Can the price of hamburgers around the world give us a clue as to the proper value for exchange rates?

APPLICATION 1: BIG MACS AND PURCHASING POWER PARITY

The Economist magazine illustrated the limits of purchasing power parity as a theory of exchange rates using a very recognizable product—the Big Mac from McDonald's. For several years, *The Economist* measured the price of a Big Mac throughout the world and checked to see whether the law of one price held. Table 19.1 contains the results for selected countries. Table 19.1 also contains the market exchange rate predicted by the theory of purchasing power parity. At this "Big Mac" exchange rate—3.81 Hong Kong dollars to every U.S. dollar—the Big Mac in Hong Kong would cost the same as in the United States. However, the actual exchange rate for the Hong Kong dollar in January 2006 when these prices were computed was 7.75 Hong Kong dollars per U.S. dollar, so the Big Mac was actually cheaper in Hong Kong. At 7.75 Hong Kong dollars for each U.S. dollar, you could buy closer to two Big Macs in Hong Kong for the amount you'd pay for one Big Mac in the United States.

19.3   The Current Account, the Financial Account, and the Capital Account

A useful framework for understanding international transactions is the **balance of payments**, a system of accounts that measures transactions of goods, services, income, and financial assets between domestic households, businesses, and governments and residents of the rest of the world during a specific time period. Let's look at the accounts that make up the balance of payments framework. There are three accounts to consider:
*   the current account
*   the financial account
*   the capital account

A country's **current account** is the sum of its net exports (exports minus imports), net income received from investments abroad, and net transfer payments from abroad (such as foreign aid). If a country has a positive current account, we say that its current account is in surplus. If a country has a negative current account, we say that its current account is in deficit. If the income from investments abroad and net transfer payments is negligible, the current account becomes equivalent to a country's net exports.

A country's **financial account** transactions include all the purchases and sales of existing financial and produced assets (stocks, bonds, real estate) by the private sector and the government. The financial account is defined as the value of the country's net sales (sales minus purchases) of assets.

A country's **capital account** transactions consist of two components. First, it includes the purchase or sale of nonproduced, nonfinancial assets, such as patents, copyrights, trademarks, and leases. Second, it also includes transfers of capital, such as debt forgiveness or migrant's transfers (goods or financial assets accompanying migrants as they leave or enter the country).

᧞ Study Tip

Here is a simple rule for understanding transactions on the current, financial, and capital accounts: Any action that gives rise to a demand for foreign currency is a deficit item. Any action that gives rise to a supply of foreign currency is a surplus item.

Let's apply the rule in the Study Tip to the current account and the financial account, taking the point of view of the United States (a similar logic applies to the capital account):

1. *Current account.* Goods imported into the United States show up as a deficit (negative) on the current account because we have to trade U.S. currency for foreign currency to buy them. Goods exported from the United States show up as a surplus (positive) in the current account because foreigners have to trade their currency for U.S. dollars to buy those products. Income from investments abroad and net transfers received are treated like exports because they result in a supply of foreign currency for dollars. Summarizing,

---

☑ Key Equation

U.S. current account surplus = U.S. exports − U.S. imports + net income from foreign investments + net transfers from abroad

---

2. *Financial account.* The purchase of a foreign asset by a U.S. resident leads to a deficit (negative) item on the financial account because it requires a demand for foreign currency. (You can think of the purchase of a foreign asset as just another import.) A purchase of a U.S. asset by a foreign resident leads to a supply of foreign currency and a surplus (positive) item on the financial account. (This can be thought of as an export.) Summarizing, we have

---

☑ Key Equation

U.S. financial account surplus = foreign purchases of U.S. assets − U.S. purchases of foreign assets

---

The current, financial, and capital accounts of a country are linked by a very important relationship:

☑ **Key Equation**

current account + financial account + capital account = 0

Any excess demand for foreign currency that arises from transactions in goods and services—that means we're looking at the current account—must be met by an excess supply of foreign currency arising from asset transactions—the financial account. Suppose the United States has a current account deficit of $50 billion, which means it is importing more than it is exporting. This excess demand of foreign currency by people in the United States can be met only by an excess supply of foreign currency that arises from the financial account—where foreign residents are purchasing $50 billion more in U.S. assets than U.S. residents are purchasing of foreign assets. In other words, the current account deficit is offset by the financial account surplus.

Let's look at the current account and financial account from a slightly different angle. Consider again the case in which the United States is running a current account deficit because imports from abroad exceed exports. (For simplicity, transfers and income earned from investments abroad are both zero.) The current account deficit means that, on net, foreign residents and their governments are the recipients of dollars because they have sold more goods to the United States than they have purchased.

What do foreign residents do with these dollars? They can either hold the dollars or use them to purchase U.S. assets. In either case, foreign residents and their governments have acquired U.S. assets, either dollars or other U.S. assets, such as U.S. Treasury bills. The value of these assets is the U.S. current account deficit. Because a sale of a U.S. asset to a foreign resident is a surplus item on the U.S. financial account, the value of the financial account will be equal to the negative of the value of the current account. So, from this perspective also, the current account and the financial account must sum to zero.

If a country runs a current account surplus—it is exporting more than importing, in other words—the country acquires foreign exchange. The country can either keep the foreign exchange or use it to buy foreign assets. In either case, its purchases of net foreign assets will equal its current account surplus. Because the financial account is the negative of the purchases of net foreign assets, the current account and financial account will again sum to zero.

Table 19.2 shows the balance of payments for the United States for 2004: the current account, the financial account, and the capital account. The current account is made up of the balance in goods, services, net investment income, and net transfers. In 2004, the United States had a negative balance on the goods account and net transfer, but a positive balance on the services and net income category. However, the large negative balance on the goods account made the overall current account balance negative.

☞ Visit www.bea.doc.gov, the Bureau of Economic Analysis Web site, for balance of payment statistics.

The financial account includes net increases in U.S. holdings abroad (negative entries in the financial account) and foreign holdings of U.S. assets (positive entries in the financial account). Because the government collects the current account, financial account, and capital account data from separate sources, a statistical discrepancy occurs. Once we include this statistical discrepancy, the current account, the financial account, and the capital account sum to zero.

In 1986, the U.S. Department of Commerce estimated that the United States had a **net international investment position** of $136 billion, meaning that U.S. holdings of foreign assets exceeded foreign holdings of U.S. assets by $136 billion. Because of its current account deficits, the U.S. net international investment position fell every year. By 2004, the current account deficit was a negative $2.5 trillion, meaning that foreign residents owned $2.5 trillion more U.S. assets than U.S. residents owned foreign assets.

☞ You may have heard the United States referred to as a *net debtor nation*. This is just another way of saying that the U.S. net international investment position is negative. As a consequence of the United States being a net debtor, earnings from international assets flow out of the United States to foreign countries. In the future, part of the incomes earned in the United States will be paid to foreigners abroad.

Let's review an Application that answers one of the key questions we posed at the start of the chapter:

2. What factors may allow the United States to continue running large trade deficits with the rest of the world?

APPLICATION 2: WORLD SAVINGS AND U.S. CURRENT ACCOUNT DEFICITS

The *2006 Economic Report of the President* directly addressed the issue of whether the United States can continue to run large current account deficits and, of course, financial account surpluses. In the report, the government recognized that the current account deficits would eventually be reduced. However, the government also highlighted a number of factors that suggested the deficits could continue for a long period of time. The report explains that the U.S. current account deficit needs to be placed in a global context. For the United States to continue to run a current account deficit, other countries in the world need to continue to purchase U.S. assets. In essence, other countries must have total savings in excess of their own investment desires in order to purchase U.S. assets. As long as there are countries in this situation, the United States could continue to run a trade deficit.

19.4 Fixed and Flexible Exchange Rates

Recall that when a country's exchange rate appreciates, there are two effects: First, the increased value of the exchange rate makes imports less expensive for the residents of the country where the exchange rate appreciated. For example, if the U.S. dollar appreciates against the euro, European watches will become less expensive for U.S. consumers. U.S. consumers would like an appreciated dollar, because it would lower their cost of living. Second, the increased value of the exchange rate makes U.S. goods more expensive on world markets. A U.S. exchange appreciation will increase imports, such as European watches, but decrease exports, such as California wine. Because exports fall and imports rise, net exports (exports minus imports) will decrease.

Similarly, when a country's exchange rate depreciates, there are two effects. First, imports will become more expensive in the United States, thus raising the cost of living in the United States. For example, if the U.S. dollar depreciated against the Japanese yen, Japanese imports would become more expensive in the United States, thereby raising the cost of living in the United States. Second, at the same time, U.S. goods would become cheaper in world markets. U.S. exports will rise and imports will fall, so net U.S. exports will increase.

To prevent the value of the currency from changing, governments can enter the foreign exchange market to try to influence the price of foreign exchange. Economists call these efforts to influence the exchange rate **foreign exchange market intervention**. In the United States, the Treasury Department has the official responsibility for foreign exchange intervention, though it operates in conjunction with the Federal Reserve. In other countries, governments also intervene in the foreign exchange market. To influence the price at which one currency trades for another, governments have to affect the demand or supply for their currency.

Figure 19.5 shows how governments can fix, or peg, the price of a currency. Suppose the U.S. and European governments want the exchange rate to be 0.8 euro per dollar. The price at which demand and supply are currently equal, however, is only 0.6 euro per dollar. To increase the price of the U.S. dollar, the governments will need to increase the demand for dollars. To do this, either government—the United States or European Central Bank—or both, can sell euros for dollars in the foreign exchange market. This will shift the demand curve for dollars to the right until the price of dollars rises to 0.8 euro per dollar.

If exchange rates are determined in free markets, we have a **flexible exchange rate system**. Under a pure flexible exchange rate system, the price of a currency will rise if the demand increases more than supply and will fall if supply increases more than demand. **Fixed exchange rate systems** are exchange rate systems in which governments peg exchange rates to prevent their currencies from fluctuating. After World War II, the countries of the world operated under a fixed exchange system known as Bretton Woods. Under this system, all countries fixed or pegged their currencies against the U.S. dollar.

Suppose the supply of a country's currency exceeds the demand at the fixed exchange rate. An excess supply of a country's currency at the fixed exchange rate is known as a balance of payments deficit. A **balance of payments deficit** will occur whenever there is a deficit on the current account that is not matched by net sales of assets to foreigners by the private sector. With an excess supply of a country's currency in the currency market, that currency would fall in value without any intervention. To prevent the currency from depreciating in value and to maintain the fixed exchange rate, the government would have to sell foreign currency and buy its own currency. As you saw from our foreign exchange intervention discussion, if a country sells foreign exchange, its holdings of foreign exchange will fall. So you can see that when a country runs a balance of payments deficit, it has decreased its holdings of foreign exchange.

An excess demand for a country's currency at the fixed exchange rate is known as a **balance of payments surplus**. A balance of payments surplus arises when there is a current account surplus that is not matched by net purchases of foreign assets by the private sector. With an excess demand for a country's currency, it will rise in value without any intervention. To prevent its currency from appreciating—to maintain the fixed exchange rate, in other words—the government will have to buy foreign currency and sell its own.

A country that faces a balance of payments deficit can lower the value at which the currency is pegged to increase its net exports, a process called **devaluation**. Conversely, a country that faces a balance of payments surplus can increase the value at which its currency is pegged and reduce its net exports, a process called **revaluation**.

In the 1970s, the Bretton Woods system was replaced by the current system—a flexible exchange rate system—in which supply and demand primarily determines exchange rates. If a fixed exchange rate system makes it easier to trade, why did it break down in the early 1970s? Fixed exchange rate systems provide benefits, but they require countries to maintain similar economic policies—especially to maintain similar inflation rates and interest rates.

This difference in their real exchange rates over time would cause a trade deficit to emerge in the United States as U.S. goods became more expensive on world markets—including in Germany. As long as the differences in inflation continued and the exchange rate remained fixed, the U.S. real exchange rate would continue to appreciate, and the U.S. trade deficit would grow even worse. Clearly, this course of events would have to be halted under an agreed-upon fixed exchange rate system.

In the late 1960s, inflation in the United States began to exceed inflation in other countries, and a U.S. balance of payments deficit emerged—just as in our example. In 1971, President Nixon surprised the world and devalued the U.S. dollar against the currencies of all the other countries in the hope of alleviating the U.S. balance of payments deficit and maintaining the underlying system of fixed exchange rates. However, the U.S. devaluation did not stop the U.S. balance of payments deficit. Germany tried to maintain the mark's fixed exchange rate with the U.S. dollar by purchasing U.S. dollars in the foreign exchange market. Germany was essentially importing inflation from the United States. With the U.S. balance of payments deficit continuing, Germany was required to buy U.S. dollars to keep the mark from appreciating. Germany bought U.S. dollars with German marks. Those German marks were then put into circulation. The German supply of marks in Germany therefore increased, and this increase in marks raised the inflation rate in Germany. Private-sector investors knew that Germany did not wish to run persistent trade surpluses and import U.S. inflation. They bet that Germany would revalue the mark against the dollar—that is, raise the value of the mark against the dollar. Investors bought massive amounts of German assets, trading their dollars for marks to purchase them because they thought the mark's value would eventually sharply increase. Their actions forced the German government to buy even *more* dollars to force the price of the mark upward and keep it pegged to the dollar. The resulting flow of financial capital into Germany was so massive that the German government eventually gave up all attempts to keep its exchange rate fixed to the dollar. Instead, it let the exchange rate be determined in the free market. This was the end of the Bretton Woods system.

The flexible exchange rate system has worked well enough since the breakdown of Bretton Woods in 1971. World trade has grown at a rapid rate. Moreover, the flexible exchange rate system has seamlessly managed many diverse situations, including two major oil shocks in the 1990s, large U.S. budget deficits in the 1980s, and large Japanese and Chinese current account surpluses in the last 15 years

Let's review an Application that answers one of the key questions we posed at the start of the chapter:

3. Why did a group of European countries adopt a common currency?

APPLICATION 3: THE FIRST DECADE OF THE EURO

On January 1, 1999, the following 11 European countries agreed to use a common currency: Austria, Belgium, Finland, France, Germany, Ireland, Italy, Luxembourg, the Netherlands, Portugal, and Spain. In 2002, euro notes and coins were put into circulation. Beginning July 1, 2002, national currencies such as French francs, German marks, and Italian lira ceased to be used. A European central bank, which is similar to the Federal Reserve Bank in the U.S., establishes a common monetary policy for all the countries that use the euro. These countries therefore can use only fiscal policy for macroeconomic stabilization. Essentially the euro zone is a fixed exchange rate system among the member countries. Fearing a possible loss of independence, the United Kingdom, Denmark, and Sweden decided not to join the euro system initially. Greece initially did not meet some of the European Union's fiscal criteria necessary to join but did become a member in 2001. It is still unclear whether adopting a common currency and monetary policy was a wise economic move for the countries that joined the new regime.

☞ For complete information about the euro, visit the European Union's euro Web site at: http://ec.europa.eu/economy_finance/euro/our_currency_en.htm

19.5 Managing Financial Crises

In 1994, Mexico experienced a severe financial crisis. In 1997, the Asian economic crisis began. The Argentinean economy collapsed in 2002. How do these crises originate? What policies can prevent or alleviate them?

Let's first consider the Mexican case. During the late 1980s and early 1990s, Mexico decided to fix, or peg, its exchange to the U.S. dollar. Mexico's goal was to signal to investors throughout the world that it was serious about controlling inflation and would take the steps needed to keep its inflation rates in line with that of the United States. Mexico also opened up its markets to foreign investors. The country seemed to be on a solid path to development. However, in some sense, the policies proved to be too successful in encouraging foreign investment. As funds poured into the country, the demand for goods increased and prices started to rise. This rise in prices caused an increase in Mexico's real exchange rate, and the rise in the real exchange rate caused a large trade deficit.

However, foreign investors started to pull their funds out of Mexico following an assassination of a political candidate and a rural uprising. At this point, the Mexican government made a crucial mistake. Instead of trying to reduce its trade deficit by taking steps to reduce prices, it allowed the trade deficit to continue. Moreover, both the government and the private sector began to find that they had to borrow in dollars because foreign investors thought Mexico might be forced to devalue the peso. If a devaluation were to occur, any lender of pesos would suffer a loss because the debt would be repaid at a lower exchange rate. Consequently, Mexican borrowers were forced to borrow in loans denominated in dollars.

Eventually, more political turmoil caused investors to pull out their funds, selling pesos for dollars. The Mexican central bank spent nearly $50 billion buying these pesos in an effort to keep the exchange rate constant. The $50 billion was not enough. Mexico ran out of dollars. Because it could no longer buy pesos to maintain the exchange rate, Mexico had to devalue, putting the peso more in line with its market value. The devaluation created even more turmoil because the government and the private sector had borrowed billions in dollars. When the peso was devalued against the dollar, the burden of these debts measured in pesos increased sharply, so more pesos were needed to pay the dollar-denominated debts. Mexico faced the prospect of massive bankruptcies and the potential collapse of its economy.

To prevent a financial collapse that could easily have spread to many other developing countries, the U.S. government (along with other international financial institutions) arranged for Mexico to borrow dollars with an extended period for repayment. This allowed Mexican banks and corporations to avoid bankruptcies and prevented a major disaster. In 1996, the Mexican government was able to pay off nearly three-fourths of the loan from the United States.

A similar crisis occurred in Asia. Economic growth had been remarkable in Asia for over 20 years. In the early 1990s, several Asian countries began to open their capital markets to foreign investors and borrow extensively from abroad. Billions of dollars poured into Asia, but there was little financial supervision and many of the investments failed. Companies in both Thailand and South Korea began to lose money. Domestic investors and world investors suddenly became pessimistic and pulled their funds out of South Korea and Thailand, among other Asian countries. The withdrawal of funds forced currencies throughout Asia to be devalued. Because many businesses had borrowed in dollars, the devaluations raised the burden of the debt and further deepened the crisis, taking its toll on other countries, including Indonesia, Malaysia, and Hong Kong. The International Monetary Fund attempted to help restore the health of these economies' financial systems, but in many cases, its policies were ineffective. Some economists, such as Nobel laureate Joseph Stiglitz, believe that the entire Asian crisis was an example of market overreaction and could have been avoided by bolder action from world organizations and developed countries.

Let's review an Application that answers one of the key questions we posed at the start of the chapter:

4.   What are the causes of financial collapses that occur throughout the globe?

APPLICATION 4: THE ARGENTINEAN FINANCIAL CRISIS

During the late 1980s, Argentina suffered from hyperinflation. As part of its financial reforms, Argentina pegged its currency to the U.S. dollar, making pesos "convertible" into dollars. To issue pesos, the central bank had to have an equal amount of dollars, or its equivalents in other hard currencies, on hand. Unfortunately, the financial and other institutional reforms worked well only in the early 1990s. As the dollar appreciated sharply on world markets after 1995, Argentina began to suffer from a large trade deficit because its currency was pegged to the dollar. Essentially, America's rising currency became Argentina's problem.   Then in 1999, Brazil devalued its currency, putting additional pressure on neighboring Argentina. Investors became doubtful that the country could repay its debts and feared its currency would be devaluated. Local citizens also became fearful of devaluation and tried to convert their pesos into dollars, further deepening the problem.   Eventually, Argentina defaulted on its international debt in 2002 and froze bank accounts. Middle-class Argentineans who still had funds in their banks suffered a sharp decrease in their wealth. A severe depression ensued.

Activity

Let's try an activity using your understanding of currency markets to see how a devaluation or a revaluation affects fixed rate systems.

Suppose that the country of Locopolis has a fixed rate system and it faces a balance of payments surplus. Would the government of Locopolis do a devaluation or a revaluation of its currency? Graphically show what would happen in the currency market.

Answer

The balance of payments surplus creates a condition where there is an excess demand of a country's currency. A revaluation would be necessary to resolve the excess demand for Locopolis' currency. Locopolis would have to sell its own currency as shown below. This would cause a shift of the supply curve to the right.

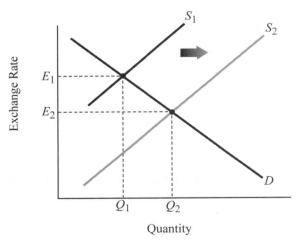

Key Terms

Appreciation of a currency: An increase in the value of a currency relative to the currency of another nation.

Balance of payments: A system of accounts that measures transactions of goods, services, income, and financial assets between domestic households, businesses, and governments and residents of the rest of the world during a specific time period.

Balance of payments deficit: Under a fixed exchange rate system, a situation in which the supply of a country's currency exceeds the demand for the currency at the current exchange rate.

Balance of payments surplus: Under a fixed exchange rate system, a situation in which the demand of a country's currency exceeds the supply for the currency at the current exchange rate.

Capital account: The value of capital transfer and transaction in nonproduced, nonfinancial assets in the international accounts.

Current account: The sum of net exports (exports minus imports) plus income received from abroad plus net transfers from abroad.

Depreciation of a currency: A decrease in the value of a currency relative to the currency of another nation.

Devaluation: A decrease in the exchange rate to which a currency is pegged under a fixed exchange rate system.

Euro: The common currency in Europe.

Exchange rate: The price at which currencies trade for one another in the market.

Financial account: The value of a country's net sales (sales minus purchases) of assets.

Fixed exchange rate system: A system in which governments peg exchange rates to prevent their currencies from fluctuating.

Flexible exchange rate system: A currency system in which exchange rates are determined by free markets.

Foreign exchange market intervention: The purchase or sale of currencies by government to influence the market exchange rate.

Law of one price: The theory that goods easily tradable across countries should sell at the same price expressed in a common currency.

Net international investment position: Domestic holding of foreign assets minus foreign holdings of domestic assets.

Purchasing power parity: A theory of exchange rates whereby a unit of any given currency should be able to buy the same quantity of goods in all countries.

Real exchange rate: The price of U.S. goods and services relative to foreign goods and services, expressed in a common currency.

Revaluation: An increase in the exchange rate to which a currency is pegged under a fixed exchange rate system.

Practice Quiz

(Answers are provided at the end of the Practice Quiz.)

1. When the dollar appreciates against the yen:
   a. there has been an increase in the value of the dollar relative to the yen.
   b. the yen also appreciates against the dollar.
   c. it takes more dollars to purchase one yen.
   d. All of the above

2. Suppose that a pound of Colombian coffee beans sells for US$0.90 in New York markets. The exchange rate between Colombian pesos and U.S. dollars is 2,500 pesos per dollar. If the exchange rate moves to 3,000 pesos per dollar, how much would a pound of coffee cost in New York markets?
   a. U.S. $0.0003
   b. U.S. $0.75
   c. U.S. $1.33
   d. U.S. $0.83

3. Refer to the figure below. In this graph, as the dollar appreciates:

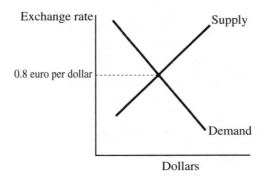

   a. more dollars are supplied.
   b. fewer dollars are supplied.
   c. fewer euros are demanded.
   d. more euros are supplied.

4. Refer to the figure below. Suppose that this is the market for dollars against the Colombian peso. The exchange rate along the vertical axis in this market is:

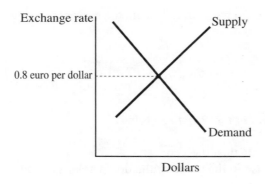

a. dollars per euro.
b. euros per dollar.
c. simply euros.
d. simply dollars.

5. Refer to the figure below. Which of the following factors could have caused the increase in supply?

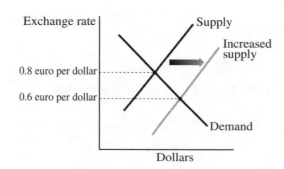

a. Lower U.S. interest rates.
b. Lower U.S. prices.
c. Dollar appreciation
d. None of the above. These are the factors that affect the demand for dollars, not the supply of dollars.

6. The price of all U.S. goods and services relative to all foreign goods and services, expressed in a common currency, is called:
a. the real exchange rate.
b. the price index for the U.S. exchange rate.
c. the nominal rate of U.S. dollar exchange.
d. None of the above. There is no such concept.

7. Greater preference for Colombian coffee, all else the same, will:
a. decrease the value of the Colombian peso relative to the dollar.
b. increase the value of the Colombian peso relative to the dollar.
c. have no effect on the value of the Colombian peso relative to the dollar.
d. increase the demand for dollars.

8. When the real exchange rate increases:
   a. a country's net exports will rise.
   b. a country's net exports will fall.
   c. a country's net exports are not affected.
   d. the multilateral exchange rate is not affected.

9. This question tests your understanding of Application 1 in this chapter: Big Macs and purchasing power parity. Can the price of hamburgers around the world give us a clue as to the proper value for exchange rates?

   The limits of purchasing power parity as a theory of exchange rates have been nicely illustrated by *The Economist*. For several years, it measured the price of a Big Mac throughout the world and checked to see whether the law of one price held. Big Macs sell for widely different prices around the globe compared to the $3.15 they sold for in the United States in early 2006.

   In Colombia, the price of a Big Mac on October 18, 2006 was 6,000 pesos, and the actual exchange rate on this date was 2,348 pesos per dollar. Based on this information, we conclude that:
   a. the exchange rate in Colombia on this date reflected the law of one price.
   b. the predicted purchasing power exchange rate based on Big Mac pricing on this date was 1,905 pesos per dollar.
   c. the price of Big Macs in Colombia is too high for purchasing power parity to hold.
   d. if we extend the results of the purchasing power parity price of a Big Mac to other goods in the economy, then Colombians should find it attractive to shop in the United States.

10. If prices in Colombia have risen faster on average than prices in the United States, while prices in Japan have risen more slowly, it must be true that the U.S. dollar has _____ value against the Colombian peso, and _____ value against the Japanese yen.
    a. gained; lost
    b. lost; gained
    c. maintained; gained
    d. gained; maintained

11. Market exchange rates simply reflect differences in the overall price levels between countries. This theory is known as:
    a. the law of one price.
    b. purchasing power parity.
    c. the real exchange rate.
    d. autarky.

12. If the sum of net exports, net income received from investments abroad, and net transfer payments from abroad yields a positive number, we say that a country's:
    a. current account is in surplus.
    b. current account is in deficit.
    c. capital account is in surplus.
    d. capital account is in deficit.

13. Fill in the blanks. Any action that gives rise to a _____ for foreign currency is a deficit item, and any action that gives rise to a _____ of foreign currency is a surplus item.
    a. supply; supply
    b. supply; demand
    c. demand; supply
    d. demand; demand

14. Since the largest component of the current account for most countries is net exports, if a country runs a current account surplus it is probably:
    a. exporting more than it's importing, and it acquires foreign exchange.
    b. importing more than it's exporting, and it acquires foreign exchange.
    c. exporting more than it's importing, and it surrenders foreign exchange.
    d. importing more than it's exporting, and it surrenders foreign exchange.

15. Fill in the blanks. When a country's exchange rate _____, imports become more expensive and the cost of living in that country _____.
    a. appreciates; increases
    b. appreciates; decreases
    c. depreciates; increases
    d. depreciates; decreases

16. After World War II, the countries of the world operated under a fixed exchange rate system known as Bretton Woods, whereby all countries fixed or pegged their currencies against:
    a. gold.
    b. the U.S. dollar.
    c. a basket of currencies from mostly developed countries: the British pound, the French franc, and the German mark.
    d. None of the above

17. Under a fixed exchange rate system, when a country experiences a balance of payments surplus, the country's currency will _____ in value. To prevent its currency from changing value, the government will have to _____ foreign currency and _____ its own.
    a. rise; buy; sell
    b. rise; sell; buy
    c. fall; buy; sell
    d. fall; sell; buy

18. Which type of exchange rate system requires countries to maintain similar economic policies—especially to maintain similar inflation rates and interest rates in order for the exchange rate system to work properly?
    a. A fixed exchange rate system
    b. A flexible exchange rate system
    c. A free market based exchange rate system
    d. All of the above

19. If Chinese savers increase their demand for U.S. Treasury bills, the demand for dollars will _____, and the value of the dollar will _____.
    a. increase; rise
    b. increase; fall
    c. decrease; rise
    d. decrease; fall

20. This question tests your understanding of Application 3 in this chapter: The first decade of the euro. Why did a group of European countries adopt a common currency?

    After ten years since the inception of the euro, what can we conclude about whether the benefits outweigh the costs of this initiative?
    a. Given the efficiencies gained by using a single currency, the benefits clearly seem to outweigh the costs.
    b. The costs appear to outweigh the benefits because the countries in the European Union no longer conduct their own independent monetary policy.
    c. We can't draw any conclusions yet. The jury is still out on whether adopting a common currency was a wise economic move for the countries that joined the new regime.
    d. The benefits of increased monetary policy independence and more tools available for stabilization clearly put the benefits ahead of the costs of having a single currency.

21. Explain the rationale behind the development of a concept known as the real exchange rate.

22. Explain the relationship between the law of one price and the theory of purchasing power parity.

23. The current account, financial account, and the capital account are linked by a very important identity: current account + financial account + capital account = 0. Explain.

24. Explain the impact of a U.S. trade deficit on the ownership of assets.

Answers to the Practice Quiz

1. a. An increase in the value of a currency is called an appreciation. When the dollar appreciates against the yen, one dollar will purchase more yen. A depreciation is a reduction in the value of a currency. If one currency appreciates, the other must depreciate.

2. b. When the dollar is worth 2,500 pesos, the equivalent of U.S.$0.90 is (0.90 x $2,500) = $2,250 pesos. So, the pound of coffee sells for an equivalent of 2,250 Colombian pesos when the exchange rate between pesos and dollars is 2,500 pesos per dollar. Now, to acquire the same 2,250 pesos when the dollar is worth 3,000 pesos, it takes 2,250/3,000 = U.S. $0.75. Therefore, if the exchange rate went up to 3,000 pesos per dollar, the pound of coffee would cost only $0.75 in New York markets.

3. a. As euros become cheaper, total spending on European goods and assets will increase. For this reason, the supply curve is upward sloping: As the value of the dollar increases, more dollars will be supplied to the currency market in exchange for euros.

4. b. The exchange rate in this market shows how many euros it takes to obtain one dollar, or euros per dollar.

5. a. If interest rates are lower in the U.S., then people will be pulling money out of the U.S. to send to other countries where higher interest rates can be earned. This means they sell dollars (increase supply) and buy the other currencies (increasing demand there).

6. a. We need to adjust the exchange rate determined in the foreign exchange market to take into account changes in prices. The real exchange rate is defined as the price of all U.S. goods and services relative to all foreign goods and services, expressed in a common currency.

7. b. If consumers in the U.S. increase their preferences for Colombian products, the demand for pesos will increase relative to the demand for dollars, and the Colombian peso will increase in value relative to the U.S. dollar.

8. b. Since the real exchange rate rises with higher domestic prices, a higher exchange rate, or lower foreign prices, those factors all cause lower net exports as well.

9. b. To obtain the market-exchange rate predicted by the theory of purchasing power parity, divide the price of Big Macs in the foreign country by the dollar price. For Colombia on this date, the predicted purchasing power exchange rate based on the price of a Big Mac is 6,000/3.15 = 1,905 pesos per dollar. The actual exchange rate for the Colombian peso on October 18, 2006 was 2,348 pesos per dollar. If the law of one price were to hold, the price of a Big Mac in Colombia would have to be the equivalent of U.S.$3.15, or 2,348 x 3.15 = 6,000/3.15 = 7,306 pesos. The Colombian price of the Big Mac, 6,000 pesos, is less.

10. a. If prices in Colombia have risen faster on average than prices in the United States, while prices in Japan have risen more slowly, this difference in inflation rates is a key reason why the U.S. dollar would have gained value against the Colombian peso, while losing value against the Japanese yen.

11. b. According to one theory of how market exchange rates are determined, market exchange rates simply reflect differences in the overall price levels between countries. This theory is known as purchasing power parity.

12. a. A country's current account is the sum of its net exports (exports minus imports), net income received from investments abroad, and net transfer payments from abroad. If a country has a positive current account, we say that its current account is in surplus; and if it is negative, we say that its current account is in deficit.

13. c. Any action that gives rise to a demand for foreign currency is a deficit item on the current account or on the capital account, and any action that gives rise to a supply of foreign currency is a surplus item on the current account or on the capital account.

14. a. If a country runs a current account surplus—it's exporting more than it's importing; in other words, it acquires foreign exchange.

15. c. When a country's exchange rate depreciates, imports become more expensive and the cost of living in that country increases. At the same time, exports will increase. Sometimes, governments try to prevent the effects of appreciation or depreciation.

16. b. After World War II, the countries of the world operated under a fixed exchange rate system known as Bretton Woods, whereby all countries fixed or pegged their currencies against the U.S. dollar.

17. a. With a balance of payments surplus and without government intervention, a country's currency will rise in value. To prevent its currency from appreciating, the government will have to buy foreign currency and sell its own.

18. a. Fixed exchange rate systems require countries to maintain similar economic policies—especially to maintain similar inflation rates and interest rates, or they will find it increasingly difficult to maintain the value of their currency at the required level.

19. a. We have seen that a key reason that exchange rates fluctuate is that in the current economy, investors seek out the best investments they can find anywhere in the world. For instance, if Chinese savers increase their demand for U.S. Treasury bills, the demand for dollars will increase, and the value of the dollar will rise.

20. c. The jury is still out on whether adopting a common currency was a wise economic move for the countries that joined the new regime, and whether having a larger market will outweigh the disadvantages of having one monetary policy for all the members.

21. Changes in market exchange rates can affect the demand for a country's goods and services. As prices change, we need to adjust the exchange rate to take into account those price changes. These adjustments in the exchange rate are based on the reality principle: what matters to people is the real value or purchasing power of money or income, not its face value. The real exchange rate adjusts for price changes by expressing U.S. prices in foreign currency and comparing them to foreign prices. Higher U.S. prices will raise the real exchange rate and the price of U.S. goods relative to foreign goods. If foreign prices fall, U.S. goods will become more expensive as well.

22. The tendency for easily tradable goods to sell at the same price when expressed in a common currency is known as the law of one price. Metals, agricultural commodities, computer chips, and other tradable goods follow the law of one price. If all goods were tradable and the law of one price held exactly, exchange rates would reflect no more than the differences in the way the price levels are expressed in the two countries. The theory of purchasing power parity states that market exchange rates simply reflect differences in the overall price levels between countries. This theory predicts that, at the market exchange rate, goods would sell for the same price if their products are expressed in a common currency. The theory does not give accurate predictions for exchange rates, however, because many goods are not traded across countries.

23. The current account represents net income flows from production, investment, and transfers. The current account is very large in absolute value for countries like the U.S. The financial account represents the net sales of financial and produced assets like land, stock, bonds, etc. The capital account represents net income flows from the sale of nonproduced items like patents or capital transfers like migrants taking assets with them. The capital account is very small for countries like the U.S. and is often ignored in this discussion for that reason.

24. A trade deficit occurs when the value of imports exceeds the value of exports. This means that we give up more dollars to buy imports than the dollars we receive from the sale of our exports. Excess dollars in the hands of foreigners are used to buy U.S. assets. In sum, a U.S. trade deficit increases the foreign ownership of assets in the United States. If foreigners use their dollars to invest in U.S. firms, the income of foreigners will rise once profits are repatriated. And, if foreigners use their extra income to buy U.S. exports, the trade situation of the United States may eventually improve. However, as long as the U.S. continues to run a trade deficit, the ownership of foreign assets in the United States will continue to increase relative to the U.S. ownership of assets abroad.